THE CIVIL WAR IN WILTSHIRE

THE CIVIL WAR
IN
WILTSHIRE

Tony MacLachlan

Rowan
Books

Published by Rowan Books,
59, Beech Grange, Landford, Salisbury, Wiltshire, England.

Copyright © 1997 by Tony MacLachlan

ISBN 0 9530785 0 7

Printed and bound by The Cromwell Press Ltd, Broughton Gifford,
Melksham, Wiltshire, England

ACKNOWLEDGEMENTS

Several people have contributed in various ways to the production of this book and it would be churlish to ignore their input. I am particularly grateful to my son, Tim, an I.T. expert, for converting my crude drawings into legible maps and conscientiously typesetting the final text.

I must also thank all those who read the text and offered advice and suggestions, most of which I accepted without argument. I am particularly grateful to Stephen Ings, a local historian, whose profound knowledge of times past and meticulous eye for detail helped me to avoid some of the pitfalls into which I would undoubtedly have fallen. Sincere thanks must also go to Bruce Purvis, local studies librarian in Salisbury, for unhesitatingly providing me with information over the telephone, and to the staff of the Wiltshire Library Service for allowing me to use certain diagrams in the text.

I have also to recognise the support offered by the owners of houses featured in the war, some of whom have allowed me to tramp unhindered over their private estates or read the letters of former residents.

Lastly, I should thank the combatants and their families, the men and women of the 17th century, whose quarrels and actions have provided the material fabric for this book. If they had chosen not to argue, I would have been forced to write about something else instead.

INTRODUCTION

An eminent military historian, Brigadier Peter Young, once told an audience that 'not much happened in Wiltshire during the civil war'. The destruction of an entire Roundhead army on the Downs above Devizes, countless skirmishes, seven action-packed sieges and the storming of four towns, some of which changed hands several times, seem hardly to be non-events, and all contributed, directly or indirectly, to the eventual triumph of Parliament over its King.

Perhaps Brigader Young did not look within the strong boxes, vaults and archives that lie forgotten in the county's aged homes or in its well-stocked libraries and public records office. Perhaps he failed to see the evidence in the cratered walls of buildings, peppered by musket ball and grapeshot, or sense the pain and sorrow of many of those who lived through those troubled times - wives deprived of husbands, children robbed of fathers, and the one-legged war veterans of Wiltshire's narrow byways . All of them speak out, in one way or the other, to those who want to hear. Their voices echo from the buildings that they left behind and their shadows seem to linger in the fields beyond. Modern Wiltshire has kept few untouched relics of former times, but those that remain have not completely shaken off the reminders of those war-filled years.

In setting out to re-create the events and traumas of the Civil War, I have visited many of the churches, farmhouses and manors where voices and swords were raised in anger. In more than twenty of these, mainly pubs today, Cromwell was reputed to have slept and in many of the barns his soldiers were billeted. The tarmac, concrete and artificial fertilizer that encases the county's surface is only superficial and the vaporous world of the 17th Century still flows out from the ground beneath.

CONTENTS

LIST OF MAPS

KEY TO MAPS

All maps have north point at the top.

☐ ☐ ☐ ▷   Routes of retreat

    ⬚
   H   Cavalry units

    ⬚
   F   Foot units

   ⊨   Position of artillery

   ✕   Site of skirmishes

1

'A resemblance of the golden age'

MARTHA Edwards was denounced as a witch for refusing to open the door to visiting Roundhead troops. Her two year old child was plunged into boiling water for his mother's crime. A year earlier an itinerant preacher was branded as the *'devil's man - and so for the King'* and murdered in a country road. And Sunday worshippers in a parish church were offered a choice by passing soldiers - either to take an oath of loyalty to the King or receive a musket ball in the head!

Events like these were to become common occurrences throughout the nation during this troubled period of civil strife. The humdrum daily routine of pre-war life would be savagely poisoned by politics and passion and rocked from its foundations by the violence of the times. Enmity, sadness, and distrust would stalk the nation's lanes, and the germs of suspicion would be implanted in everyone.

Wiltshire was no less torn than any other county in the nation's south and west. One who knew Wiltshire at the time paints a landscape of near Arcadian charm and near-perfect tranquillity.

> *'The turf is of a short sweet grass, good for the sheep, and delightful to the eye, for its smoothness like a bowling green and pleasant to the traveller; who wants here only a variety of objects to make his journey less tedious, for here is...not a tree, or rarely a bush to shelter one from a shower...the innocent lives here of the shepherds do give us a resemblance of the golden age.'[1]*

---

[1] Aubrey, John. 'Antiquities of Wiltshire'.

1

He was speaking of the vast and featureless plain of chalk lying between the Kennet and Ebble, perhaps two-thirds of the county's area. Scorched unmercifully by the summer sun and iced by winter's chills, it was inhabited only by hardened shepherds and the flocks that were in their charge. Hares and rabbits in profusion cropped the short grass, and birds of prey hung motionless overhead. It was a landscape that had changed little in a thousand years, and the remnants of earlier men lay undisturbed on the land's gentle contours.

The valleys that crossed this open landscape were more densely peopled, and here mixed farming, mainly subsistence, was practised on the open fields that were the legacies of medieval times. Wheat and barley were widely cultivated, mainly for the production of bread and beer. John Aubrey, connoisseur of such things, comments on the quality:

> 'The wheat and bread of this county, especially south Wilts, is but indifferent; that of the Vale of White Horse is excellent. King Charles II, when he lay at Salisbury, in his progress, complained that he found neither good bread nor good beer. But for the latter, twas the fault of the brewer not to boil it well; for the water and malt there are as good as any in England.'[2]

Here, too, the more affluent lived, controlling the destiny of their chalk-land estates from their manorial homes and dictating the pace and tenor of local politics.

The clay land to the north, the remaining third of Wiltshire, hugged the Avon valley, and was a very different world. Wet and damp by contrast with the chalk, this was the cheese country where field enclosure had been almost completed by the early 17th century:

> 'In the dirty claey country,' wrote Aubrey, 'they feed chiefly on milk meats which cools their brains too much

---

[2] Aubrey, John. 'Antiquities of Wiltshire'.

and hurts their inventions. These circumstances make them melancholy, contemplative and malicious.' [3]

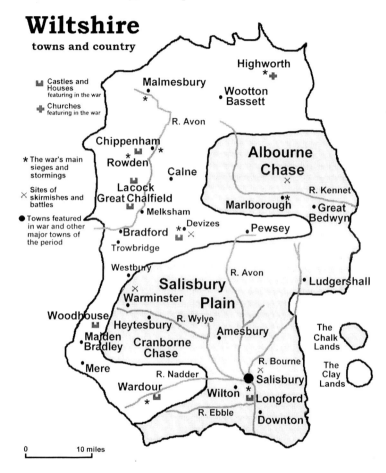

Wiltshire

towns and country

Castles and Houses featuring in the war

Churches featuring in the war

* The war's main sieges and stormings

× Sites of skirmishes and battles

● Towns featured in war and other major towns of the period

Highworth

Malmesbury

Wootton Bassett

R. Avon

Chippenham

Albourne Chase

Rowden

Calne

R. Kennet

Lacock
Great Chalfield

Marlborough

Great Bedwyn

Melksham

Devizes

Pewsey

Bradford

Trowbridge

Westbury

R. Avon

Ludgershall

Salisbury

Warminster

Plain

Woodhouse

R. Wylye

Heytesbury

Amesbury

The Chalk Lands

Maiden Bradley

Cranborne Chase

The Clay Lands

Mere

R. Bourne

R. Nadder

Salisbury

Wardour

Wilton

Longford

R. Ebble

Downton

0   10 miles

[3] Aubrey, John. 'Antiquities of Wiltshire'.

Small tenant farms prevailed, edging the villages of the Avon, and here lived a conservative society of dairy farmers treading contentedly in the paths of their fathers. Aubrey is critical of their sluggish ways.

> *Our husbandmen go after the fashion; that is, when the fashion is almost out, they take it up, so our countrymen are very late and very unwilling to learn or be brought to new improvements.*[4]

Not far beyond were the prosperous woollen towns of the Avon, particularly Bradford, *'the pretty clothing town...made all of stone.*[5] This time-tested industry, dependent on the flocks of sheep that roamed the chalky plains, had transformed life since the Middle Ages, swelling poor hamlets into some of the nation's most affluent towns. Other settlements had grown rapidly as commercial or religious centres, and perhaps 1 in 10 of Wiltshire's people no longer depended entirely on the land for sustenance.

Yet this outward picture of stability disguised the enormous strains of the pre-war years. Agriculturally, socially and industrially, Wiltshire was being slowly forced to adapt to the headaches of post-medieval life. The trauma of the Reformation had been followed by the rise of mercantilism and the market orientated economy, and the old closed-knit system of subsistence and parochialism had been rapidly eroded. The lands of the monasteries, perhaps 30% of the county's surface area, had been sold to royal courtiers and favourites, and a host of new imported men had begun to play a major role in the county's social life. William Sharington, the master of Henry VIII's mint in Bristol, had purchased the abbey lands at Lacock at a fraction of their estimated value. Sir William Seymour and Sir William Herbert did just as well, the former obtaining monastic lands at Edington and Maiden Bradley, while Herbert took possession of the monks' estates at Wilton. For a while little obvious change might have been

---

[4] Aubrey, John. 'Antiquities of Wiltshire'.
[5] Ibid.

noticeable: clerical lords had been replaced by secular, but the estates continued to operate on commercial grounds. Great houses arose from the monastic ruins and the age of materialism was born. Many of the enthusiastic purchasers of clerical property were the self-made men of Wiltshire's cloth industry. The industry had made Wiltshire the nation's sixth richest county, in the decades preceding the war. Disposal of abbey lands at bargain prices had spawned a lively market and the chance to speculate. But such men had been active in pre-Reformation times, and the Wiltshire countryside was studded with the proofs of their success. Thomas Tropenell erected Great Chalfield Manor in 1467 while Westwood Manor, the home of the Bradford clothier Thomas Horton, is about 40 years younger. Tall towered churches followed. St Mary's at Steeple Ashton is said to be the county's finest, the gift of the clothier Robert Long. By 1600 Hortons, Longs, Methuens and Yerburys, to name just some of the age's millionaires, had left the cloth trade, preferring to enjoy the charms of gentrification and exert an almost semi-feudalistic control over their immediate sphere of influence. Beside these meteors in the social firmament, the older established families glowed with lower magnitude. The Hastings, the Stourtons and the Willoughby de Brokes, although still possessing several manors, had lost political influence and few were to play any prominent part in the troubled events of the 1640's. In contrast, the new made men, titled and otherwise, would provide the bulk of the county's M.P.s and military leaders.

But the cohesive fabric that had been stitched around this post-Reformation order was beginning to unravel, tugged by new economic forces beyond the ability of any one man to control. Rapid demographic growth was partly to blame. The population of Wiltshire in 1620 was about 80,000 and growing annually by 3%. Land, the means for sustenance as well as social advance, was in short supply and a resulting rise in food prices became inevitable. A run of poor harvests made the situation still worse. Between 1626 and 1630 the price of wheat rose 40%. Since more money had now to be found for the purchase of cereals, there was little left over for cheese, meat and the clothing produced in the mills of the

Avon. Unemployment rose, not just in the woollen industry, but also amongst the farmers of the clay. The rise in population caused deforestation and reclamation of land from the waste, but those forced to farm these more marginal lands were denied the right to self-sufficiency and so rapidly joined the ranks of the poor. Subdivision of holdings, the consequence of large families, commonly made farms uneconomic, and rendered them vulnerable to purchase by the rich. Acres of chalk downland and clay vale were snatched from the common man and became the haunt of the imported gentry. Royal forest land, too, was up for sale, available at a price to those with the ready money to pay. Land, for some, was the golden path to greater wealth, but for others, forced to exist on what was left, it was the thorny ground to economic ruin.

Worse was to follow. Aggravating this rural upheaval was the enclosure of the common field, the age old system through which medieval man had farmed the village lands. Sheep runs required less labour than crop cultivation, and profit minded landlords were quick to take advantage of the period's beckoning opportunities. Seemingly callous men, with no thought for their tenants, were turning their rolling acres into vast pastures, displacing whole communities in their zeal to widen their sources of profit. Soon the evicted would throng the Avon's highways and another cause of poverty and vagrancy was born. Forests, too, were enclosed and grazing rights destroyed. Melksham and Pewsham forests, ancient hunting lands of medieval Kings, virtually disappeared in the first three decades of the century. From Trowbridge to Amesbury, and Marlborough to Malmesbury, it was to be much the same: exploitation of the lower folk in the quest for financial gain.

The prosperity of the cloth industry, was threatened too, this time by forces from outside the county. Wiltshire's industry had long felt the shadows of competition, particularly from Devon and Somerset. But hasty and unwarranted interference from London was doing most damage. In 1614, James I granted Cockayne, a London Alderman, the right to dye and finish cloth before its export to the continent. Unwisely he supported this grant of a monopoly by banning the export of undyed cloth, the product on which Wiltshire's exporters largely relied. Additional resentment was caused in the 1630's by the appointment of government inspectors to examine the quality of cloth. One such appointee, Anthony Wither, too zealous in his work, was thrown into the Avon during a bout of Wiltshire stubbornness. The Thirty Years War on the Continent, by virtually closing the avenues for exports, stoked the unemployment. This, of course, came as a godsend to the recruiting sergeants. Many of those worst affected, the urban middle men, like the Salisbury clothier, Edmund Stephens, joined the King's or Westminster's armies out of sheer financial necessity. Yet behind all this turmoil is a picture of hard work, of industrious spinners, weavers and fullers employed in the mills of the Avon and Nadder valleys, and probably impervious to the politics of the time.

Religious discord was to play its part. Controversy had been endemic in England since the Reformation and none were immune from its consequences. The ideological debate might have been beyond the comprehension of many, but the organisational changes that took place at parish level had affected the poor as much as the rich. The Elizabethan prayer book had instilled conformity in Sunday worship and helped to marginalise both Papism and Puritanism. Those who refused to attend church could be fined a shilling a week and might additionally suffer the disapproval of their God-fearing neighbours. For a while at least, something approaching religious uniformity returned and the muddy waters of spiritual upheaval began to calm.

But twenty years before the outbreak of war, it had begun again. In 1635 William Laud had been appointed as Canterbury's Archbishop and a new bout of reform was unleashed. Determined to elevate the image of the parish priest and deepen the mysticism of church worship, he had ordered the railing of altars in an attempt to separate the parson from his flock. Interpreted as a deliberate swing towards Catholicism, this ill-timed move caused the Puritans to rush to the barricades of religious defence and another cause of war was slowly hatched. The licensing of Sunday sports, another of the age's religious innovations, was fiercely opposed in the more puritanical areas in the county's north-west.

Attempts to improve the standards of education of the parish priest were greeted more sympathetically. The poet George Herbert, a distant relative of the Pembrokes of Wilton, and rector of Bemerton from 1630 to 1633, had advised priests to become: *'all to their parish, and not only a pastor but a lawyer also and a physician'*, while parishioners were encouraged to say their amens thoughtfully and not in a *'slubbering fashion, gaping or scratching the head or spitting'*.

Upheavals in town and countryside led to protest. Petition, not riot, was to be the chosen weapon. In 1620 unemployed Wiltshire cloth workers petitioned Whitehall for redress of their grievances, but spoke the language of moderation in their letter to the King: *'To starve is woeful, to steal ungodly and to beg unlawful'*.[6]

This appeal was largely ignored. In the countryside, however, protest was sometimes more than vocal. Enclosure by agreement had been reluctantly accepted, but a spate of arbitrary enclosure in the 1630's and the continued sale of forest lands became too much for local men to endure. Events on the common land outside Malmesbury were typical of the decade's incidents. Leasing the land from the town, the enclosers were suddenly faced by a crowd *'of the meanest and beasest sort of people'*. Led by a baker and a blacksmith, the protesters assembled and *'threw down gates and stiles, pulling down hedges and fences'*.

Levelling and destruction of hedges became increasingly common. At Winterslow some yeomen pulled up 83 lugs of quickset and 180 of dead hedge in just four hours. And at Great Wishford a group of levellers, adorned with red feathers, paraded for a day in a disputed field. But only minor damage was reported, and everywhere protest was generally spasmodic and largely ineffective.

In such circumstances, the distant clouds of impending war were long ignored as an irrelevant and insignificant distraction.

---

[6] 'Petition from the men of Wiltshire'. Wiltshire Public Records Office.

The local politics of change, threatening the livelihood of local people, were of far greater concern. Only for the county's M.P.s and men of social station did events in London have any meaning. Carried back from the capital by returning squires, the nation's bitter rows and squabbles would be eventually mimicked in regional versions within Wiltshire's scattered towns, and laid on parlour tables for men to share. Inevitably the moods and opinions of those most involved would at last rub off on their tenants, and simpler folk might then take sides.

For this the social structure of the time was largely to blame. Pre-war society was hierarchical, glued by respect for superiors and knitted in unquestioned subservience. *'As it is a thing required by law and reason that children bear the honour and reverence to their natural parents which is commanded'*, Thomas Beard had written in 1597, *'so it is necessary...that all subjects perform that duty of honour and obedience to their Lords, Princes and Kings'*.

Yet that society was never rigid. Wealth, not birth, provided the means and avenues for social advancement, and those with ambition could generally ascend. Wiltshire's own experience in the preceding 100 years had amply demonstrated how rapidly the successful tradesman could acquire the styles and comforts of the upper classes - and even vie with the aristocracy for public office. Ownership of one's own coat of arms became the ultimate goal, enabling those who reached the highest pinnacles to distinguish themselves from those they left behind. Ennoblement might even follow, permitting the favoured to strut like lordly peacocks in the company of the Earls of Pembroke and Hertford, the two principal peers of the county, and themselves only second generation aristocrats. Jealous Lord Stourton, member of a much older Wiltshire lordly family, but bypassed in the Tudor distribution of honours, would sound his horn derisively whenever he passed the gates of Wilton. Such men might then become obsessed with preserving their marks of status, complaining bitterly of anything that could blur their lofty stature. In 1621 a Hampshire M.P. opposed legislation that obliged the families of gentry to wear broadcloth in winter. *'So little betwixt us and our servants,'* he moaned, *'...a gentleman should not know his wife from his chambermaid'.*[7]

Social mobility could also be downward. The unlucky and imprudent could fall with a crash into the quagmire of pauperism, and become almost indistinguishable from the landless masses. This lowly sector of society, estimated at less than 10% of the county's population, and expanding almost daily as a result of enclosure and industrial unemployment, was becoming increasingly costly to support. The Elizabethan Poor Law had made parishes responsible for the sustenance and relief of the poor, placing the burden on the parish officials to find the means and methods. Faced by the rising cost and numbers on its lists, these officials normally refused to assist those who were unable to prove either birth or connection with the parish, and even more of the unfortunate classes were found on the county's lanes.

Vagrancy and poverty might be a frequent fate for the less fortunate, but generally the inhabitants of towns were better shielded against the vicissitudes of earthly life. Greater ranges of employment and apprenticeship would offer some protection against complete impoverishment. But trade downturns could always intervene, rocking the affluence and stability of even the most solid urban communities. Salisbury, ranked at the end of the 16th century as the 16th wealthiest town in the nation, had a population of about 8,000, most engaged in the cloth industry and associated trades. Deliberately planned around its chequer blocks, it lacked the winding street pattern of most medieval towns and seems to have been regarded as a generally pleasant place to live. The Reverend Pelate, chaplain to Lord Coleraine, the owner of nearby Longford Castle, is more than complimentary in his description, sounding more like a modern travel brochure than a portrayer of fact:

> *'The city is well inhabited, and as well provided for by markets and fairs with all things foreign and domestic. It*

---

[7] Carlton, C. 'Going to the Wars'.

*has been styled the English Venice (as Venice the Italian
Salisbury) from its rivers running along every street and
exceeds Venice in its church tower and prospect.'* [8]

Within this lattice work of streets weavers, fullers, dyers,
drapers and the craftsmen of a dozen other trades lived in close
proximity. Cloth was stretched after fulling or hung to dry in the
tiny yards behind the tenements, and the horizons of these men
seldom stretched beyond the outer edges of their city or the
concerns of their particular trade. Working life was controlled and
directed by the Guilds, who increasingly came to dominate the
city's political life. Here was a parochial world, as limited as the
rural village and just as unchanging.

But the countryside was never far away. In all but the most
congested central areas of the city, men grew fruit and vegetables
on intensively farmed allotments, while pigs and cattle were kept in
urban stalls. On market days animals from the grazing land that
fringed the city would be driven through the streets and penned for
sale in the large open space that is still the hub of Salisbury's busy
centre. Monitoring the whole process, like a vigilant school
prefect, was the tall spire of St Mary's Cathedral and the clerical
world of the Close.

Devizes and Marlborough were considerably smaller,
numbering no more than 2,000 souls apiece. Both had grown up as
market towns in the shadow of castles and both revealed the same
urban vibrancy as their much larger counterpart in the south.
Marlborough, one of the homes of the Seymour family, Wiltshire's
political giants, was the more elegant, a fact which Celia Fiennes,
writing later that century, was keen to point out:

*'Marlborough looks very fine, with a good river that
turns many mills: its buildings are good and compact, one
very large street where stands the Market Place and*

---

[8] Pelate, H, The Rev. 'The Longford MSS'. Archives of Longford Castle.

Town Hall;....it's of a great length including the two parishes and the town stands itself on a high hill. [9]

Wiltshire's other boroughs had fared less well. Places like Bedwyn, Hindon, Downton and Heytesbury, with few advantages apart from their earlier clerical or lay patronage, had decreased in size. Chippenham, Warminster and Trowbridge vied with the larger towns as centres of the county's social and economic life. Wilton, in the shire's south and partly eclipsed by Salisbury's rapid growth, had once been the Wessex capital.

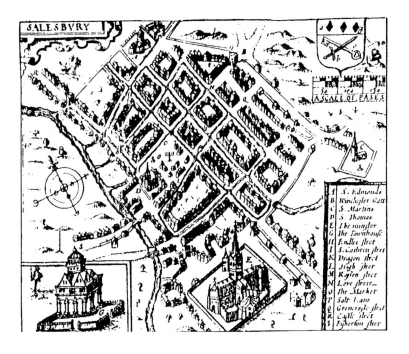

17th century map of Salisbury

---

[9] Fiennes, Celia. 'Through England on a side saddle in the time of William and Mary'.

The age old routines of town and country were about to be disordered by the arrival of this sudden war. For the victims of pre-war economic change, war would appear as a God-send, the solution to unemployment and distress. Men joined the new armies for a variety of reasons: political, social and personal. But for many, the motives would be less lofty, the chance to start afresh and fill their empty bellies. The lanes and highways of Wiltshire would be suddenly cleared of the casualties of progress, and unemployment nearly disappeared.

But adverse effects would soon be felt. Fields were forsaken, workshops deserted and trade disrupted. The parsonage at Cholderton would be typical of many. Abandoned by its war-going incumbent, it was rendered almost uninhabitable by neglect. Rectors would be forcibly ejected from Parish pulpits for preaching a disfavoured creed. A shortage of horses made ploughing impossible. And soon the bitter cry of widowed women would ring through Wiltshire's hamlets, and the lanes would be thronged by a new batch of paupers and the wounded men of other counties' battles.

Yet life would not be permanently altered by the struggle. The seasons would continue to pass with immutable regularity, water wheels still turned, and countless ambitions would remain unfulfilled, much as they had done for centuries past. Memories of civil war would eventually fade and become interred beneath a new crop of spring grown corn. War, despite the upsets of the time, was to be little more than a hiccup on a landscape of solid resilience.

---

[9] Fiennes, Celia. 'Through England on a side saddle in the time of William and Mary'.

2

'With many libellous invectives against the state'

'*EVERY county has its civil war*[1], Lucy Hutchinson's comment is as valid in Wiltshire as in any other of England's divided shires. In every county, with the possible exception of distant Cumbria and the more fortunate regions of East Anglia and the Thames estuary, the fabric of society was to be torn apart by political and religious issues beyond the comprehension of many and equally beyond the ability of any one man to solve.

Initially, it seemed to be nothing more than the age old squabble amongst the ruling classes. But when at last it seemed that only a military solution would be possible and the need for muscle became apparent, the argumentative factions cruelly played upon the fears of lesser men, and used their social status and powers of persuasion to call upon the lower orders for support. Ultimately the ploughman and the carpenter would be as much involved as the aristocrat and his lady.

Soon this all enveloping conflict would start to challenge society's existing norms and codes, throwing into question some of the established values of the time and creating less acceptable standards of behaviour. Faced by the horrors of war and largely concerned with self-survival and the protection of personal property, men would become more bestial and instinctive in behaviour. The quarrel would sadly pit brother against brother,

---

[1] Hutchinson, Lucy. 'The Life of Col. J. Hutchinson'. Page 121.

father against son, and split the ordered society of pre-war England into two irreconcilable halves:

> *...Parents and children, brothers, kindred, I and dear friends have the seed of difference and division abundantly sowed in them.....I have heard foul language and desperate quarrelling even between old and entire friends, and how we can thus stand and not fall, certainly God must needs work a miracle!'* [2]

Henry Oxinden, a Kentish landowner, wrote to a London friend in June 1642. His comments were as true in Wiltshire as any other troubled county.

Even before war had become inevitable, these leaders of the county had begun their personal war of words, employing the Sunday pulpit and the eloquence of fiery preachers to purchase the hearts and minds of the masses. Puritanical speakers railed at their congregations for hours, instilling the virtues of Parliament's cause and reminding their listeners of their spiritual duty to resist God's enemies. Most favoured amongst the biblical texts employed to implant the seeds of insurrection in the slumbering masses were two apparent calls to arms, ingeniously misquoted but used with effect. One, from Exodus, was utilised to justify intra-family strife and condone both patricide and fratricide in the service of God:

> *'Consecrate yourselves today to the Lord, even every man upon his son and upon his brother; that he may bestow upon you a blessing this day.'* (Exodus Ch.32, v.29)

The other attempted to infuse guilt into those who remained inactive:

> *'Curse ye bitterly the inhabitants thereof; because they came not to the help of the Lord, to the help of the Lord against the mighty.'* (Judges Ch.5, v.23)

---

[2] Gardiner, D. 'The Oxinden and Peyton Letters'. Page 174.

Fed in large handfuls to the gullible and God fearing, these clarion calls were largely successful, but were promptly condemned by the other side, amongst them Lord Clarendon.

> *'These men...infused seditious inclination into the hearts of men against the present government of the church, with many libellous invectives against the State too...they contained themselves with no bounds, and as freely and without control inveighed against the person of the King...to incense and stir up the people against their most gracious sovereign.'* [3]

Equally, the King's men, arguing in support of God's anointed government, extolled the virtues of the rule of law and an ordered church where each man knew his place.

A county's ultimate allegiance, therefore, was largely dictated by its administrative and cultural leaders, the landed aristocracy and the lesser gentry who dominated the shire's affairs. In East Anglia, a region strongly influenced by the puritanical zeal of the Netherlands, Parliament dominated the debate and support for the King was minimal. But in England's far west, susceptible to the influence of the Irish Catholics, Royalism was the dominant hue. The counties in between, split almost equally between two rival philosophies, became fractious debating grounds - and ultimately the battle ground where the conflict would be settled militarily.

In Wiltshire, the feud was to be more personal than political and religious, and the national conflict would be partially distorted by the long-standing rivalry between the county's two most influential families. The Seymours, headed by William, Marquis of Hertford, had risen to royal favour in the reign of Henry VIII, providing that insatiable monarch with one of his six wives. Custody of his son Edward, had been conferred on Edward Seymour, 1st Earl of Hertford and Duke of Somerset. As Lord Protector, he had become the most powerful individual in the kingdom. The family's

---

[3] Clarendon, Earl of. 'The History of the Rebellion and Civil Wars in England'. Vol II, Bk VI, Page 370.

fortunes had been eclipsed following the ambitious man's execution, but time and fortune had restored them to a position of significance.

The 3rd Earl, enjoying the full favour of the Court despite some earlier indiscretions, served the King as governor of the household of the Prince of Wales. His qualifications for this honoured position, according to Clarendon, were entirely suitable. Hertford, it seems,

> '...was a man of great honour, great interest in fortune and estate, he had carried himself with notable steadiness from the beginning of the Parliament in the support and defence of the King's power and dignity.....he was of an age not fit for much activity and fatigue, and loved, and was even wedded so much to, his ease that he loved his book above all exercise; and had even contracted such a laziness of mind that he had no delight in an open and liberal conversation.' [4]

In 1640, in recognition of his service, he was created Marquis of Hertford, and in February 1642 offered the Lord Lieutenantship of the county, a position previously normally enjoyed by members of the rival family. He declined this position, largely on the grounds that Charles had not accepted the Militia Bill, the controversial measure by which Parliament had unilaterally taken responsibility for the nation's security. This rejection of further regally bestowed honours encouraged the Parliamentary leaders to hope that Hertford would emerge as one of their champions. They were, however, to be disappointed: in the early summer he climbed down from the fence and joined the King at York.

His brother, Francis Seymour, had served the county as one of the shire M.P.s for twenty years. During his early career in the Commons, he had strenuously opposed the King's wilder policies and earned the monarch's anger. But his swing from the

---

[4] Clarendon, Earl of. 'The History of the Rebellion and Civil Wars in England'. Vol II, Bk VI, Page 385.

parliamentary party in the months following was violent and articulate. Now openly supportive of the King, he was rewarded for his loyalty by a peerage in 1641 and took his seat in the Lords as Baron Seymour of Trowbridge. Active thereafter on behalf of the King, he effectively abandoned Wiltshire for national concerns, leaving his wife and daughter at the family home in Marlborough.

The influence of these two men was to a large extent neutralised by the Herberts of Wilton, holders of the Earldom of Pembroke and Montgomery. Philip, the 4th Earl, had equally enjoyed the King's favour. For much of the reign, until his hasty dismissal in July 1641, he had served as Lord Chamberlain, but had lost that office as a result of his open opposition to Strafford. Throughout his tenure, he had displayed rare skills of self-survival, a cocktail of resilience and affability that earned the respect of even Clarendon.

> *'He was exceedingly beloved in the court, because he never desired to get that for himself which others laboured for, but was still ready to promote the pretences of worthy men.'* [5]

Others claim that he was foul mouthed and bad tempered. He apparently broke his staff of office over the head of a courtier. Experience of the King's caprices, however, and the shock of passing events perhaps eroded some of this man's earlier self-constraint and he becomes a victim of events as much as a champion. Both Houses had then nominated him for the vacant post of Lord Steward, but this had been vetoed by the unforgiving King. From then on, Pembroke marched in Parliament's camp, guided not so much by Roundhead sentiments as by personal ambition and hostility towards his Royalist rival in Wiltshire. In February 1642, after Seymour's refusal, Parliament appointed Pembroke as Wiltshire's Lord Lieutenant, a post that his family had held almost without interruption until 1640. In March he was a member of the Parliamentary delegation visiting the King at

---

[5] Clarendon, Earl of. 'The History of the Rebellion and Civil Wars in England'. Vol II, Bk VI, Page 388.

Newmarket in a vain attempt to gain his consent to recent measures passed by Parliament. But he was a Parliamentarian by default, not by conviction, a point that Clarendon was at pains to emphasise:

> *'When the decrees of the Star chamber...were called in question...his fear, which was the passion always predominant in him above all his choler and rage, prevailed so far over him, that he gave himself up into the hands of the Lord Say to dispose of him as he thought fit.* [6]

Behind these powerful families ranged the county's lesser nobility and many of the gentry. Charles had the undying support of Thomas, 2nd Lord Arundell of Wardour, and his wife, the Lady Blanche. Convinced Royalists in every respect, they had responded in 1639 with £500 to the King's request for money and troops with which to fight the Scots. They were to be just as generous in the weeks ahead, eventually turning up at the King's war court at York with a troop of horse recruited entirely at their own expense. Few others would be as lavish in their support. The Longs of Wraxall in Somerset would be the exception. Sir James, amateur entomologist and naturalist, kept his sword in his hand throughout the war and was appointed Sheriff of Wiltshire for his efforts. His uncle, Sir Robert, enjoyed the Queen's personal favour and served as secretary to the Council of the Prince of Wales. Beside these shining champions, the remaining adherents were colourless paintings in a gallery of inactivity: the Thynnes of Longleat, Talbots of Lacock, Scropes of Castle Combe, and the recently ennobled Leys of Teffont Evias, now Earls of Marlborough. The Penruddockes of Compton Chamberlayne were to rouse from their sleep after the King's execution. Poor Sir John lost his head years later for leading a rising against Cromwellian iron rule.

---

[6] Clarendon, Earl of. 'The History of the Rebellion and Civil Wars in England'. Vol II, Bk VI, Page 400.

If aristocratic sentiment was predominantly Royalist in Wiltshire, the allegiance of the county's 34 M.P.s was overwhelmingly Roundhead in sentiment. Only 12 were openly Royalist and, of these, only 2, Walter Smyth of Bedwyn and George Lowe of Calne, are known to have served in the King's Oxford Parliament, the rival body that sat throughout the war in support of the King. Of the rest, only Robert Hyde, cousin of the great historian, Lord Clarendon, made any energetic attempt to win Wiltshire to the Royalist cause.

Many of the remaining 22, however, assumed positions of importance in the Parliamentary camp, either serving as local generals in the field, or else representing their county in the deliberations at Westminster.

Sir Edward Hungerford, one of Chippenham's two M.P.s, would emerge as the county's military commander, but his role was frequently challenged and was ultimately to be usurped by more capable soldiers. Most vociferous of the Westminster politicians was Sir Henry Ludlow, shire representative, a man of outspoken views and unbending principles. In May he was rebuked by the Speaker for claiming that Charles was not worthy to be King. Royalist wits immortalised this in verse:

'Who speaks of peace, quoth Ludlow, hath neither sense nor reason.

For I ne'er spoke in this House but once, and then I spoke high treason.' [7]

At his back, offering more tacit support, were Sir Neville Poole of Malmesbury and John Evelyn, representing Ludgershall in the Long Parliament, both of whom were to play prominent parts during the coming months. Yet all this is still some way in the future. Until early July 1642, when isolated sparks in distant regions threatened to ignite a national bonfire, it was still possible to believe that a peaceful settlement might yet be secured. The thoughts and opinions of those about to arm lie buried in Wiltshire

---

[7] Quoted in Waylen, J. 'The History of Marlborough'.

beneath the dust of time. Choosing which side to support was often a long and arduous process and an encyclopedia of factors might have governed the eventual decision. A deep conviction in the sanctity of kingship, fear of social change and upheaval, and dread of puritanism provided three powerful magnets to the regal cause. But there were many in the kingly ranks who did not adhere to all three, and some were strongly opposed to the wild arrogance of the King and the religious practices which he had espoused. Sir Edmund Verney, a sincere and deeply religious man who later carried the King's standard at Edgehill, probably voiced the feelings of many.

> *'I do not like the quarrel, and do heartily wish that the King would yield and consent to what they desire. Yet I have eaten his bread, and served him near 30 years, and will not do so base a thing as to forsake him, and choose rather to lose my life.'* [8]

He did. Killed during the fury of the fighting, Verney continued to clutch the standard in death as firmly as in life. To rescue the flag, Captain John Smith had to hack off the dead man's hand. Verney was just one of many martyrs for a cause in which they only partly believed. Similarly there were Episcopalians on Parliament's side, men who saw the rash excesses of Charles' rule as far more dangerous than Puritanism, and nowhere was social class the main determining factor in securing eventual allegiance.

Then, like condemned men waking on the morning of their execution, the factions had time to reflect on their deeds and shudder in the dawn of expected war. In February the leading men of Salisbury petitioned Westminster *'for redress of grievances for those whose throats were exposed to the sword of the savage and barbarous foe.'* [9] Fears of change and the upheavals that war would bring were paramount in the minds of thoughtful men. The

---

[8] Gardiner, S.R. 'History of the Great Civil War'. Vol I, Page 4.

[9] Uncatalogued document in Wiltshire Local Studies Library, Trowbridge.

The Allegiance Of Wiltshire's Members

For the King	
Name	Constituency
Sir Walter Smith	Bedwyn
Richard Harding	Bedwyn
George Lowe	Calne
Sir Edward Griffith	Downton
Robert Reynolds	Hindon
William Ashburnham	Ludgershall
Anthony Hungerford	Malmesbury
Sir James Thynne	Shire
Sir Francis Seymour	Marlborough
Sir William Saville	Old Sarum
Robert Hyde	Salisbury
William Pleydell	Wootton Bassett

For the Parliament	
Name	Constituency
Hugh Roger	Calne
Sir Edward Baynton	Chippenham
Sir Edward Hungerford	Chippenham
Sir Henry Ludlow	Shire
Robert Jenner	Cricklade
Thomas Hodges	Cricklade
Sir Neville Poole	Malmesbury
Alexander Thistlethwayte	Downton
Colonel Edward Baynton	Devizes
Robert Nicolas	Devizes
Thomas Moore	Heytesbury
Edward Ashe	Heytesbury
Thomas Bennet	Hindon
Sir John Evelyn	Ludgershall
Sir Henry Vane	Wilton
Sir Benjamin Rudyard	Wilton
John Franklyn	Marlborough
Robert Cecil	Old Sarum
Edward Poole	Wootton Bassett
Michael Oldsworth	Salisbury
William Wheeler	Westbury
John Ashe	Westbury

Earl of Pembroke was just one of many to anticipate the destruction of the old social order.

> *'We hear every fellow say in the streets as we pass by in our coaches, that they hope to see us on foot shortly,....and be as good men as the Lords, and I think they will....if we take this course.'* [10]

Others were equally ashen about the loss of comfort. Those about to fight would be obliged to give up soft beds for the damp soil of a windy hillside and fine food for scraps of bread and ditch water. Those they left behind were concerned about the absence of tenants and non payment of rates. And pamphleteers were in no doubt about the consequences of war. One is particularly full of foreboding.

> *'And let thy tears run down,*
> *To see the rent,*
> *Between the robes and Crown,*
> *War like a serpent, has its head got in,*
> *And will not end as soon as it did begin.'* [11]

But then the eloquence, oratory and self pity had to stop. In April Sir John Hotham refused to allow the King to enter Hull. The physical dispute over ownership of the nation's fabric was about to commence. The sword would now replace both the mouth and the pen.

---

[10] Sidney, R, Earl of Leicester. Sydney Papers. Ed. R.W. Blencone (1825) Page XXI.

[11] Warburton, E.G.B. 'Memoirs of Prince Rupert and the Cavaliers'. (1849) Vol I, Page 226.

3

'Tosspots and ruffians, rogues and vagabonds'

THE leading men of the county would now become the pivot of support and the recruiting sergeants by which men would be found to fill the ranks of the opposing armies. The problem was to find legal methods of procuring the required numbers, of somehow compelling men to join the ranks without resorting to impressment. And always there was a shortage of money with which to pay and arm these unready followers of Mars.

The most concrete source of soldiers was the Trained band, the local defence force based upon the Saxon fyrd. Since those distant times, all the able bodied men of the county had been obliged to attend musters, theoretically once a month, at assembly points chosen by the Lords Lieutenants and their deputies, and there drill and train for the defence of their home county. Those called were usually expected to provide equipment and weapons, a harsh demand on people often unable to provide even the most essential requirements of life. Theoretically a county assembly of the trained bands could produce impressive numbers: a muster role for Wiltshire in 1639 includes more than 5,000 names! Both sides, anxious to raise troops at short notice, jockeyed to gain control of these local militia. Nationally, Parliament triumphed, having secured the allegiance of most of the Lord Lieutenants, the only men able to officially muster the groups.

But these trained bands were impressive on paper only. Such forces could not be compelled to serve outside their county's boundaries, providing a limitation to their effectiveness as mobile armies. Secondly, the activity on the village green was often little more than a showy pantomime, a comedy performed by disinterested amateurs. Discipline was frequently poor and military skills absent, even amongst the officers of the corps. A contemporary report gives an idea of what sometimes happened:

> '...officers love their bellies so well as that they are loath to take too much pains about disciplining their soldiers......after a little careless hurrying over of their postures.....they make them charge their muskets, and so prepare to give their captains a brave volley of shot at his entrance to the inn.' [1]

Few accounts exist of the activities of Wiltshire's bands. Some speak of ill-discipline, disunity and a sad lack of Wiltshire pride. In October 1631, for instance, 20 men of Warminster were called out to assist in the eviction of a troublesome tenant from lands near Corsley. The Privy Council later wrote to the Earl of Pembroke, complaining bitterly of the men's behaviour.

> '...Directions have been so far neglected that the service could not be performed. For there was sent only one company of four score men under Captain William Wallis, but the pikemen without corslets and only four of the shot well provided, the rest wanting either powder, or bullets, or both, and their match not fit for service.' [2]

Clearly incapable of providing even a policing action within their own borders, these men could hardly be relied upon to win a war. The arguing factions would need to look for securer means of raising the numbers required.

Both sides, therefore, relied instead on the recruitment zeal of their supporters, men who could use their status in the county to raise whole regiments of horse and foot. Invariably a member of

---

[1] Carlton, C. 'Going to the Wars'.

[2] Kerridge, E. 'The Revolts in Wiltshire against Charles I'. Wiltshire Archaeological Magazine.

the gentry would act as recruiting agent, offering to raise and equip a stated number of men from amongst his own retainers or men of the immediate neighbourhood. Those summoned to his colours found it difficult to refuse. With something of a semi-feudal hold over these lesser beings, the county's leaders were able to bring considerable pressure to bear upon their tenants. In an age when obedience and subservience formed the glue which held the social fabric in place, few men had the gall to resist their betters' demands and threats of eviction from homes would generally persuade the most reluctant to conform.

But the raising of private armies was illegal and a lawful way of recruiting had first to be found. The King's chosen device was the Commission of Array, a medieval procedure with a document in Latin, which was impressed with the Great Seal. One was issued for each county or major town and contained the names of all leading men who it was anticipated would be prepared to raise troops for the regal cause. Heading the list of regal commissioners in Wiltshire were Lord Hertford and Sir Francis Seymour. Those addressed were summoned to a meeting at the home of one of the named, where the following instructions were read to the assembled men.

> 'Charles by the grace of God...To our trusted and well beloved...greeting. We do hereby constitute and appoint you to be Captain of one company of foot in the regiment of our trusty and well beloved Colonel...You are forthwith to impress and retain of such as will willingly and voluntarily serve us for our pay, and for the defence of our Royal person, the two houses of parliament, the Protestant religion, the law of the land, the liberty and propriety of the subject...to bring them to our standard, and to cause them to be duly exercised in arms...'[3]

Armed with this authority, Lords Stourton and Arundell managed to raise about 100 men from their Wiltshire estates while

---

[3] Uncatalogued document in Wiltshire Local Studies Library, Trowbridge.

George Vaughan raised an entire regiment in the county's south. Hertford and his brother, however, met with so much opposition in their own scattered lands that the *'marquis considered his own personal safety endangered, and accordingly repaired towards Somersetshire'* [4]. On August 12th, he was appointed as the King's Lieutenant\General in the west with instructions to raise an army within the western counties. Markedly more successful in the bordering county, he soon put together the Cavaliers' first army in the south, a force composed of almost no Wiltshire men.

This, however, hardly removed the danger, a fact which John Ashe, a landowner on the Somerset border, was quick to point out. Writing to the Speaker of the Commons on the 8th, he concludes:

> *'..very probable it is that they go about to get more strength to come into Wilts,...and a strong report hath been these ten days that they will very speedily put their commission in execution about Sarum and Warminster....Sir, we are lost and spoiled if we have not commanders; for though the country people be stout and resolved, yet we are not able to maintain the cause and support our courage without expert men.'* [5]

Parliament chose to rely on an equally dubious procedure. In the Spring M.P.s, hurried through a Militia Ordinance, snatching control of the militia from the King and appointing their own Lords Lieutenants in place of the King's earlier nominees. In July Sir Edward Hungerford and Sir John Evelyn were sent down from Westminster to execute this ruling, and they were followed in August by the Earl of Pembroke, Lord Lieutenant and now Governor of the Isle of Wight as well. Like the King, Parliament chose to issue commissions to individuals, instructing them to raise companies or even whole regiments, or alternatively to accept the offers of sympathetic gentry who volunteered to recruit at their own expense. But, unlike the King, Westminster offered financial

---

[4] Waylen, S. 'History of Marlborough'.

[5] Waylen, S. 'History of the Devizes'.

inducements: each commissioned captain who undertook to raise a full troop of horse was paid £1,100 'mounting money', enough to purchase horses, arms and equipment for the troops. Officers of foot units were paid similar sums of 'levy money', most of which was spent on wages for their men.

Impressment was a less favoured method of raising numbers. Rarely used at the start of war, it would become more fashionable later when the supply of volunteers began to dwindle. But Wiltshire's recruiting officers were ever active at the roadsides and taverns, and many of those in the ranks at the start of the war were less than willing to join. All too often those impressed were the dregs of society as one near contemporary admits:

> *'When service happens,'* he explains, *'we disburden the prisons of thieves, we rob the taverns and alehouses of tosspots and ruffians, we scour both town and country of rogues and vagabonds.'* [6]

Such men made impressive numbers but uninspiring soldiers. But numbers in the Wiltshire ranks were never great. Perhaps 2,000 men, just 3% of the county's population, were in arms at the start of war. The total was never to rise much above that level. War would remain a minority pastime and the humbler sorts were to become mere tokens, playing pieces of little intrinsic value in a game of lordly virtues. The hearts and souls of loved ones and families would be torn apart as they watched their men depart and the sorrowing would then commence.

Parliament's efforts and the failure of the bibliophile Lord Hertford to execute the King's Commission had effectively placed the county's main towns in Parliament's hands. 400 foot, completely armed, were mustered at Marlborough, denying the Royalists any access to the town's store of weapons, and a similar body of men paraded provocatively in the streets of Devizes. Simultaneously John Hungerford assembled a company of infantry at Chippenham. Only Salisbury seemed to be in any overt danger.

---

[6] Carlton, C. 'Going to the Wars'.

At the end of July, Thomas Lawes, the city's mayor, received a message from the King with instructions to publicly read it to the community. Unsure about what to do, he asked Sergeant Robert Hyde, the town's active Royalist M.P. for advice. A faithful adherent to the King's cause, he reminded the mayor of his duty and prompted the official to publish the royal proclamation.

A sudden pawn in a game of immeasurable proportions and uncertain consequences, poor Thomas was imprisoned for his misdemeanour. But Hyde was ultimately to pay the penalty. A certain Whateley, having openly labelled the Parliamentarians as rebels and traitors, was sentenced by the justices and jailed within the city. Instantly he appealed to his M.P., who personally intervened and bailed the outspoken man. Reported to the Commons, this single-minded M.P. was summoned to Westminster to answer for his actions. The mayor eventually testified and Hyde was imprisoned in the Tower. To prevent any further Royalist seeds from germinating within the city, a company of hastily raised volunteers watched over Salisbury until troops commissioned by Pembroke arrived to police the city's streets.

With Hertford's departure into Somerset and the first clashes of the two field armies in the midlands, partisan activity in Wiltshire became less evident and something of the pre-war tone of life returned. But passions were now too inflamed and opinions too divided to allow a peaceful settlement. In late September, when distant fields had already been stained with English blood, the Royalists of Wiltshire issued their first public declaration of support for the King:

> *'...we hold ourselves most especially bound and engaged to defend and maintain with our lives and fortunes, according to our utmost ability, the Protestant religion....and also his Majesty's royal person and prerogative....These things being taken into our serious consideration, and the times now requiring us to declare ourselves, since we can no longer be at peace,...we profess to all the world that we cannot see or find any*

*other lawful way to free ourselves from the distresses we
are in, than by our best assistance of his Sacred Majesty
against all that oppose him.'* [7]

In October, the Commons, attempting to put the county and its
neighbours on a sounder wartime footing, appointed Pembroke as
their general in the west. But more a politician than a military man,
he was soon relieved of this arduous responsibility, and his place
was taken by Denzil Holles, one of Dorset's more active M.P.s.
The Parliamentarians kept constant vigil over the towns and
villages, reporting any signs of disturbance to the Commons, and
drilling the county's tiny militia. On November 2nd, Charles,
belatedly responding to the September declaration of support from
the Wiltshire Cavaliers, published another proclamation, offering
'grace, favour and pardon' to the people of the county, but
expressly excluded Sir John Evelyn of West Dean, Walter Long,
Sir Edward Hungerford and Sir Henry Ludlow from this generous
amnesty:

> *'Whereas we have taken notice that by the malice,
> industry and importunity of several ill affected and
> seditious persons in our county of Wilts, very many of our
> weak and seduced subjects of that our county have not
> only been drawn to exercise the militia, under colour of a
> pretended ordinance, but have made contribution of plate,
> money and horses towards the maintenance of the army
> now in rebellion against us...we do hereby offer our free
> and gracious pardon to all the inhabitants of our said
> county of Wilts for all offences concerning the premises
> committed against us.'* [8]

But in the closing days of November, just when the county's
inhabitants had resumed their earlier pace, the storm clouds at last

---

[7] 'Declaration to His Majesty'. Wiltshire Local Studies Library, Trowbridge.

[8] 'The Agreements made between His Majesty and the knights, gentlemen, etc of
Wiltshire'. Wiltshire Local Studies Library, Trowbridge.

built up and gathered menacingly above Marlborough. The deadly game of war would at last begin.

4

'A large silk flag with a red cross, and two lions passant'

ON August 22nd King Charles raised his standard on Nottingham's castle hill, *'with little other ceremony than the sound of drum and trumpet'* [1]. An eye witness has left an account of the event that marked the official birth of the war.

> *'...His Majesty came into the castle yard, accompanied with the prince (Rupert) and Maurice his brother, the Duke of Richmond, and divers other courtiers and cavaliers, and finding out the highest pointed hill in the yard...the standard was brought in there and erected. At which time all the courtiers and spectators flung up their caps and whooped, crying, "God save King Charles and hang up the Roundheads".'* [2]

But the war which burst into bloom that day had already started, nurtured through the summer months in a sequence of regional quarrels and localised fighting. On April 23rd, Sir John Hotham, Parliament's governor in Kingston upon-Hull, had refused the King entry into the city, and the war's first siege lines were consequently formed. At the opposite end of the country, a similar stubborn streak produced another of the war's early heroes: Lord George Goring, who refused to surrender Portsmouth to Parliament's

---

[1] Hutchinson, Lucy. 'The Life of Col. J. Hutchinson'.

[2] Ibid.

Hampshire agents. He was not ejected until September 7th, two weeks after the war's official start.

In the period between these two coastal sieges, full-scale war rocked Dorset and Somerset, a region where unbridled Puritanism and ardent Royalism had found it difficult to co-exist. On 4th August a skirmish had taken place at Marshall's Elm in Somerset, the first setpiece action of any size in the south. It was followed a month later by more sustained fighting at Sherborne and Yeovil, this time by almost fully fledged armies that had grown like summer mushrooms on Somerset's damp levels. Leading the Royalist forces in this early contest of strength was Ralph, Lord Hopton, one of the county's M.P.s, and the Wiltshire magnate, Lord Hertford. Opposing them was William Russell, the Earl of Bedford, a man with considerable battle experience but few local connections.

Circumstance, not superior strategy, placed the laurels of victory in Bedford's lap. On 19th September, Hertford, *'having found just cause to discontinue the prosecution of such service, and being desirous to save the effusion of blood that must necessarily be spent',*[3] agreed to surrender the castle at Sherborne. Three days later, permitted to leave with his force untouched, he divided his command at Watchet, withdrawing his infantry and guns across the Bristol Channel into Wales while Lord Hopton with 50 dragoons and 160 horse marched west to assist Cornwall's leaderless Cavaliers.

These Royalist setbacks, occurring in quick succession at the very moment in which Charles was recruiting in Nottingham, robbed the King of much of his earlier optimism. Less than 300 men had joined him during his time in that city, a rate of recruitment so low that Sir Jacob Astley, later commander of the King's foot regiments, warned his master that: *'he could not give*

---

[3] Propositions propounded by the Marquis of Hertford to the Earl of Bedford'. MSS, BM.

any assurance against his Majesty being taken out of his bed, if the rebels should make a brisk attempt to that purpose.' [4]

In the days following, midlands men began to trickle in, brought to Nottingham in response to further calls. On 13th September, hoping to tap the more ardent Royalism of the Severn's valley and the Welsh borders, Charles set out for Derby at the head of just 4,500 men. A week later, he reached Shrewsbury. In those few days, his army had almost doubled in number, swollen by the loyal energies of his Cheshire and Shropshire supporters. Here then was recruited the army that was to fight at Edgehill, the first major battle of the war.

The army that opposed the King on that late October day was recruited in much the same way, drawn largely from the counties of the east. On September 9th, Robert Devereux, Earl of Essex, appointed to the command of Parliament's army, joined his men at Northampton, and the clash of the Titans seemed imminent.

But more than 6 weeks of cat and mouse manoeuvring were first to take place in the midlands, with the timing and direction of movement controlled and decided largely by the King. Worcester, the vital crossing point of the Severn and a link with the Cavaliers of Wales, was the King's next gain, occupied by his forces on 16th September. Powick Bridge, fought in the yellowing meadows to the south of the city just one week later, was a chance encounter and the war's first true battle. An undoubted Royalist victory, it sent shivers down the Parliamentary spine, and accounts of the action were wildly exaggerated:

'We had such a terrible report of this last night,' wrote Colonel Arthur Goodwin, a Roundhead officer, *'that I know not how many of our men were killed, and how many of our officers and commanders, that we were*

---

[4] Clarendon, Vol III, Bk I, Page 194.

all commanded to stand to our arms and watch all night in the field.' [5]

In fact, only 28 Roundheads had died in the battle, many of them as they tried to recross the river to safety. It had been a brief engagement, short by comparison with most of the war's later actions. But for those involved, men with no experience of fighting, it had been little less than a glimpse of Hell and a taste of the hereafter.

Powick, however, was to be a hollow victory. Worcester was almost indefensible and a Royalist evacuation soon followed. Only a small detachment of the Parliamentary army had been involved at Powick, and the bulk of Essex's slow moving force was near at hand. At noon on the 24th, Essex paraded his army through Worcester's streets. The cathedral and its contents were desecrated that evening in an orgy of religious fervour, and Roundhead soldiers dressed up in the torn surplices of the clergy.

Charles, fuelled by success at Powick, was anxious to reclaim his capital. More cautious hearts attempted to deflect the King, pointing out the dangers of leaving an enemy army unbeaten in his rear. But equally compelling reasons existed for striking towards the east. Capture of London, as well as giving the King access to the city's wealth, would sever Essex from his base of supplies and bring the City Roundheads tumbling to their knees. No amount of counter reasoning could dissuade him from his chosen path, and on 12th October, the royal army set out from Shrewsbury, heading south-east towards his target on the Thames.

Essex, unsure of the King's intentions, chose to remain at Worcester, and so failed to close the road to London. During those wasted days of inactivity, the King's army continued to grow. On the 19th, Charles was joined at Kenilworth by regiments from Lancashire and Wales, bringing his strength to almost 15,000.

---

[5] Carte MSS, Bodleian Library, No. EEEE 42.

Beyond lay the unguarded road to London and the reclamation of his throne.

News of his advance reached the capital, creating a whirlwind of panic in the city's streets. Chains were placed across the main thoroughfares and the trained bands were on almost constant vigil. Royalist sympathizers, wearing red ribbons on their hats, were just as active, parading in the city's streets and preventing a mob from pulling down the organ in St Paul's Cathedral. The dominantly Puritan hue of London and southern England seemed in danger of being washed away and replaced by the brighter colours of reviving Royalism.

On the 19th, stung by criticisms of his lethargy and poor judgement, Essex at last set out from Worcester, and, for a while, the two armies marched in parallel in a race towards the capital. Both armies moved equally slowly, averaging no more than ten miles a day. Beyond Warwick, the Royalists turned south-east towards the Thames, still a day's march ahead of the hunters, with their mood of optimism growing.

Now the paths at last began to converge. But the huntsmen were as blind as the hunted. Until the night of the 22nd, when a sudden meeting in the streets of Wormleighton caused a brief skirmish, neither commander had the slightest idea of the whereabouts of his adversary. The battle of Edgehill on the 23rd was fortuitous, the result of an unplanned collision between two armies engaged in a frantic rush to London.

Nearly 30,000 men stood in arms that day, one of the largest engagements fought on English soil. The King's army, each of its constituent regiments dressed in the fanciful colours of its colonel's choice, had occupied the ridge above Radway for most of that autumn morning. Essex's army, just as multi-coloured, lay a mile to the north-west, cautiously holding the lower ground near Kineton. The Parliamentary general was reluctant to strike the first blow, aware that this would be an unforgivable act of rebellion. But soon after 1 p.m., the Royalist army descended the ridge and minutes later the cavalry on both wings were thundering westwards in a furious assault on Parliament's unsure lines.

Essex's ranks melted in the heat of that steely charge. Within minutes, it seemed that Royalist arms had already triumphed: half the Roundhead army had left the field. But so too had much of the Royalist horse, intoxicated by success into wild pursuit of the fleeing enemy. The battle would be decided by those that remained: the entire Royalist infantry and seven shaky regiments of Parliamentary foot.

In the next few minutes, near defeat became near victory. For, finding themselves supported by thirteen troops of almost untouched horse who had remained detached at the edge of the field, the Roundhead lines were suddenly galvanised into a force of resistance by Thomas Ballard and John Meldrum, commanders of the foot. The Royalist euphoria, fed by their earlier success, was turned into panic by the unexpected Parliamentary advance that unexpectedly hit the infantry of the Royalist centre.

By 5 p.m., the field was smothered in darkness and the last sounds of battle slowly faded. Soon that tiny piece of rural England would again be silent, the stillness of the night broken only by the calls of the wild and the cries of the wounded. The war's first battle had ended in stalemate.

Edgehill was a national affair: men from the kingdom's more distant shires fighting alongside those from nearer home. Slowly reports of that dreadful battle and its casualties would filter through to those far off places, and the suspense and torment of waiting loved ones would commence. The emotions of the battle's survivors and their families lie unrecorded, but their feelings are as ageless and tender as those caught up in the agonies of later wars. Yet, in an age of snail-like communication and uncertain reporting, their ordeal was possibly worse.

Some accounts suggest that 5,000 were killed or wounded that day. But such figures are insupportable when measured against the total number of men engaged, and a figure of 1,000 dead and 2,000 wounded is far more probable. Whatever the number, the blood at Edgehill confirmed that men were prepared to die for their convictions. From now on, people would rely upon the power of the sword and pike to resolve a dispute that fine rhetoric and reasoned argument had sadly failed to settle. On the 25th, after a day of sabre rattling, Essex withdrew to Warwick. Both sides were quick to claim a victory. For the Royalists, still in possession of the field, there is some justification. The road to London remained open and, Essex's blooded regiments, their cohesion gone, were reduced to shadowing the King's proud force.

Banbury fell to the Royalists on the 27th, and two days later the King entered Oxford. Both towns were to remain in Royalist hands until the war's end, the latter serving throughout as the practical and spiritual capital of Royalism. Now just Windsor with its small Roundhead garrison stood in the way of a Royalist pounce on London.

The opening days of November were probably the most favourable moments for the King in the entire war. A triumphant entry into London at the head of a victorious army would have been enough to catapult the Parliamentary leaders into headlong flight. But this would require a more positive move and advance, a willingness to throw caution to the wind. In the event, Charles was to throw away his God-sent advantage, and the opportunity of taking London was to never re-occur.

On November 1st, Rupert's troops, choosing a more northerly approach to the capital than the rest of the Cavalier army, entered Aylesbury. The Buckinghamshire militia, far too weak to resist, appealed to Sir William Balfour, whose brigade of horse was stationed further north. Rupert, advanced to meet this tiny force and clashed with the enemy at Holman's Bridge.

The skirmish that followed scorched Rupert's princely feathers. Accounts of the battle claim that Rupert lost 600 men and was sent scurrying back to Oxford with his tail between his legs. The Parliamentary victory at Aylesbury would be a powerful tonic in the days following Edgehill.

Surprisingly, Essex won the race to London. On 8th November, having struck almost directly south-east from Warwick via St Albans, the Roundhead army reached the capital and prepared to defend its western approaches. 8,000 of the city's trained bands paraded in arms at Chelsea, and sections of Essex's army took up positions at Brentford. By contrast, the Royalist approach was circuitous and casual, pursuing a path that followed the winding meanders of the Thames. Denzil Holles' regiment of redcoats, about 700 men, guarded the road to Hounslow, while Lord Brooke's purple coats lay behind barricades in the riverside town.

But even at this eleventh hour, peace proposals were being whispered in the King's ear. Infused by the panic that had struck London when reports of the Royalist approach first reached the capital, Parliament sent Algernon Percy, 10th Earl of Northumberland and three supporting commissioners to Charles' camp at Colnbrook by the Thames. In the petition presented to the King on the 10th, they asked that the King: *'...appoint some convenient place, not far from the city of London, where your Majesty will be pleased to reside until committees of both Houses of Parliament may attend with some propositions for the removal of these bloody distempers and distractions.'* [6] This, however, was mere posturing, an act of emptiness which the King both perceived and matched. Ostensibly agreeing to consider these proposals, he would continue to pursue his claim by purely belligerent means.

Parliament's field commanders were briefly deluded, naively confident that the Colnbrook talks would succeed. Late on the 11th, the Westminster members, Lords and Commons, labouring under the same delusion, sent a messenger to *'...know the King's pleasure concerning a cessation of arms during the time of this treaty.'* But the message was never delivered. On the morning of the 12th, in heavy autumn mist, Rupert attacked Parliament's Brentford lines. Within minutes, the lone regiment of redcoats had almost ceased to exist. It had been a brief fight, savagely intense and conducted, *'...almost to handy-gripes, and to the sword point, and to the butt end of our muskets.'* [7]

---

[6] Chippendale, N. 'The Battle of Brentford'. Partizan Press (1991).

[7] Lilburne, S. 'State Trials'.

Fragments of the regiment fell back to the barricades, buttressing the purple coats' defence of the town. But it was to be just as hopeless: a wave of whooping Royalist horsemen passed over the flimsy barriers, and many of the fleeing defenders were drowned as they tried to escape across the Thames. Washer women at the river's banks witnessed their plight. *'We lost many precious young saints, and brave resolute soldiers, who now wear their victorious palms in Heaven'*, wrote John Vicars, chronicler of the wars.[8] Yet the most cautious accounts suggest that fewer than forty died, a happy contrast with the toll of Edgehill. Many lie in an unmarked grave in the grounds of St Lawrence's church.

The town was unmercifully punished for siding with the rebels. For months to come, the Parliamentary chroniclers, spoke of the following day's barbarity, infusing indelible fear into the minds of Londoners about the likely consequence of a Royalist occupation of the capital. *'Their plundering was so universal,'* wrote one, *'that even divers of the richer, as well as the meaner sort, were, and to this day still are, inforced to live off the charity of the Earl of Essex his soldiers, the Cavaliers leaving scarce one piece of bread or meat in all the town: it would pierce a heart of flint, to see, the tears dropping from the old men's eyes, in expressing their sad condition.'*[9]

But delay at Brentford cost the King his victory. On Sunday 13th November, the day of the sack of Brentford, Sir James Ramsay with 3,000 men hurried south to procure the bridge at Kingston and the Earl left London to inspect his assembled troops on Turnham Green. Swelled by the arrival of the London Trained bands, this army now numbered 24,000, nearly twice the size of the King's tired force. Slowly withdrawing his men from Brentford,

---

[8] Vicars, S. 'England's Weeping Spectacle'. Thomason Tracts in British Library.

[9] 'A true and perfect Relation of the Barbarious and Cruell Passages of the King's Army at Old Brainford', Thomason Tract.

Charles drew up his lines at Turnham Green to confront the peer, but the mood of optimism had gone.

Both sides spent the day in silent observation of the other. At about 3 p.m. Essex ordered his artillery to open fire. The Royalist guns remained silent. At one point during the day, the King sent a messenger galloping towards the enemy lines with proposals for negotiations. But before Essex could pen his reply, gunfire was heard somewhere to the south. He immediately accused the King of treachery and the poor messenger was unfairly arrested. Royalist guns in Syon House, the peacetime home of the Earl of Northumberland, had opened in anger on two barges, laden with ammunition for the use of Ramsay in Kingston. Just for once, the King seems not to have been guilty of treachery.

This might have been one of those stretched and suspended preludes to a great battle. Line upon line of muskets and fluttering colours faced each other across the broad expanse of Turnham Green, now part of the tarmac and concrete of London's western suburbs. The ground was unsuitable for cavalry action, the arm of warfare in which the King's army excelled, and his infantry were outnumbered by two to one. It had become a war of nerves, not tactics, and it was the King who gave way first. With hardly a gesture of defiance, the regal colours fell back to Hounslow during the night and a general retreat seemed about to begin.

The King's next move, therefore, was not anticipated, and came as a response to sudden Parliamentary caution. Essex, although his Kingston detachment might have been used with effect against the King's southern flank, had ordered Ramsay to fall back to London Bridge. His motive might have been strategically sound, but his timing was flawed. Charles, instead of withdrawing west as expected, advanced on Kingston and set up his headquarters at Oatlands. Believing that this signified an attempt by the King to link with his sympathizers in Kent before a march on London from the south, Essex hastily arranged for a bridge of boats to be constructed over the Thames at Putney to enable his forces to cross and deploy quickly on the other side. The King had again been checked.

This was to be the nearest that Charles ever came to reaching his capital. He remained at Kingston for five days and his reluctance to advance or retreat is open to different interpretations. Indecision was the most likely reason. On the 19th, having gained almost nothing by this immobility, he fell back to Reading and the threat to London was at last removed. A few days later, Charles retired to Oxford, leaving Sir Arthur Aston with two regiments of horse and six of foot to fortify the Berkshire town. With winter rapidly approaching, it seemed that the war and its players might be about to hibernate.

5

'A town the most notoriously disaffected'

ROYALISM had withdrawn to its Oxford lair, recoiling like a snake after the first real clash of arms. Expecting eventual punishment for his recent attempt on London, Charles ordered the erection of a ring of garrisoned points around his new capital, and the King's 'heartland' was born, from Banbury in the north to vulnerable Reading at its southern tip. Almost isolated within a world of Parliamentary dominance, the heartland's survival would depend upon forging strong links with Royalist Wales and the Cornish peninsula, the sources of both supplies and men for the King's army.

With Wales, this became much easier after the fall of Worcester on November 5th. The Parliamentary garrison had evacuated the city immediately after Edgehill and it was promptly retaken by Royalist forces. Beyond lay the rich recruiting grounds of the upper Severn Valley and a corridor of support that led as far as Chester and the Irish Sea.

But Royalism still needed to throw out a lifeline to the south-west, and just as the first full frosts of winter began to bleach the Wiltshire countryside, the war came spilling across the county's northern border: Marlborough had become the target of renewed Royalist ambitions.

Its main fault was that it lay in the way of Royalist expansion, like an unintentional guardian of the pathway to Cornwall, and its early occupation by the King's soldiers was desirable. But without proper defences and in a region of pronounced Parliamentary sentiments, it was hardly the ideal place in which to house a garrison. Possession of the town, however, would rob the county's Roundheads of their northern bulwark, a point which Clarendon is quick to emphasise in his description of Marlborough's varying qualities.

> '...a town the most notoriously disaffected of all that country, otherwise, saving the obstinacy and malice of the inhabitants, in the situation of it very unfit for a garrison...this place the King saw would prove quickly an ill neighbour to him, not only as it only as it was in the heart of a rich county, and so would straighten him, and even infest his quarters.' [1]

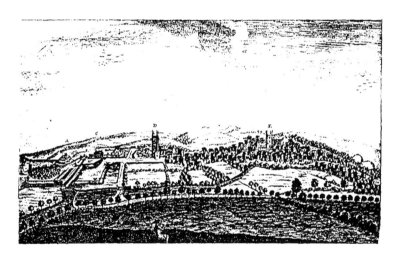

View of Marlborough in 1723

At the very centre of this potentially troublesome town lay the home of Sir Francis Seymour, previous M.P. for the town and now one of the King's most loyal supporters. Serving the King in

---

[1] Clarendon, Vol II, BK VI, Page 156

Oxford, he had left his wife and daughter at his Marlborough mansion, and concern for their safety might have prompted the decision to assault. The townspeople, anticipating an early attack, had organised their defences as well as they could and appointed Sir Neville Poole, one of the town's current members, as their commander. But he had no more than 150 local men at his back and few substantial points behind which to shelter. The men of Marlborough, more adept at plying the chisel and spade than wielding the pike, had been picked to serve as Parliament's first champions in Wiltshire's war.

George, Lord Digby, left Oxford at the head of 400 horse on 24th November, heading directly for the Wiltshire town. Reports of his advance preceded him, instilling both fear and doubt in the minds of the defenders, and eroding their will to resist. His unhesitating appearance in force outside the town that day would have rocked the defenders' house of cards and sent it crashing instantly to the ground without a fight.

But he chose to parley instead. The following morning he drew up his men on the town's common and sent his trumpeter to offer terms. The road nearby was already thronged with the inhabitants of the surrounding countryside, arriving to attend the weekly market. Few looked up at the massed lines on the common beyond. Tight lipped and silent, they continued their way as if warfare and armies had little relevance in their daily lives. And in the precious hours that followed, Poole was able to steady nerves and augment his tiny force, recruiting from the countrymen that chose to stay and join his thickening ranks. Almost casual in his handling of the ultimatum, he delayed in sending a response until his defending force numbered nearly 700. Then, backed by untidy rank of poorly armed men, he issued his bold reply, as defiant as any in the war, and similar in its ambivalence to that thrown back at the King from the walls of Hull.

'...the King's Majesty,' he declared, *'providing he were attended in royal and not in warlike wise, should be as welcome to that town as ever was prince to people; but*

as to delivering up the good town of Marlborough to such a traitor as Lord Digby...they would sooner die.' [2]

Ten musketeers ceremoniously advanced towards the Royalist lines and fired their muskets. Poole, despite his words of loyalty to his monarch, had picked up the gauntlet of the King's weak champion. Digby, taken back by their impertinence, withdrew to Aldbourne. The cavalier commander had made his second mistake. Spirited by the Royalist reaction, the men of Marlborough attacked his quarters during the night, forcing the peer and his men to pull back as far as Wantage. This gave the defenders yet more time for breath. In the respite allowed, they wrote to the Earl of Essex at Windsor, asking him to spare what troops he could for the defence of Wiltshire's northern borders. He sent just two officers, a small return for their entreaties, but a valuable commodity in terms of military experience. One of these was the veteran Scotsman, Colonel James Ramsay, who now superseded Poole as commander of the defence. Within hours of his arrival, he had barricaded the main entrances and ordered the construction of horn works north of the town, with a linking curtain wall. The river, however, was regarded as sufficient defence in the south and only light works were built on the water's lapping banks.

The Commons had issued orders to the local people to supply the town with provisions, promising all those that delivered to the town would be paid in full. John Franklyn, Marlborough's other member, was probably the bearer of this message. Inspired by the townspeople's sense of purpose, he volunteered to remain in his constituency and fight at their side. Choosing first to serve as a mediator, he sent a messenger to the Cavaliers to ask on what terms they would agree to depart. Digby, pointing to his assembled ranks, replied:

---

[2] Waylen, J. 'History of Marlborough'.

'Get your ways then to your friends, and tell them what you have seen. If they throw down their arms and submit themselves to His Majesty, they shall be used like friends.'

The respite had also allowed the Royalists' force to swell. On 2nd December, Lord Henry Wilmot joined Digby at Wantage, their combined force totalling nearly 4,000 men. Late on that day, Lord Grandison and Colonel Grey arrived with a further two horse regiments from Basing, a troublesome outpost within the Parliamentary south. The following morning this fattening force was seen on the downland above Marlborough, the packed lines of men colourless and featureless against the grey winter sky.

A day of inactivity followed, probably intended by the Royalist commanders to unnerve the inexperienced yeomen and market stallsmen who manned the town's gossamer barricades. But soon after noon the Royalist force split, the Basing regiments disappearing briefly, only to re-emerge in new positions south and east of the threatened town. A sudden spirited sortie drove them back, scattering the besiegers in the direction of Okebourne. Some of the more adventurous infantry even probed as far as Mildenhall, but here Roundhead blood was to be spilled at last. Savagely punished by a cavalry detachment quartered in the village, the raw recruits of Wiltshire's northern villages would be hardened into steel by this brief exposure to the heat of battle.

In possible reprisal, Royalist scouts and light detachments approached the town that night and cheekily fired on the town's watchful sentinels. The greeting was instantly returned and a brief skirmish took place. In the morning, the defenders picked up a gauntlet, cap and bloodstained handkerchief at the scene of attack.

On the 5th, the Royalist lines were again on the move, splitting and reforming in a display of military precision which sent shivers down the watching men of Marlborough. It continued for much of the morning, a seemingly purposeless manoeuvre on the downlands north of the town. Then the lines slowly compacted and the long anticipated advance began. Grandison's and Wentworth's cavalry regiments, supported by Grey's dragoons, slowly rode forward and drew up within musket shot of the town's northern defences, while Digby deployed his men along the river front south of Marlborough. The Royalist brigades again became motionless and silent, waiting, it seemed, for the short words of command that would send them hurtling to the attack.

But the silence was broken by a distant rumbling, an indistinct noise from the north. The men of both sides strained to listen, trying to identify its source. Brief hopes of relief flitted through the minds of the defenders, hopes that the army of Essex was marching to their assistance. The rumbling became more audible, translating itself into the sound of wagon wheels and the tramp of soldiers' feet. Then the awful truth dawned on Marlborough's men: additional units of infantry under a Colonel Blake and a train of artillery had joined the Royalist masses on the hill to the north.

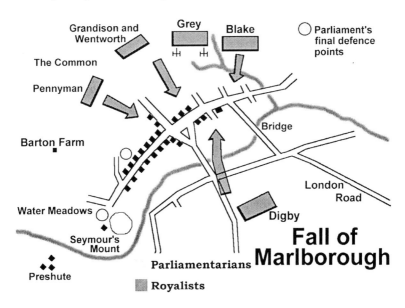

The guns were given the responsibility of starting the attack, and a sudden salvo of cannon shot roared out. But, placed above the roofline, the barrels could not be lowered sufficiently and most of the shots which followed passed over the houses, doing almost no damage. If the guns had been placed on the lower ground to the south of the town, the carnage and destruction would probably have been far greater.

The assault began soon afterwards. On the north-east, the cavalry and foot attacked simultaneously. Colonel Blake's infantry got within musket shot, protected by high hedges, and peppered the defenders without mercy. Lord Rivers' regiment and Grey's dragoons moved in to second this Royalist probe, and hand to hand fighting took place on the broken earthworks. Almost miraculously, the defenders got the better of this close-hauled fighting and the Royalist regiments were driven back with considerable loss.

View of Marlborough from the north

On the northwest, they should have fared better. The regiment of the two Pennymans, Sir William and Sir James, assisted by a company of dragoons, assaulted a post held by only twenty-four Roundheads. But again the Royalists were held, and it is stated that not a single defender was felled. Three hours of fighting had gained the Royalists very little ground and the defenders held on, like a stubborn wall in a night of storms. Yet as so often in the annals of fighting, a lucky shot or the sudden initiative of an individual transforms events. Whether by chance or by design, a nearby barn was fired, forcing the Roundhead defenders in the immediate vicinity to retreat in disorder. A group of attackers passed through the smoke without injury and demolished the unmanned barricades beyond. Patrolling cavalry followed and Marlborough's northernmost thoroughfares were suddenly in Cavalier hands.

In the south, where the river's banks offered natural defence, the defenders had been less hard pressed and few Royalist units had even crossed the river. But the defenders now found their rear threatened and turned to face the invading cavalry. In those moments of distraction, Digby's cavalry swept forward, crossing the river without interruption, and falling on the defenders from behind. Yet even now, with the town in enemy hands, the will of the Roundheads to resist had not entirely gone. Little knots of men fought from behind hastily barricaded doors and windows. Ramsay, with a few musketeers, retreated into the church and briefly fought off the hungry wolves at the stout oak door. Neville Poole and a few pikemen withdrew to Seymour's Mound, Lord Seymour's family home, taking possession of Lady Seymour and her pretty daughter. Seeing the two ladies as possible bargaining counters, the Parliamentarians made lifesize effigies and placed them on a hill in full view of Wilmot's men, hoping to entice the Royalists into a chivalrous rescue.

But the victors were content with what they had gained and seem to have made no immediate effort to take the Mound. Instead they turned to pillage, punishing the townsmen for their partisanship and rewarding themselves for their efforts.

'What they spared in blood, they took in pillage', states Clarendon, *'the soldiers inquiring little who were friends or foes.'* [3]

Property was needlessly destroyed that day, a senseless desecration that would only serve to make the town even less tenable as a garrison point. Fifty-three houses were made uninhabitable and the homes of many inhabitants were partially consumed in fire. One eyewitness, writing in later years, describes the Royalists as *'all hungry, gaping thieves'*, while a contemporary poet writes sadly of the town's virtual destruction.

'That trusty town they plundered in a rage,
'Cause they opposed them; that ('tis thought) an age
Of years can hardly ever its repair,
To make it half so flourishing and fair' [4]

The Mound, sacrosanct home of a Cavalier dignitary, was left alone and it seems that Poole and his tiny band might have escaped punishment. He was certainly not among the captured. The ladies were presumably released. But 120 less fortunate of the defenders were taken alive, amongst them John Franklyn, and imprisoned for the night in a local barn with a dead horse for company. The next morning they were led in chains to Oxford, a long procession of men stooping in humility and exposed to the dispassionate gaze of local inhabitants. At Lambourn a sympathetic villager attempted to relieve them, bringing water to quench their raging thirst and wash their grimy faces. Further on, some of the weary men stooped to pick up ice, but were struck in the face by their merciless guards. It

---

[3] Clarendon. Vol II, Bk VI, Page 157.

[4] Waylen, J. 'History of Marlborough'.

was reminiscent of the journey to Golgotha, just as pathetic, and prompted by a similar desire for revenge. Not one account of events portrays the Royalists in a favourable light. One claims that the victors, in order to augment the number of the captured, took men from the fields as the procession passed.

> *'They take up men, they ask not whom, to make up this number...some from the plough in the fields, some from their doors, some as they came to look upon them as they passed'.*[5]

Whatever the number that reached Oxford, the poor men's treatment never improved. Lodged in the castle under the care of the provost-marshal, the prisoners were forced to drink the water used by the guards to wash their hands. Here they remained, forgotten by their side until a petition reached Westminster the following March, smuggled from Oxford in a draper's cart. Ironically, forty of the men were to escape two days later by making a hole in their prison wall and hiding until nightfall in a baker's yard. Swimming the Isis, they eventually made their way to London and entertained the politicians with tales of their treatment.

This was undoubtedly some of the harshest treatment of prisoners in the entire war, seldom paralleled in the coming weeks. High ranking prisoners were normally regarded as bargaining counters, frequently exchanged for officers captured by the other side, and there are consequently few records of abuse. The episode caused justifiable indignation in London, and a letter was immediately sent to the Earl of Essex, instructing him to enter into negotiations with the King for the release of the remaining men. He had already been severely criticised for unforgivable lethargy in

---

[5] Waylen, J. 'History of Marlborough'.

A TRVE
RELATION
Of the approach of P R I N C E
RVPERT
To that good Towne of MARLBOROW:

And how he was refifted by the Townef-
men, with the ayd of the faithfull *Militia* of Wilt-
fhire, till Serjeant Major *Skippon* arriv'd there
with fome of his EXCELLENCE
the Earle of *Effex* Forces,

With which he gave the faid Prince *Rupert* Battell, and obtained of him and his Cavaliers a glorious victory.

With a Speech made by the faid Serjeant
Major *Skippon* to his fouldiers before the faid
Battell, truly certified in a Letter from thence
to a Citizen of good credit in *London*,
and fo publifhed.

L O N D O N, Printed for *Iohn Matthewes*.

**Frontispiece to a contemporary account of the capture of
Marlborough.**

53

marching to the garrison's rescue. A swift advance, it was suggested, might well have saved the day:

> '...it might have been prevented,' states a letter from the town on the 9th, 'if the solicitation of Mr. White, of my Lord general and the council of war could have prevailed to have sent us forward to their relief in time; but when it was too late, then we were sent.'[6]

Blood had been shed at Marlborough and buildings destroyed. But for little purpose. On 8th December, the Royalists evacuated the town, convinced that the place was untenable. One report, however, suggests that the King's men were still in occupation when a Parliamentary relieving force arrived during the following night.

> '...about eleven or twelve we marched towards the town,' claims a contemporary pamphlet, 'and drew up in a field before it, into the ankles in clay. About nine or ten, in the evening, we fell in upon them; ... some twenty of our horse were sent in amongst them, who slew their sentinel, charged a whole troop, and safely returned with the loss of only one man. Then six or seven companies of dragoons were sent in, who, every step, went up nearly to the tops of their boots; and yet went on with such courage and cheerfulness, though exceedingly wet, weary and dirty, as though they had been in the most delightful garden walls.'[7]

London's propaganda machine might have chosen to distort the truth. Too ashamed perhaps to confess the loss, the Roundhead press produced yet another version of what happened, altering both

---

[6] Waylen, J. 'History of Marlborough'.

[7] 'A True Relation of the approach of Prince Rupert to that good Towne of Marlborough'. MSS in Wiltshire Libraries.

the date of the action and turning disaster into victory. More poignantly it places different actors on the stage and reveals Rupert as the defeated Cavalier commander, a probably deliberate attempt to discredit the prince in the eyes of a gullible world. Sergeant-Major Philip Skippon emerges as the Roundhead hero, ultimately driving away the Cavalier hordes, like beaters at a summer hunt.

Prince Rupert is said to have demanded the town's surrender on the 18th, threatening them with *'all the imminent ruins of approaching destruction'*. Unimpressed by his colourful display of strength on the common above, the town's leaders refused, mocking the prince's messengers and sending them scuttling back towards the distant lines.

> *'...and so dismissing the Vant-currers of the Prince's forces with a cheerful and deadly volley of musket shot, which lighting among the thickest of his horse squadrons, sent divers of them with their riders to the earth. The Prince, gall'd with this unexpected resistance and sudden charge, rid up himself to the very ditches of the works, discharging his petronels among our men.* [8]

He dismounted his cavalry and launched them in support of the foot in an attempt to scale the works, *'which they attempted with all the fury of desperate ruffians'*. They were repulsed by the defenders with considerable loss and Rupert recalled his troops as the winter night fell.

The ditches surrounding the town, however, were filled with Royalist dead, providing the living with a human platform from which to assault the earthworks the following day. To facilitate this new aggression, Royalist engineers worked throughout the cold winter night *'like moles casting up their trenches in the darkness'* and using the excavated soil to create a bulwark on which they

---

[8] 'A True Relation of the approach of Prince Rupert to that good Towne of Marlborough'. MSS in Wiltshire Libraries.

mounted four cannon. Few men would have slept that night: the cold, the excitement and the sound of pickaxes had drained away the desire to sleep.

Accounts of events now begin to differ markedly. Skippon, a man who had risen to prominence in the defence of London, arrived at the head of 5,000 men. Drawn by the flicker of campfires on the common, the Roundhead commander probed the Royalist outguard and caused alarm in the Prince's camp. Dawning daylight exposed the two sides drawn up in battle order, the prince's men extended in line across the common in an attempt to outflank the Parliamentarians, but with a large contingent left in the newly made trenches to face the men of Marlborough.

Skippon apparently addressed his troops, his words and sentiments amongst the most poignant of the war.

'...We are engaged, the more the pity, not against any foreign enemy, but against domestic and intestine foes...that being broken, so much more deadly and desperate will be the enmity towards us...we being to fight for our lives, our friends and liberties, against a race of vipers, that would eat the passage to their ambitions through the entrails of their mother, the Commonwealth; tis for our King, our lives, and the Parliament we fight, Gentlemen, and 'twere a dishonour to you valours to bid you be valiant, I know you are so; let us on therefore in heaven's name, and either live conquerors for our country, or die its martyrs.'

Something approaching a full-scale battle apparently evolved. Both sides discharged their cannon, the regular overture to a long day's fighting. Rupert then launched one of his furious charges on the Parliamentary right while Skippon, wielding a battle-axe at the front of his troops, countered with an advance against the Cavalier left. This unanchored section of the Royalist force was soon forced back towards its trenches, disordered and unled. Here it was immediately set upon by the townsmen who, seeing the Royalist

MARLEBOROVVES MISERIES,

OR,

ENGLAND turned IRELAND,

BY

The { Lord *Digbey*, and *Daniel Oneale*.

READE and IVDGE,

This Being

A

Moſt Exact and a true Relatior

OF THE

Beſieging } { Pillaging, and
Plundering } { Burning part of the ſaid Towne.

Written by *T. P. W. B. O. B. J. H.* who were not onely Spectators, but alſo Sufferers in that moſt unchriſtian action.

Dedicated to all ENGLAND, and directed to the City of *LONDON*, to ſhew the abuſe of the Subjects, Liberty, and Priviledges of their owne goods.

Fælix quem faciunt aliena pericula Cautum:

Jan: 13. 1642.

Printed by one that Prints the Truth. 1643.

Frontispiece to contemporary account of the storming of Marlborough

discomfort, had chosen this moment to join the fight. Grabbing the four Royalist guns as they passed, the men of Marlborough turned the weapons on their former owners and pushed the displaced Royalists back towards the scene of battle.

The fighting ended minutes later. Attacked from front and rear, the Royalist infantry fled from the field and Rupert's putative attempt to take Marlborough had apparently collapsed.

The town was to play only a limited role during the rest of the war. Probably impossible to garrison anyway, it was rendered indefensible by the Royalist sacking and was generally ignored by the military strategists of both sides. Malmesbury and Devizes, better points from which to defend, were the keys to unlocking Wiltshire.

6

'Confidence in roaring boys'

'You may see what confidence is to be put in roaring boys'[1]

MERCURIUS Aulicus, the Royalist newsheet acidly commented on January 11th. It had euphorically reported the dramatic results of a personal rift between two of Parliament's key commanders in Wiltshire.

The squabble between the two Sir Edwards, Baynton and Hungerford, had simmered almost unnoticed since the previous Autumn and seems to have evolved from personal jealousy and a dose of mistrust. But as long as both shared equal responsibility for the county's defence, this rivalry would remain self-contained, evident only in their private correspondence and in a few terse public remarks. It had developed, however, at a time when Parliament's cause in Wiltshire could least afford to be weakened by internal strains and bickering. The storming of Marlborough and early Royalist success in Devon and Cornwall had opened two new fronts on Wiltshire's borders and was threatening to scar the county's level fields with the indelible furrows of war.

Parliament had no obvious strategy for dealing with this sudden Cavalier aggression, preferring to rely upon the individual initiative of the men on the spot and the courage of communities lying in the path of the enemy advance. But on January 10th, the Houses placed Wiltshire under a unified command, appointing Baynton as Commander-in-chief. The two Edwards were instructed to raise two regiments of horse, each of four troops, and one regiment of

---

[1] Mercurius Aulicus. 'Royalist Newsheet'. January 1643.

1,000 dragoons. Baynton's regiment was given custody of Malmesbury and Devizes, the two towns most at risk from a sudden Royalist advance, while Hungerford seems to have based himself in Cirencester beyond Wiltshire's northern border.

To place any confidence or responsibility in either of these men was an act of naivety, almost bordering on stupidity. Both were too concerned with self-enhancement, and neither had the vision nor the qualities required. Events were to confirm that their confidence was misplaced. For while Hungerford was to prove fickle and unreliable, Baynton was to become stridently provocative, unwittingly pushing men into the opposing camp as effectively as sheep before a dog. An anonymous letter complains of his behaviour while he was in command at Devizes:

> *'Sir Edward Baynton hath lorded it with such an equisite tyranny that he hath converted more to the King's side by persecution than I have been able to win either by my rhetoric or reason.'*[2]

At some time during his winter stay in the town, Baynton arrested the mayor, Richard Reeve, for publishing the King's proclamation. Releasing him a few days later, he warned the official against reoffending. Reeve, ardent Cavalier that he was, replied: *'If you offer injury to me who am (sic) the King's deputy, you offer it to the King.'*[3] Many of Devizes' leading men proclaimed their loyalty to the King in the days following.

Only a company of foot guarded Malmesbury, probably too few to guarantee the town's security in the face of a sustained Royalist assault. But flanked by two defensive rivers and with substantial man made defences, this ancient settlement seemed capable of weathering the immediate storm. Piqued by constant sniping at his authority, Baynton, whose activities on behalf of Parliament had

---

[2] Baynton, E. 'Letters to Earl of Pembrokeshire'. Lords Journals.

[3] Ibid.

previously placed his loyalty beyond dispute, now began to appear lukewarm in his zeal, a mere shadow of the enthusiast that he had been at the time of the war's birth. Only one day after his appointment to high command, *'some passion overcame'* him, and he spontaneously abandoned the town, drawing back his troops to Devizes in a gesture of pusillanimity. The citizens, dangerously exposed to the winds of invasion, appealed to Hungerford, at Cirencester.

Responding as promptly as a soldier should, Hungerford dispatched forces to Malmesbury, taking personal charge of the new garrison later that day. Baynton, hearing of Hungerford's arrival, sent a Lieutenant Edward Eyre with 140 dragoons, ostensibly to assist in the defence of the town. But Eyre's real mission was less honourable, and later that night he burst into Hungerford's chamber and took him prisoner. Reports of this strange deed filtered through to Cirencester, only seven miles distant, and three troops of horse were immediately sent to rescue the knight and administer punishment to Baynton and those responsible.

Baynton had returned to Malmesbury that same night, and was there when the horsemen arrived. He, in his turn, was to be taken into custody in exactly the same manner as his rival. *'They came to me pretending a great deal of friendship,'* complains Baynton in his account of events. *'But on the sudden seized upon me in my lodging, plundered me and my soldiers of all that we had, and the next morning carried me and Captain Edward Eyre to Cisseter, with as much ignominy as possible, upon two dragooners.'*[4]

Both parties then made an appeal to the Commons for judgement, supporting their testaments with hints of intended treachery by the other. Baynton's explanation for his behaviour lives on, and bears all the imprints of a man fighting his corner, lashing out with fanciful and ill-founded accusations: *'They say*

---

[4] Baynton, E. 'Letters to Earl of Pembrokeshire'. Lords Journals. (Journals of the N. of L. Vol V, Page543).

likewise that I had seized upon Sir Edward Hungerford,' he continued in his letter to the Earl of Pembroke, *'which I had just cause to do; for besides the correspondence between him and my Lord Seymour, which I can bring pregnant proof of, he sent twice to my Sergeant Major; to command him to draw up my forces to such places as he should appoint, pretending that he had an order from the Parliament for it.'*[5]

It all seemed faintly ridiculous, and the Commons clearly thought so too. They decided in Hungerford's favour and voted to remove Baynton from his position of seniority. On January 31st, Hungerford was made Commander-in-chief of the Wiltshire forces, with virtually sole authority to direct the militia and to commission regiments as he thought fit.

His authority and determination were soon to be tested. Edward Massey, commander of the Roundhead garrison in Gloucester, had established daughter garrisons in Tewksbury and Cirencester as part of his ring of defence, and an attack on each had long been expected. The Marquis of Hertford had visited Oxford at the end of December, offering personally to lead an expedition against Cirencester, but command of the forces that set out the following week was shared with Rupert and Maurice, both of whom wanted to take any credit for the advance towards the west. On January 7th, the trio had summoned Cirencester. They received a blunt reply. Unclear about what to do, the Cavaliers hovered outside the town until darkness fell, their earlier eagerness apparently dulled by God's intercession.

'...It pleased God of his mere mercy to discourage their bad resolutions', crowed one Roundhead pamphlet, *'...that they all retreated to their night quarters...the next*

---

[5] Baynton, E. 'Letters to Earl of Pembrokeshire'. Lords Journals. (Journals of the N. of L.) Vol V, Page 543.

morning they only showed themselves again to the town,
and so departed without making one shot at it. [6]

It was to be only a temporary reprieve. On February 2nd 1643, the Royalist forces stormed the town, attacking from north and west. The county's Parliamentarians could no longer view Wiltshire's war as self-contained; the struggle had become universal, and Wiltshire men were drawn like moths into someone else's fight. Perhaps 1,100 prisoners were taken that day, the majority herded into the parish church like branded cattle. The townspeople, braving the Royalist curfew, broke the windows of the church and passed bread to the imprisoned men. Days later, the captives were paraded through the streets of Oxford. One, totally naked, lay stretched across a horse, too injured to feel embarrassment. A townswoman swore at him as he passed, unkindly reminding him that he had received his just reward. The poor man was seen to lift his head, utter an inaudible reply and then promptly die. This incident, a frequent occurrence in later stages of the war, indicates how deeply the venoms of passion and hatred had become infused even in the veins of non-combatants.

Hungerford, operating so far in self-declared autonomy, but anxious not to receive the full blame for any coming disasters in the county, now attempted to distribute responsibility for the defence over broader and more competent shoulders. Amongst those who took subordinate positions of authority were Edmund Ludlow, son of Sir Henry. He undertook to raise a troop of horse and assist in developing new strategies of defence. On February 13th, Hungerford and his new lieutenant visited Salisbury, searching for George Vaughan, the county's High Sheriff and a known Royalist troublemaker. While there, they apparently liberated a boy who had said that he would kill the King. Mercurius Aulicus, notoriously unreliable in its reporting of events,

---

[6] Mercurius Academicus.

claims that this Parliamentary duo stole money and plate and demanded £500 from the citizens to spare the town from plunder.

More controversial perhaps, and a desperate reaction to the fall of Cirencester was Hungerford's unilateral decision to abandon Malmesbury. The Gloucestershire town's fall removed the hastily erected dam behind which the Wiltshire Parliamentarians had hopefully huddled. Unable to shore up the abbey town's defences in time to halt the Royalist tidal wave, he withdrew his remaining forces and awaited events, symbolically but pointlessly leaving a Major Traill and just six soldiers to greet the new Royalist landlords.

Malmesbury was immediately garrisoned by Colonel Herbert Lunsford with a troop of horse and 400 foot, units of the Oxford army. Involved in some of the war's first clashes and frequently drunk, he and his two brothers, Henry and Thomas, had become the targets of Parliament's abuse. Fact and fiction became entangled, and it became fanciful to believe anything that might be said about these men. It had now become fashionable to portray them as cannibalistic, with a particular appetite for young children. One rhyme depicts them more as monsters than as blackened knights:

> *'From Fielding and from Vavasour,*
> *Both ill-affected men,*
> *From Lunsford eke deliver us,*
> *Who eateth us children.* [7]

This swift sequence of actions pitted the two sides in a frenzied struggle for the domination of North Wiltshire, a battle which the most determined, not necessarily the strongest, would win. Thomas Hungerford, Edward's brother, was another of the armchair generals, resolute on paper but not in the field. Writing to the Earl of Essex immediately after the fall of Malmesbury, he talked bravely of reversing the tide:

---

[7] Parliamentary Hymn, Collection of Loyal Songs. Vol I, No. 17, Page 38.

'There are not two hundred (Royalist) soldiers at Malmesbury, not five hundred at Ciceter,....But you must needs spare a troop of horse which, with the horse I have, ought to guard the avenues thence towards Ciceter. If you have any intention of assisting me in this design, then to keep it as private as possible [8]

Sir Edward Hungerford's own reaction to Lunsford's arrival on his doorstep was to summon a rendezvous of the county's gentry to a meeting in Salisbury, where he attempted to force them to sign a declaration of undying loyalty to Westminster and its cause. But most of those present voiced their fear of Gloucestershire's Royalists and consequently would not sign a document which committed them to treachery. The meeting faded as quickly as mist on a summer's morning. Without the solidity of the gentry at his back, and in utter despair, he *'shifted for his own safety'*, evacuating Devizes on 23rd February, and falling back to Bath with the remnants of his regiment.

Two days later, Perfect Diurnal, the Parliamentary newsheet, responded to reports of the town's evacuation, lightly censoring Hungerford for his weakness: *'it being much to be wondered at that the Devizes should be so easily won, so well provided it is with the Parliament's forces'.* [9]

Lunsford did not immediately take advantage of this withdrawal. He chose instead to bully the town into making a cash payment. Some of the inhabitants tried to buy his mercy by presenting him with quantities of stolen plate. William Thurman, a draper, and the brains behind this bribery, was later charged with theft. A few days later, Lunsford sent 200 horsemen clattering into

---

[8] Letter from Sir Thomas Hungerford to the Earl of Essex. Lords Journals.

[9] Perfect Diurnal. Parliamentary Newsheet. 25 February 1643.

Devizes and demanded an immediate payment of £400. With their arrival, town and castle passed effortlessly into Royalist hands. The militia, left behind to hold Devizes when Hungerford slipped away, followed his example and melted into the surrounding countryside. Three Wiltshire towns were now in Royalist hands and poor Parliamentary strategy had been partly to blame. A thick veil of pessimism, as opaque as the smoke at Cirencester, descended over Wiltshire's Parliamentarians, preventing them from perceiving any long term path towards victory.

But external forces again intervened, this time from the east. During Parliament's saddest moments, when it seemed that much of the nation's south would crumble to Cavalier pressure from Oxford, Parliament's new champion emerged, pushing inexorably towards Gloucestershire after a winter of successful campaigning in Sussex and Hampshire. William Waller, one of the Andover M.P.s, had made his reputation at Portsmouth and Chichester, wresting both cities from Royalist clutches. On February 11th 1643 he had been made commander of the Western Association and given the task of relieving the hard pressed Roundheads of Gloucester and Bristol.

Advancing rapidly through Salisbury, and deciding his targets as he progressed, he relieved Bristol and then turned his attention towards Malmesbury. Hearing that a punitive force of Cavaliers was attacking Sir Edward Hungerford's home at Rowden, near Chippenham, he sent a Major Burghell with 100 horse to intercept this merciless party. On 20th March the two units clashed at Sherston, producing a quick and decisive action in which twenty-five Royalists were taken and the rest dispersed. Almost simultaneously a small Royalist detachment in Chippenham was driven out and that night Waller's army rested at Tetbury, preparing to confront Lunsford in Malmesbury at the earliest opportunity.

Malmesbury's Cavaliers seemed ambivalent about their ability to hold the abbey town and had chosen to rely largely on natural defences. Two rivers, the Avon and the Ingleburre, enclosed the settlement, and the only really vulnerable point was the West Port, where earthworks and trenches had been hastily constructed. Within the town were Col. John Owen's regiment *'400 men, whereof not 200 armed. Col. Bampfylde 120, not 60 armed'* and just 26 pikes. In a sudden tone of wobbling confidence, John Innes, one of the garrison officers, penned a letter on March 17th to Rupert in Oxford, requesting immediate reinforcements:

Portrait of William Waller

67

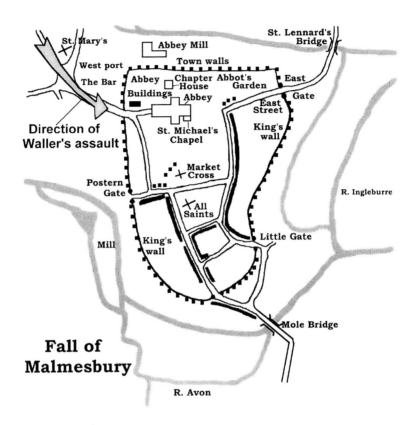

St. Lennard's Bridge

Abbey Mill

St. Mary's

West port

Town walls

The Bar

Abbey Buildings

Chapter House

Abbot's Garden

Abbey

East

East Gate

East Street

Direction of Waller's assault

St. Michael's Chapel

King's wall

R. Ingleburre

Postern Gate

Market Cross

Mill

King's wall

All Saints

Little Gate

Mole Bridge

Fall of Malmesbury

R. Avon

'See that the enemy being stirring this way, my request to your Highness is that you would be pleased to send some regiments that is arrived, and I doubt not that we shall be able to withstand any opposition they shall dare to make.'[10]

---

[10] Letter from Sir William Waller to Earl of Essex of 'a great victory he obtained at Malmesbury'.

Crossing the single road into the town, the Abbey Row, was a spar of wood, 14 feet long with iron spikes, known as the Bar, and this was to be the central feature of the early Royalist defence. On 22nd March, Waller's men pushed in narrow columns across the Stane Bridge and deployed to confront the Cavalier defence. Sober for once and clearly anticipating attack, Lunsford had posted a sizeable force of musketeers at the Bar and these succeeded in holding Waller's first assault. Half an hour later Waller withdrew, leaving a dozen dead and wounded in front of the Bar.

'This business cost us hot water. As we fell on we advanced two Drakes and under that favour our musketeers possessed themselves of some houses near the Port (West Port) from whence we galled the enemy very much', wrote Waller in his account of the action. *'If our men had come out roundly we had then carried it, but the falling of some cooled the rest, and so the first assault failed after a fight of near half an hour'.*[11]

At some point during this skirmish near the Port, Royalist cavalry seemed to have appeared outside the town, but were driven off by Arthur Heselrige's "Lobsters", the curiously armoured cavalry regiment that took part in nearly all the early battles in the south. Waller's second attack was not launched until nightfall. Part of the explanation for this long delay might have been the absence of the Roundhead ammunition train, curiously delayed, causing Waller's men to be short of ammunition. Yet he redressed the situation by deploying his men for a nocturnal assault. Waller takes up the story again:

'I caused all the drums to beat, and trumpets to sound, drawing both horse and foot into the streets: as in

---

[11] Letter from Sir William Waller to Earl of Essex of 'a great victory he obtained at Malmesbury'.

preparation to an assault...which gave the enemy much apprehension, that immediately they sent out a drum and craved a parley'.[12]

At 8 a.m. on the 23rd, the Parliamentary army entered the town. Most of the supporting Royalist cavalry that had hovered outside the town and launched the sudden assault on the previous day had long since disappeared. Considerably outnumbered, Lunsford had little choice but to capitulate and accept whatever terms were offered.

Abbey Row, Malmesbury

Cirencester had been partly avenged. But the punishment meted out at Malmesbury was not nearly so severe and hardly offended

---

[12] Letter from Sir William Waller to Earl of Essex of 'a great victory he obtained at Malmesbury'.

the laws of pre-war decency. 300 prisoners were taken, amongst them irascible Colonel Lunsford, and these were sent to Bristol. There is, however, no record of ill treatment or harsh words. Parliament, in its kid-glove treatment of the captives, had elevated the rules of war.

Waller committed Malmesbury to the care of Sir Edward Hungerford, providing him with a company of dragoons to assist his own regiment of infantry. Yet within 48 hours, *'for reasons best known to himself'*, Sir Edward had abandoned Malmesbury for the second time that year and fled to Bath, leaving a Sergeant-Major Clifton and a handful of men to serve as a token garrison.

Of course he gave his reasons, citing one in particular as an excuse for his withdrawal. Waller had left large numbers of prisoners in Malmesbury's jail, but too few troops to serve both as jailers and defenders of the town. His journey to Bath had not been flight, but an attempt to remonstrate with Waller or Massey.

On March 25th, the town was reoccupied by the Royalists and Colonel Bampfylde appointed governor. And in curious contradiction of Hungerford's own testimony, Mercurius Aulicus, the Cavalier newsheet, claims that eleven colours, eight guns and large supplies of ammunition were found within Malmesbury, while upwards of 400 soldiers were taken prisoner. In the weeks to come, Malmesbury was to change hands three more times.

7

'A mother weeping for her children'

WILTSHIRE'S future was to be largely dictated by events taking place outside the county. Reading, midway along the Thames Valley between London and Oxford, had been garrisoned by the Royalists since the previous autumn. The Earl of Essex, commander of Parliament's main field army, had hibernated throughout the winter near London, earning severe rebuke for his unjustified inactivity. Now at last he had stirred, pushing his army towards Reading in a partially conceived plan with no obvious objectives. Positioning his army outside the town on April 15th, he had commenced a formal siege.

This sudden Parliamentary aggression set off shock waves in Oxford. The King, perhaps believing that Oxford was the next target, began to collect his scattered forces for the capital's defence. Malmesbury was just one of the frontier towns that was to be evacuated as a result.

Now that the regal cat had again been cornered, the Parliamentary mice could grow far bolder. Parliament's new initiative was to be personally engineered by Hungerford. Hurt by recent criticism of his leadership, he was probably searching for ways of removing some of the verdigris that had tarnished his earlier silvery reputation, and saw salvation in a campaign of his own creation. In April, Sir Edward returned to Wiltshire at the head of 700 men, and positioned himself at Mere.

This town lay in an area of inflamed Royalist passions, fuelled by the ardent Cavalierism of Lord Thomas Arundell of Wardour and his distant neighbours, the Thynnes, of Longleat. These

72

gentlemen had emptied their coffers in aid of the King, and their lands were vulnerable to Parliamentary reprisal. At the end of April, Hungerford mischievously seized Arundell's livestock on Horningsham Common and simultaneously sent a Captain Jones to plunder Thynne's park at Longleat. Both parties returned, rewarded by theft. Arundell's animals filled the bellies of Roundhead soldiers for weeks to come, and amongst the booty carried by Jones and his men was a green velvet saddle with tassled plumes.

But this was just a playful prelude to more serious intentions. On Tuesday, 2nd May, Hungerford approached Wardour Castle, *'a receptacle of Cavaliers and malignants'*. What followed was a contest of unequals, the tiny garrison of just twenty-five holding out briefly against a Parliamentary force of nearly 1,300. At the head of this David like force stood Lady Arundell, holding the castle in her husband's name during his absence in Oxford. Solid as an oak tree in a sudden gale, she refused Parliament's first summons, haughtily reminding her would-be assailants that she had been commanded by her husband to hold the castle until his return. Sheltering behind her verbal defiance and untested strength were her daughter-in-law and three young grandchildren.

Five days of bombardment followed, the Roundhead cannons placed within musket shot of the main entrance. Two mines were also sprung, one into an external vault of the castle, the other more precariously penetrating the foundations themselves. But psychological weapons were to be more damaging and hastened the surrender. Robbed of sleep and forced to constant vigilance at window openings and tower tops, the handful of defenders were now: *'distracted between hunger and want of rest, that when the hand endeavoured to administer food, surprised with sleep, it forgot its employment; the morsels falling from their hands while they were about to eat'.*[1] When Hungerford's men placed petards

---

[1] Mercurius, Aulicus. No. 5.

on the garden doors and threw wildfire into the broken windows, the threads of resistance finally snapped and the defenders asked for terms.

The conditions of surrender were hardly honourable, and robbed Lady Arundell and her daughter-in-law of property and dignity. Despite a worded promise in the articles that the house would be safe from plunder, the castle was cruelly looted and even the owner's wardrobe was ransacked. But money buried at the foot of a tower was never discovered. A valuable chimney piece was defaced and paintings were torn from frames. The veils of decency had been openly ripped to pieces. In the gardens surrounding the castle, fruit trees were hacked down and lakes drained away.

The two ladies and the young children were conveyed to Shaftesbury, about five miles from Wardour. But the cruellest lash of the punitive whip was yet to fall, a wound too harsh for any family to endure. While the fate of the women was decided, Lady Arundell's two grandsons, just seven and nine years old, were dragged from their mother's protecting arms and taken as captives to London.

> '*In vain do the children embrace and hang about the neck of their mother,*' wrote Mercurius Aulicus, '*...but the rebels, having lost all bowels of compassion, remain inexorable. The complaints of the mother, the pitiful cry of the children, prevail not with them, like ravenous wolves they seize on the prey.*'[2]

Lord Arundell, hearing of this crime, wrote to Sir William Waller, a man known for his compassion and warmth of heart, asking him to restore his sons to freedom. The M.P.'s reply is politically correct, but exonerates him from any involvement in the sad affair.

---

[2] Mercurius Aulicus. No. 5.

'...it is my unhappiness that I am not capable of performing your command, they being by order from the Parliament removed to London. I was a mere stranger both to their taking and removal, and therefore I presume your nobleness will impute nothing to me in either.'[3]

Hungerford was presumably responsible. So anxious to rise in the esteem of his peers, his cruel and heartless action had taken him crashing downward into an abyss of infamy from which it would be difficult to rise again. He now effectively disappears from Wiltshire's see-saw war, preferring the greater certainties of campaigning in Somerset. His place was eventually taken by Edmund Ludlow, appointed by Hungerford to the governorship of Wardour Castle. In early May, while Hungerford lay before Wardour, this energetic man, mirroring his father's outbursts in the Commons, patrolled with his troop of horse on Wiltshire's furthest frontiers. Hearing that cavalier raiders had ransacked the family home at Maiden Bradley, he determined to take swift revenge.

'I conceived that I might take some stragglers,' he explains in his memoirs, *'therefore I went thither after night with about forty horse, when I could hear of no man, yet I found much provision which a gentlewoman had obliged the people of the town to bring together, and which she was preparing to send to the King's army, amongst which was half a dozen pasties of my father's venison, ready baked.'[4]*

This man's later defence of the castle during the period of prolonged Royalist supremacy in the county lifts him to the pinnacle of the admired, placing him near the head of the Parliamentary leadership in the county. His steady ascendancy

---

[3] Clarendon. MSS. No. 1719.

[4] Ludlow, E. 'Memoirs'. Ed. C.N. Firth (1894). Page 36.

takes place during the chapter of Royalist domination, a time when Parliament's fortunes were to sink to their lowest ebb. For more than a year following Hungerford's barbarity at Wardour, Wiltshire was to lie in the King's shadow and the county which had been so predominantly Roundhead in its earlier declarations had become part of the King's western domain. Yet Wardour, by a twist of circumstance, was to be the mirror reverse of events and trends. Held by the Royalists during the moments of early Parliamentary dominance in the county, it was taken by Parliament at the very moment when Royalist ascendancy bloomed.

For the uninvolved men of the county, however, domination by either party was of little relevance. Both sides were to bleed the county's resources equally. Wherever the King's or Parliament's writ was heard and their soldiers patrolled, tax assessors were sure to follow, and the effects were identical.

Initially King and Parliament had depended on voluntary contributions. Charles had relied on the generosity of the Arundells, Stourtons and Seymours to fuel his war machine while Parliament drew on the wealth of the woollen industry and the contributions of individual capitalists. Charles had then issued a series of appeals to individual people or towns, offering forgiveness to communities who paid without fuss. But each of these appeals was to be watermarked with a threat. In February 1643, for instance, the Penruddockes of Compton Chamberlayne received a royal demand for money with more than a veiled hint of the consequences of refusal.

> *'Though we are unwilling in the least degree to press upon our good subjects, yet we must obey that a necessity such compels...We must therefore desire you forthwith to send us the sum of One hundred pounds for our necessary support and the maintenance of our army...And of this service we cannot doubt since if you should refuse to give us this testimony of your affection you will give us too*

great a cause to suspect your duty and inclination both to our person and the peace.'[5]

There is no record of whether poor Sir John paid up. Only Salisbury's Close and its clerical Cavaliers seem to have contributed voluntarily.

Parliamentary control of Wiltshire in the early months of war enabled the county's Roundheads to develop a more reliable method of securing contributions. In November 1642 the Commons had appointed a Committee for the Advance of Money, its prime task being to negotiate a loan from the City of London. But this was to be a forced loan, the City merchants obliged to contribute 20% of the value of their personal property. Taxation in principle, if not in name, it was to be the basis by which Parliament would now bleed money from the areas which it controlled. On 24th February 1643 Westminster passed an ordinance *'for the speedy raising and levying of money for the maintenance of the army'.* Each county would be obliged to pay a certain amount weekly to commissioners appointed for the purpose. All persons and corporations were to be assessed for ability to pay, and only church ornaments, servants' wages, people with annual income below £10 or with property worth less than £100 would be exempt. On these criteria, Wiltshire was ordered to contribute £725 weekly to London. Anyone convicted of tax evasion or falsifying the value of his estate would have his bill trebled!

This hastily passed measure was immediately condemned by the enemy as illegal. Yet an almost identical system was soon installed by the King's men and, passed by a Parliamentary rump sitting in Oxford, was constitutionally no more legitimate than the London decree. But taking up arms against one's monarch was hardly lawful, and the moods and opinions of the time were unlikely to be influenced by legal niceties. Twelve Commissioners were

---

[5] Letter to Sir John Penruddocke. Wiltshire Public Records Office.

appointed in Wiltshire, amongst them the two Edwards, Baynton and Hungerford.

This cumbersome machinery operated too slowly and in May 1643 another ordinance was passed to speed collection. Two persons only were needed in each county. In Wiltshire Sir Edward Hungerford and the morally upright Edward Goddard of Upham were selected for this task. The politically 'sound', often the constables of the hundreds, were chosen by both sides as the agents of collection, and the chance existed for the dishonest and unscrupulous to line their pockets. Able to rely on locally billeted troops to enforce their demands, such men might become tyrants in their own communities. Something of their power is portrayed in this rhyme from the Welsh borderlands:

**Wiltshire's County Committee
February 1643**

Edward Ashe
Edward Bainton
Sir Edward Baynton
Sir John Evelyn
Edward Goddard
Sir Edward Hungerford
Robert Jenner
Thomas Moore
Edward Poole
Sir Neville Poole
Alexander Thistlethwayte
Edward Tucker

---

*'Here is the sealed demand of a saint, pray
Pay without delay.
Lest the saint (his lust he conceals not)
becomes an angry devil.* [6]

---

[6] Carlton, C. 'Going to the Wars'.

The Cavalier tax system was apparently never as harsh as that of its rivals. Known Parliamentary supporters were naturally taxed most heavily, robbed of as much as 40% of the value of their estate. Yet wholesale confiscation of property was a thing of the future, and most Parliamentary estates remained untouched - apart from the fleeting visit of passing regal horsemen and the shallow probes of inquisitive officers. The burden of contributions fell equally upon town and county. The Oxford Parliament, assessing Wiltshire's share towards the King's finances at £500 weekly, set a 10% rate on income and property, and appointed regional administrators to collect what was due. But the Royalists were generally more sensitive to local government machinery and seemed anxious to remove the cause of grievance. Grand juries or county meetings were often appointed at which the taxed could air their views.

Little knots of defiance, however, did occur. Refusal to pay taxes, particularly in the woollen towns of the Avon, was the commonest symptom of unrest, and the homes of Parliamentary sympathizers were constantly watched. Bromham Hall near Chippenham and Deane House, residences of two of the most troublesome Roundhead M.P.s, were robbed during a brief pulse of Cavalier vindictiveness. But for the countrymen as a whole, the periodic clatter of Royalist hooves on village cobbles would be enough to force compliance.

In the winter of 1642, parts of Wiltshire were paying to both parties. The men of Chippenham and Malmesbury groaned audibly of the iniquities of double taxation, the taxmen of both sides visiting the towns on the same day (and sometimes at the same time) to collect their dues. In December 1642, Chippenham paid three contributions to Edward Hungerford at Malmesbury and to the King's itinerant commissioners, as well as a fine of £200 for assisting Parliament. Collectors sometimes charged double as a punishment for paying tax to the other side! John Nicholas of Winterbourne Earls was regularly visited by the commissioners of both sides. In May 1643, fearing another visit from the rapacious

Roundheads, he hid amongst the droppings in his pigeon loft to avoid a meeting.

But even these painful extractions from people hardly able to afford the necessities of life failed to fill the bottomless coffers of war. In desperation, the insatiable cormorants at Oxford and London looked for other sources of income. Trade and commerce, the basis of the nation's life, was still an untapped reservoir. On July 22nd 1643 the House of Lords approved a new ordinance which would give almost unlimited powers to Parliament's excise officers. A governing committee was set up in London with offices in all the major towns and ports within Parliament's empire. Local officials were then responsible for registering tradesmen within their regimes and the commodities on which they depended. Almost at will, these men could decide the rate to be levied on goods for sale. 3d on a bale of raw wool, 6d on finished cloth and 4d on a barrel of salted freshwater fish were typical rates. The Royalists were far more selective in how they operated. For a long time the tin mines of Cornwall and the flow of money from foreign sympathizers kept the monetary pipeline full. The capture of Bristol in the summer of 1643 handed the resources and wealth of this major port to the King, and taxing of the nation's interior trade was then less necessary.

In time, the excise was to emerge as the second largest source of income, exceeded only by the direct taxes on income and property. Frequently it was double levied. Merchants might be taxed on their raw materials and then obliged to pay again on the finished product. And periodically they would be plundered on route, their wagons held until the duty was paid. In the course of a journey, a tradesman could be relieved of his merchandise by both sides.

No village could now feel detached from the reach of war. What had started as the politicians' war, a struggle for national mastery, had somehow soaked into the fabric of community life, like toppled oil on old rags. But taxation was only one of the growing unpleasantries of war. Men lost more through plunder and the theft of passing soldiers than any tax man could ever hope to take. Plundering, after all, was one of the age old conventions of war, the accepted prize for success at arms. Soldiers rarely joined the colours through dedication to the cause and most had enlisted for the rewards that soldiering offered as the following lines from a contemporary ballad imply:

*'I come not forth to do my country good
I come to rob and take my fill of pleasure.'*[7]

Every besieged house or war visited town in Wiltshire fell victim to passions as intoxicating as drink and as endemic as any disease. Much was senseless destruction. Whole forests were uprooted, waterways fouled and cattle maimed out of pure devilment. Other desecration was apparently purposeful, perpetrated in the belief that they were serving their cause or performing the Lord's holy work. Parliamentary zealots destroyed church fabric and denounced certain poor women in public as witches. Royalist soldiers, less motivated by religious fervour, had less justification for their actions. But their atrocities were just as extreme. Soldiers staying overnight in a Salisbury inn during the Spring of 1643 chose to destroy the beds they had slept on. Others overran a butcher's shop and threw freshly slaughtered pigs into the Avon. Property was destroyed on the mere supposition that its owners had once favoured the Parliamentarians.

War plundered hearts as much as property. It had torn away the menfolk, leaving wives and widows to sob alone at night on the hearthside mat. Family values had been pulled apart, and father had fought son in a confusion of principles and political rhetoric. Castles and homes, drained of their material goods, could be restored and reparations made, but broken hearts could never be made whole. And the bitterest legacy of all was the wail of fatherless children, the most innocent victims of this impassionate war. Deprived of their menfolk's brawn, the women could do little

---

[7] Carlton, C. 'Going to the Wars'.

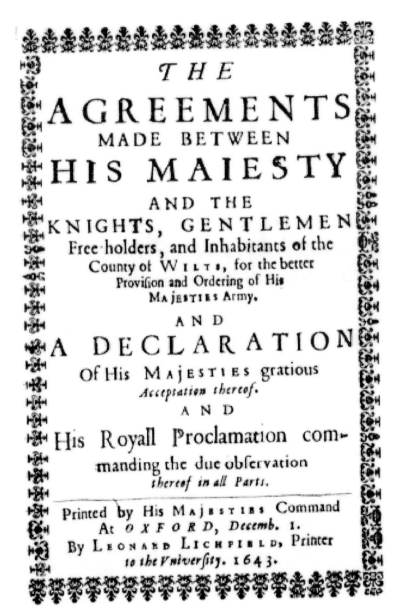

Frontispiece to a contemporary document

Caricature of a plundering soldier

to repel the bailiffs, and a life of destitution might begin. Then the roads were full again, the armies of the displaced as large as the armies of the conquerors. And with rents unpaid, the landlords, too, came face to face with impoverishment. Spiritual plunder, the rape of the soul and the draining of hope, was as heavy to bear as any desecration of wayside property.

But plundering was often necessary to feed the bodies of those passing troops. The payment of troops was frequently in arrears and the supply of food and provisions erratic. Faced by hunger and deprivation, men relied upon their own resourcefulness and stole from the community. Local justices could do little. Offenders were subject to military law and not civil discipline. Moreover, they were rarely caught. And judicial sessions had been severely disrupted by war's arrival. In January 1643 the Salisbury Grand Jury were unable to meet, requesting the Justices to *'take into their consideration that these troublesome and dangerous times have been the cause'*. Law and order in town and country was breaking down as rapidly as military discipline.

Military commanders often did little to enforce discipline within their own ranks. Unprincipled generals frequently encouraged wild behaviour in the belief that soldiers would fight more energetically if the chance for spoils lay beyond. But, as a weapon of war, plunder could be double edged: it could quickly erode military discipline and alienate the local population. More enlightened commanders gradually saw order and civility as a speedier way to win the war, and military conduct began to improve. Hungerford's merciless treatment of the Arundell children had plunged military behaviour to an unacceptable depth. People as well as property had become the targets for revenge. Measured against this, behaviour and standards could only improve.

8

'As unmovable as a rock'

W AR was now to be like a sequence of intermittent tides breaking periodically on a sun strewn beach. In between these sudden flows, life could almost resume its regular monotony, untouched by matters military or political. Men and women, unconsciously programmed to be part of Wiltshire's social or economic life, might listen with disinterest to the distant rumblings of war or look up briefly from their daily work when a sweat covered horseman galloped through their village. For most of the county's inhabitants, governed by the changing seasons and the demands of nature, the war was an alien quality, the prerogative and plaything of the warring classes. War had so far failed to be all-embracing, except for those few who chose to let it be.

Yet when the wave did break, it was to transform the fragile and idyllic lifestyle into a swamp of sudden activity and personal acrimony. The sound of distant hoof beats became louder, cascading into the villages or towns like the waters of an uncontrollable flood. Those exposed to its path would have only minutes in which to consider the safety of their property and loved ones. The innocent of Wiltshire were like the fox cubs of Spring: safe for most of the time from the huntsman's long reach, but subjected within seconds to the terrors of the pack.

The Spring of 1643 was a period of distant rumblings. War had receded, translated into irrelevant arguments in Cornwall and the Midlands, and hardly touching the affairs of Wiltshire. Cannon fire at Wardour seemed equally external, a squabble between passionate neighbours that must soon subside. Only the brief appearance of a Royalist force in Salisbury in May shook this state of near tranquillity.

But this was not an army of occupation. Salisbury was merely a convenient resting place for soldiers on the long haul between Oxford and the west. In early May, Charles despatched the Marquess of Hertford to his former haunts, hoping that his appearance in Wiltshire and Somerset would activate the slumbering gentry into active Royalist support. With Hertford was Prince Maurice and the youthful Robert Dormer, the Earl of Carnarvon, spirited adventurists with a flair for attack. At their backs were two entire regiments of horse and two regiments of foot[*]. On 25th May, this mounted force left Oxford and rested for a few days at Salisbury, its intention being to combine with Ralph Hopton's western army somewhere in the levels of Somerset.

> *'The Marquess of Hertford is retired back to Salisbury, where he now remains among his old friends that invited him thither, who are heartily sorry to entertain such a guest the second time,'* wrote a Salisbury resident to a friend in London, reflecting the mood that probably prevailed, *'and they would willingly now give him £2,000 to be gone.'*[1]

The Cavalier regiments appear to have been quartered in the Close, the only openly Royalist area of the town, and seem to have interfered very little with the city's daily routines. But Dutton, the mayor, was arrested for his autumn failure to read the King's declaration of pardon. Unguarded artillery outside the council house was snatched for the King's use, and a few silent supporters were rewarded for their loyalty. Salisbury, largely neutral in its

---

[*]   The Earl of Carnarvon's and Colonel Thomas Howard's regiments of horse, Lord Hertford's and Prince Maurice's regiments of foot.

[1]   'Letter to an absent friend in London'. Wiltshire Public Records Office.

attitude and without defensive walls, had little to attract the King, and the decision to move out was made.

The Royalist commanders dined that night at Wilton, home of the absent Parliamentarian, the Earl of Pembroke. Then, parading their forces in an intimidating show of strength on Cranborne Chase, and plundering the Earl of Salisbury's nearby house, they set out for Chard on June 4th, and the mood of dislocation within the town began to subside.

With Hertford's departure, the immediate threat of conflict in S. Wiltshire departed too. The presence of so many Cavaliers within Salisbury had teased the countryside, driving small numbers of men into opposing camps and increasing the chances of localised friction. But this had been a spontaneous reaction, not a carefully engineered demonstration of force. Collapsing as quickly as it had blossomed, this brief activity merely confirmed that support for both sides was as transitory as gossamer.

At Chard on the 4th, two Royalist armies combined. Ralph Hopton, with 500 horse and 3,000 foot and fresh from a victory at Stratton in Cornwall, had taken considerable risk in leaving Cornwall and agreeing to march through untamed Devon to a union with Hertford and Maurice. Hovering at Bath, ready to pounce on any un-coordinated Royalist movements, lay William Waller, the energetic Parliamentarian whose rapid movements had elevated him to the status of a legend in the minds of his enemy. But this placed him too far north to assist the Somerset Roundheads, and only local initiatives could stem the Royalist advance. Frantic activity followed the news of the Cavalier union; the country's able bodied were ordered to assemble at Taunton or join the muster at Wells. These levies, gathering in impressive numbers, were far inferior in quality to the seasoned troops which they were expected to oppose, and the Royalist conquest of Somerset was consequently rapid. 7,000 men left Chard on the night of the 4th, heading relentlessly towards the shire's chief town.

Taunton was surrendered within less than 12 hours. Edward Popham, the town's Roundhead governor, decided to offer no resistance, and wisely fell back to Bridgwater, where he could combine with the North Somerset Parliamentarians and possibly with Waller. Unable to move all his heavy ordnance in time, he ordered them to be sunk in the castle's moat. Bridgwater was to follow in rapid sequence, just part of Parliament's collapsing house of cards. The soldiers of the garrison, unseasoned men without adequate defences, were seized by panic and abandoned the town as soon as they heard that Taunton had been taken. Also caught up in the infectious panic was Thomas Luttrell, commander of the garrison of Dunster Castle, who promptly surrendered to Hertford's troops. As a shield to Waller's waiting army, Colonel Edward Popham, one of Somerset's energetic Roundheads, managed to weld the scattered forces of East Somerset into a significant force at Glastonbury. Remnants of the Taunton and Bridgwater garrisons joined him there, swelling the human screen's total to nearly 3,000 men. On the 11th, the Royalists reached Somerton, only 6 miles across the levels from the Parliamentary positions. The following morning a small force of Parliamentarians attacked the enemy camp, a gesture of defiance and little more. It did nothing to stop the Royalist advance, which resumed that day and pushed without further interruption towards Glastonbury.

Similar scenes took place on the road from Glastonbury to Wells, constant harrying of the Cavaliers by small groups of musketeers placed behind the road's flanking hedges. Thereafter the scene changed: instead of the flat levels across which deployment and movement of forces had been easy, the road now rose steeply to the scarp of the Mendips. In place of those protective hedges, the landscape lay open and wild, inevitably exposing the retreating Parliamentarians to the dangers of a sudden charge. To forestall this, William Strode, the Parliamentary commander, prepared a brief stand across Nedge Hill, hoping to purchase sufficient time for his main force to gain the top of the Mendips and deploy in a more extensive manner on the level land behind.

This brought on the battle of Chewton Mendip, a two stage engagement which was hardly more than a confused skirmish. The Cavalier foot, tired after the strain of the long day's chase, took up quarters in Wells, and the horse prepared to do the same. But Maurice, keen for adventure and aiming to copy his brother's reputation for dash, led his cavalry through the town and encountered the Parliamentary rearguard stretched arc-like across the road beyond.

The villain or hero of the moment was to be the 33 year old Earl of Carnarvon, *'an excellent disarmer and pursuer of advantage'*. Impulsively he charged at the head of his regiment, scattering in an instant the Parliament horse drawn up on Nedge Hill. His delighted horsemen rode into the village of Chewton Mendip in pursuit and captured many of the enemy's ammunition wagons. Infused with the same impetuosity as their young commander, the regiment then followed the scattered enemy towards the gates of Bath.

An evening mist had begun to descend, disorientating the pursuers and breaking them into small groups. Drained of their exuberance by the speed of the chase, the glory-seeking horsemen were suddenly confronted by Waller's silent cavalry, placed like a solid wall across the road. The first of Carnarvon's men almost collided with the motionless wall, their mounts skidding to a halt on locked hooves within feet of Waller's forward ranks. But the wall remained impassionate, hardly reacting to the Royalist discomfort and merely watching as the embarrassed Cavaliers, carbines or swords in hand, hurriedly turned their horses and galloped back to the safety of their lines. Minutes later the Parliamentary wall moved forward, ordered into a gallop by the regimental commanders. The predators had now become the hunted.

Somewhere south of the village lay a similar wall of men, this time the solid ranks of Maurice's men, and fortunes were to reverse again. The sequel was to be fought in the deepening mists, a strange silent world in which it would become almost impossible to distinguish friend from foe. Reacting instantly to this sudden threat, Waller's cavalry deployed in two divisions while the dragoons lined the hedges on either flank. The mist, however, had become a fog. Lost in the swirling moisture, the troops of both sides fell silent, listening for the sounds that would pinpoint the positions of the enemy. For a while, it was almost as if the war and the foe had ceased to exist, and nature had somehow become the only foe. The Roundhead dragoons' nerves broke first. Imagining themselves to be surrounded on all sides, they fired wildly into the fog before remounting their horses and fleeing for safety.

This triggered the main engagement, a fleeting skirmish with no real pattern or clear result. The Royalist horse charged what they believed to be the main Parliamentary positions. Within minutes they had routed one wing, but the other, under less intense assault, countered and somehow wrapped itself around the Royalist rear. In the confused fighting, Maurice received a head wound and was taken prisoner. His captors, however, failed to recognise him and he was left almost unguarded on the field. Despite the close locked fighting, Carnarvon managed to organise another charge which fell upon Parliament's rear and drove their men from the field. Maurice was freed in the process, provided with a horse in his hour of need by a Royalist soldier and escorted hurriedly from the field.

The next morning, safe in the Cavalier camp at Wells, the prince remembered his anonymous saviour:

> *'The prince told me he would not part with the horse, till he saw the man that horsed him, if he were alive,'* wrote Richard Atkyns, one of the prince's officers, *'...and when he came to the Prince, he knew him, and gave him 10 broad pieces, and told him withal, that he should have any preferment he was capable of'.*[2]

---

[2] Atkyns, R. 'The Vindication'. Page 16.

Fifteen years later, Atkyns met the man begging in the streets of London, his face and body wasted with disease.

The London Press reported a slightly different version of events:

> *'The truth is they were utterly routed and scattered;*
> *lost all their carriages, but a party being sent out by Sir*
> *William Waller soon recovered most of the carriages, and*
> *pursued the enemy within three miles of Wells, and there*
> *skirmished with them, did good execution upon them, took*
> *divers prisoners, many horse, and so with honour*
> *retreated to Bath, and not in a pelting chase. (At this time*
> *Prince Maurice received two sore wounds, was beaten off*
> *his horse, and narrowly escaped from being taken*
> *prisoner) as Mercurius Aulicus would bear the world in*
> *hand; but we must pass by his insolence, seeing his pen is*
> *so accustomed to publish notorious untruths that with the*
> *common liar he is justly suspected even when he stumbles*
> *upon a truth.* '[3]

Soon after the skirmish, Hopton, an old friend of Waller's, wrote to his rival and proposed a private meeting. War, the divider of families and the framework for many acts of shameful violence, might leave untouched those deep sentiments of honour and friendship that beat within the hearts of decent men. Waller's gentle reply exhibits literary skills and stoic reality:

> *'Certainly my affections to you are so unchangeable,*
> *that hostility itself cannot violate my friendship to your*
> *person. But I must be true to the cause wherein I*
> *serve...that great God who is the searcher of my heart*
> *knows with what a perfect hatred I detest this war without*
> *an enemy...we are both upon the stage, and must act such*

---

[3] 'A true Relation of the great and glorious victory etc'. Document in Wiltshire Local Studies Library, Trowbridge.

*parts as are assigned us in this tragedy. Let us do it in a
way of honour and without personal animosities.* [4]

The pace of war now slowed again. Abandoning the strategy of
rapid movement of the previous days, the Royalists took root,
attracted to the glittering target of Bath like moths to a candle. For
several days, they remained inactively at Wells, and a new
Parliamentary strategy was allowed to evolve. Waller's army lay
camped on Claverton Down, a point from which he could move in
any direction to screen Bath and maintain his links with Bristol.

At the end of June, the Royalist army advanced from Wells to
Frome. This triggered a new bout of skirmishing, mainly brief
stands by the retreating Parliamentarians in Somerset's narrow
lanes. On 2nd July, the Cavaliers reached Bradford on Avon,
spilling the war across the border into Wiltshire. Having secured
the crossing of the Avon, Maurice and Hopton lay within 6 miles of
their target.

Waller had been outwitted! Most of his force still lay south of
the Avon across the previously expected avenue of the Royalist
advance. In an attempt to block the chosen Royalist approach from
the east, he constructed a bridge across the Avon at Claverton and
placed a substantial force on high ground near Monkton Farleigh.
On 3rd July, the Royalists began to outflank this exposed position,
forcing Waller to withdraw towards Batheaston. The approach to
Bath had now been cleared and Maurice ordered his forces to push
along the Avon valley towards Bathford. That same evening the
Parliamentary detachment holding the Claverton crossing was
overpowered and Waller's defence strategy lay in tatters.

He had been forced into a role in which he had few skills.
Waller was a man of movement, a brilliant strategist of the forced
march and the lightening strike. Nothing in his military career had
taught him the skills of standing still or the arts of defensive
campaigning. This intrinsic weakness, not the brilliance of the

[4] Atkyns, R. 'The Vindication'. Page 19.

Royalist generals, had allowed the enemy to approach to within five miles of Bath.

Maurice, by contrast, was a practical opportunist. With an eye for the exploitation of any sudden advantage, he could react to events and force open any obvious chinks in the enemy's defensive armour. He now ordered his forces to move along the Avon valley towards Bathford. That evening, the 3rd, the Parliamentary troops holding the crossing at Claverton were overpowered and, with their defeat, Waller's attempts to halt the Royalist advance on the far side of the Avon were ended.

The next few hours saw Waller at his best. Correctly surmising that the enemy intended to assault Bath from the north, probably from the commanding heights of Lansdown Hill, he withdrew his forces from Batheaston in a bid to be the first to reach the hill. For a while, the opposing armies were marching in parallel lines, racing to seize the favourable ridge whose eastern end lay only 3 miles from the city. The major engagement for which both sides had jockeyed for so long seemed now inevitable.

Fate and personal ideologies had placed Waller and Hopton in opposing camps. Yet these personal commitments alone could never sour the friendship that had cemented the two in happier times. Both now saw the war as little more than a new chapter in that friendship, a chance to spar in public like two young bear cubs frolicking outside their den. The victor in the coming battle would doubtless be congratulated by his rival and the endless rounds of chess would begin again.

Waller won the opening bid, snatching the hill before his opponent's arrival. By the evening on the 4th, the Parliamentary army was ranged along the south-eastern edge of Lansdown Hill, with most of the Royalist army moving slowly over the rough terrain from Bathford. Just before midnight, Hopton assembled his officers to discuss the feasibility of launching a night assault. The Royalist positions, however, were clearly exposed to a possible probe from Bath, and the cautious Cavaliers, leaving only small units to hold the base of the hill, fell back to Batheaston Bridge.

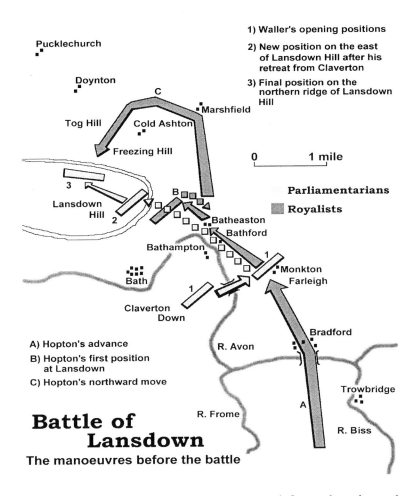

1) Waller's opening positions

2) New position on the east of Lansdown Hill after his retreat from Claverton

3) Final position on the northern ridge of Lansdown Hill

Pucklechurch

Doynton

C

Marshfield

Tog Hill

Cold Ashton

Freezing Hill

0   1 mile

3

Lansdown Hill

2

B

Batheaston

Bathford

Bathampton

1

Bath

Monkton Farleigh

Claverton Down

1

Bradford

Parliamentarians

Royalists

A) Hopton's advance

B) Hopton's first position at Lansdown

C) Hopton's northward move

R. Avon

Trowbridge

A

Battle of Lansdown

R. Frome

R. Biss

The manoeuvres before the battle

The next morning Hopton's army surged forward again, and occupied the grassy meadows between the Avon and Lansdown slopes. A whole morning was spent in indecision. Above, Parliament's guns lined the summit, silent but threatening. The grey sky behind was spiked by pikes, and small groups of men could be seen in discrete movement amongst the masking trees. In contrast, the Royalist ranks lay in the open. An attack uphill was clearly impractical and the call to retreat was sounded.

94

The Parliamentarians watched in fascination as the questioning lines of Royalists fell back and momentarily disappeared in the direction of Bathford. Waller, acting like a barometer to a change of weather, and with all the fluidity of quicksilver, instantly redeployed his army along the hill's northern slope. For, having penetrated his rival's mind, he correctly interpreted the withdrawal as tactical, a swing north towards Marshfield in a bid to find a more favourable position from which to storm the hill. This perspicacity, more than any previous intuition, earned him the admiration of his opponents, and the Royalist Slingsby's description of Waller as the *'best shifter and chooser of ground'* is particularly appropriate. So despite Hopton's masterful manoeuvre north towards Marshfield, his enemy awaited his arrival from behind a line of breastworks and interspersed guns.

The northern slopes were equally favourable for Parliament. Waller's flanks were covered by thick woodland in which he placed detachments of musketeers. Behind the main line lay a strong reserve of horse and foot. Commanding the more open northern slopes and vale beyond, it was one of the best defensive positions imaginable, a source of envy for the opposing commanders. All night the waiting soldiers rested at their posts, the Roundhead campfires a line of gold in the dark night sky.

Soon after first light on the 6th, Waller sent a strong scouting force towards Marshfield, hoping to discover the location of the slowly moving Royalists. This managed to surprise a body of breakfasting horsemen and spread brief panic in the Cavalier camp. But by 8 a.m. the entire Royalist army turned south at Tog Hill after their northward detour. At Freezing Hill, Hopton's soldiers caught their first view of the impressive enemy positions. Minutes later, they were teased by sudden showers of Parliamentary dragoons, little groups of fast moving men who played like lightning on the moving flanks of the enemy, and then evaporated almost as quickly as the morning dew.

In mid-morning, the Royalist army solidified for almost two hours, an apparent attempt to tempt Waller from the ridge and

95

contest the issue on less favourable grounds. Parliament's cavalry chose instead to probe the immobilised enemy lines, but were held by the musketeers. In the early afternoon, Hopton, realising that the wily fox on the hill top had no intention of falling for the bait, ordered his army to return to Marshfield prior to a march to Oxford.

This was to be a far more successful bait. Waller, seeing the first signs of retreat, sent Colonel Robert Burrell with 1,000 horse and dragoons in an attack on the Royalist flanks and rear. At about 1 p.m. they fell upon the enemy rearguard and successfully routed two entire regiments. Atkyns, watching from the safety of Tog Hill, was impressed, publicly recording his admiration for Burrell's action.

> *'And this was the boldest thing that I ever saw the enemy do; for a party of less than 1,000 to charge an army of 6,000 horse, foot and cannon, in their own ground, at least a mile and a half from their body.'* [5]

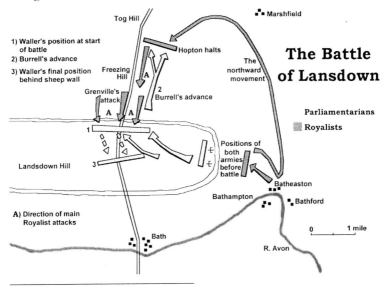

[5] Atkyns, R. 'The Vindication'. Page 19.

But a body of musketeers, which had been ordered to protect the army's flanks, remained firm despite the flight of the Cavalier horse. In fact, they were still firmly positioned when Hertford's and Carnarvon's regiments of horse, well forward in the line of withdrawal, returned to counter the Parliamentary aggression. This punitive attack, coming without warning like Valkyries from the north, was impossible to resist. The Parliamentarians, tiring after the prolonged skirmishing, were instantly hurled back towards the slope from whence they had come. Elated and now possibly able to determine the shape of battle, the retreating ranks of Royalist foot halted. Colonel Nicholas Slanning, commander of one of Hopton's veteran regiments of Cornishmen, was the first to turn, his 300 musketeers hurrying to engage the dragoons on the flanks. Simultaneously, Carnarvon and Maurice, acting in complete unison, unleashed their regiments on the horse in the Parliamentary centre.

So started the battle which both sides knew to be inevitable. But for Waller, the able chooser of ground, both the timing and venue were not of his choosing. For almost 24 hours, he had rigidly held the high ground, hoping to suck the enemy towards its wooded slopes. Now he found himself on terrain of no advantage, witnessing the discomfort of his cavalry in the face of unexpected enemy aggression. With less than his usual composure, he sent two further regiments to Burrell's assistance, unwisely committing almost his entire equestrian force to the conflict on that lower ground.

By 2 p.m., the Royalists were back in their earlier positions on Freezing Hill, the position that they had vacated just two hours previously. Circumstances had robbed Hopton of the chance of retreat and the survival of his army now depended upon total victory. In front were the rudderless units of Roundhead horse, fragmented by the ferocity of the Royalist counter attack. Another assault on the same scale would probably cause the disintegration of Waller's cavalry, and might even drive the watching infantry from their positions along the ridge. A withdrawal to Oxford, on the other hand, would merely enable the Parliamentary horse to recover and would expose the Royalist army to attack from the rear - at a time and place of Waller's choosing.

The key to the Parliamentary positions was a narrow lane, still existing, that led due south to the crest of the ridge. Most of Waller's demoralised horse were now struggling to ascend, forcing their way up this tiny corridor without any semblance of military order. Maurice, seeing the opportunity for increasing the confusion, advanced his horsemen across the meadows flanking both sides of the lane, and ordered them to open fire at close range. The quarry, caught in the narrow defile, was little better than a beached whale, and relatively few of the horsemen survived intact. The collapsing units coalesced in the lane, struggling to compress their ranks into the narrow opening, and hardly a shot was fired at the Royalists in retaliation.

Behind the cheeky Cavalier horse surged the seasoned Cornish musketeers, all anxious to participate in the partridge shoot and gain some of the credit for Parliament's defeat. On the crest above, however, Parliament's seven big guns began to fire. But this merely angered the Royalist infantry below and infused them with a quest for glory. Here at last was a chance to protect their homelands. Sir Ralph had reminded them frequently of the need to destroy Parliament's western army, and the dangers to Cornwall of leaving the enemy army intact. Only the nervous lines of Parliamentary infantry on the ridge above lay between the Cornishmen and a triumphal return to their distant homes.

Just after 3 p.m., the Royalist musketeers began their flank advance, ascending the hill in close formation to tackle the enemy in the woods above. Simultaneously, massed horse and pike pushed up the central roadway, a tactic without precedent, relying on sheer force of weight to topple the defenders from the hill. The characteristic dispositions of an attacking force were reversed: the horse were now in the centre with the foot on the wings.

The battle developed without form or plan; neither side's commanders had intended it this way. Folly and precipitate action had replaced all previous Royalist strategy and weight had taken the place of precision manoeuvring. The Parliamentary guns, lowering their barrels to the level of the roadway, were able to sweep the approach, and here the advance was held. Waller, in an attempt to encourage the enemy to over-confidence, withdrew some of his forces to give the impression of defeat. This had the desired effect: Sir Robert Welsh asked Maurice to place him in command of a body of horse with which to pursue the enemy. Recklessness had become the hallmark of the day and reasoned thinking was now the art of armchair strategists only.

Welsh and his men gained the summit, most galloping up the winding road to where the Parliamentary lines had first been seen. Expecting to find nothing but the enemies' backs, he was confronted by an almost solid wall, a mass of Roundhead infantry and closely packed horse. Waller's forces, far from retreating, were standing as firm as before.

This brought on the fiercest engagement of the day. Five times the Parliament's horse charged the insurgents, breaking the ranks and hurling them down the hill. According to Hopton's own account, at the end of the day barely 600 of his cavalry force of 200 remained, the rest having fled the field and ridden to Oxford with reports of defeat.

They might have been forgiven for so thinking. Pushed back from their tenuous toeholds and pounded by the enemy guns, the Royalist army seemed almost to have collapsed. Men scrambled in both directions, some upwards in quest for glory, others downwards, all guided by a desire to *'shift for themselves'*.

One man, however, was about to save the day and pluck victory from certain defeat. Sir Bevil Grenvile(or Grenville) of Stowe, one of Cornwall's M.P.s, and the stalwart of Hopton's western campaign, led his regiment of foot from Freezing Hill against the very centre of Parliament's positions. Positioning some horse to cover the open ground on his right and musketeers on his left, he led his solid body of pikemen towards the narrow lane. For a while, his closely packed pikes were protected by the steepness of the slope and the bend in the road. But near the top, they were exposed to the full fury of the enemy.

'As I went up the hill, which was very steep and hollow,' writes Atkyns, performing the role of war correspondent for the Royalist press, *'I met several dead and wounded officers brought off, besides several running away, that I had much ado to get up by them. When I came to the top of the hill, I saw Sir Bevill Grenville's stand of pikes, which certainly preserved our army from a total rout...they stood as upon the eaves of an house for steepness, but as unmovable as a rock: on which side of this stand of pikes our horse were, I could not discover; for the air was so darkened by the smoke of the powder, that for a quarter of an hour together (I dare say) there was no light seen, but what the fire of the volleys of shot gave, and twas the greatest storm that ever I saw.*[6]

Three times the Cornishmen were charged. From this wall of resolution, the Parliamentarians fell back, and their line was punctured at last by the granite men of Cornwall. The ecstasy of the moment, however, was drained by the death of Sir Bevil, killed in the final moments of the last charge, and today a monument marks the spot where he allegedly fell. On either flank the Royalist musketeers took advantage of the enemy's dislocation to secure their positions on the scarp slopes. Heavy fighting followed in the woods and soon the entire ridge top was in Royalist hands.

The Roundhead forces fell back to a stone wall that crossed the road about half a mile south. But darkness was now falling and the two sides collapsed into inactivity, the victors of the day precariously balanced on the edge of the ridge, and the defeated cowering behind the protecting sheep wall. The Royalist right took the opportunity of creeping forward during the night into some

---

[6] Atkyns, R. 'The Vindication'. Page 19.

disused pits, so securing more stable positions from which to strike at the enemy in the morning. Neither side could expect to sleep much in spite of the day's exertions. The Royalists, forced to remain alert from fear of being attacked and rolled like stones down the hill, and the Parliamentarians aware of the consequences of surprise. Waller, despite his still strong positions and the existence of an unused reserve in his rear, seemed strangely demoralised, and had already decided upon a retreat to Bath. Ironically the general, whose position was most secure, was the first to withdraw while the other, balanced precariously on the ridge's edge, chose to hold his ground.

Soon after 1 a.m. the Royalists were alerted by movements in the enemy camp. Scouts were eventually sent forward to discover the cause and these, approaching the wall, found only lighted matches and upright pikes: the Parliamentarians had withdrawn while leaving the impression that their men still manned the walls.

Parliament's accounts of the day's battle are brief. One, despatched to the Commons immediately after the action, makes little mention of the storming of the hill and Grenville's glorious stand.

> *'The enemy (enraged by the wounds of their chief commanders from so small a party of ours) charged up to our ground, which ground after a hard dispute was yielded unto them partly by force, partly voluntarily upon good advice,...both armies being on the plain, charges grew so hot on both sides, as the like was never seen in England. Yea, some old soldiers said that the furious fights in France were but a play in comparison of this.* [7]

Features of that summer battlefield still remain unchanged. The wooded slopes, the lane and the daytime colours have so far defied the northward expansion of Bath's suburbs. Yet if man destroys,

---

[7] 'A true Relation of the great and glorious victory'.

he also adds: on the left of the road near the scarp top stands the immortalised reminder of the death of Sir Bevil. Sounds of that day still whisper, somehow caught in the rustle of leaves and the freshening wind. Imagination, knowledge and a little romanticism are all that is necessary to reconstruct the day's savage action.

Perhaps Clarendon should be allowed to have the final word:

> '*He was a gallant and a sprightly gentleman,*' he fondly says of Grenville, '...*and by the gentleness of his spirit, accompanied with courage and authority, had restrained much of the licence, and suppressed the murmur and mutiny, to which that people were too much inclined...all men exceedingly lamented his loss at the time he fell.*'[8]

The Royalists had won a victory. But they had lost one of their most charismatic leaders. With him went the soul of the Cornish army on which Hopton and Prince Maurice would so depend. Ironically, it was to be the Parliamentarians who performed the rites of victory: almost immediately after the departure of the Royalists, Waller's army reoccupied the heights of Lansdown Hill, and Hopton commenced the retreat to Oxford, a route which would take him across Wiltshire's northern border.

---

[8] Clarendon, Earl of. 'The History of the Rebellion and Civil Wars in England'. Vol III, Bk VII, Page 108.

9

'The soul of that army ... believed to be dead'

L ISTED amongst the acclaimed Royalist victories, Lansdown was curiously to usher in one of the deepest and most prolonged periods of Cavalier despair in the early months of war. Within 24 hours of the fighting, Parliamentary forces had again congealed on Lansdown Hill, their army ranks intact and full of optimism. The Royalists, by contrast, were in full retreat towards Marshfield, the first leg of their journey to Oxford, displaying all the characteristics of a defeated army. Colonel Henry Slingsby, one of those in the Cavalier ranks, measured the depth of this mood of despair.

> *'Our horse was bad before but now worse,*
> *Our foot dropped for their Lord Hopton,*
> *and that they had no powder left to defend them for...*
> *we had but nine barrels*[1]

The death of Grenville might have triggered this episode of self-inflicted despondency. It was to be deepened on the day after the battle by an even greater tragedy, one that temporarily extinguished their guiding light. During the early stages of retreat, an ammunition cart blew up, killing or injuring those nearby. Amongst the maimed was Ralph Hopton, *'by the blast of the powder thrown from his horse'*, and for some time he was to be

---

[1] Hopton, Lord R. 'De Bellum Civile'.

rendered incapable of motion or leadership. It was a savage punishment for his soldiers' audacity on Lansdown's slopes, and a cruel reminder that God was an undoubted Roundhead. The loss of two leaders in one day, and almost all that remained of their ammunition, was too much for the army to bear. The tragedy for the Royalists was equally a tonic for the Parliamentarians.

> *'When Sir William Waller had intelligence of this blowing up of the powder, of which he well knew there was a scarcity before, and of the hurt it had done,'* writes Clarendon, *'he infused new spirit into his men, and verily believed that they had no ammunition, and that the loss of Sir Ralph Hopton (whom the people took to be the soul of that army, the other names being not so much spoken of or so well known, and at this time believed to be dead), would be found in the spirits of the soldiers.'*[2]

Almost catapulting themselves in delight from the heights of Lansdown, they set out in pursuit of the enemy, threatening the Cavaliers' every move. On 8th July the Royalists left Marshfield, heading towards Chippenham on a circuitous path to Oxford. The road through Malmesbury would have been far more direct. But the town had been recently re-occupied by Parliament's troops, and now Colonel Thomas Nicholas Devereux, the garrison commander, hungrily watched, his insubstantial force being enough to deflect the Royalists from this shorter route. Somewhere in the sad line was Sir Ralph Hopton, carried deferently in a litter and valued almost as a demi-god by those in his command.

The Royalist fugitives were soon in the exposed uplands of the Southern Cotswolds, pushing their way east through Wraxhall and Giddeahall across the border into Wiltshire. Just outside Chippenham, scouts reported that Waller's cavalry had ridden through Box and Pickwick, and were threatening the rear. The

---

[2] Clarendon, Earl of. 'The History of the Rebellion and Civil War in England'. Vol III, Bk VII, Page 110.

Royalist commanders immediately halted the Cornish regiments and sent messengers to Waller, offering to contest the issue afresh on the level land between Biddlestone and Chippenham. Waller, despite his new found optimism, respectfully chose to decline. Both sides spent the night of the 8th in arms, bivouacking almost within talking distance of one another in the fields west of Chippenham.

For the inhabitants of this Wiltshire town, war was a novelty, a scarcely talked about matter that had so far only taken place in other people's back yards. Although never far from the tramp of armies, Chippenham had not yet been visited in anger, and the seasonal pattern of daily life had seldom been affected. Now the townsfolk were to be entertained throughout that summer night by the unfamiliar sound of cannon, a grumbling dialogue between two invisible foes pitched somewhere in the unenclosed countryside that lay towards Corsham. In the early hours of morning, however, detachments of Parliamentary cavalry rode hurriedly through the town, like fleeting phenomena from another world. Two or three hours later, the Parliamentary commander himself, with his brimmed hat and stern face, passed through the town with the body of his army, and disappeared towards the rising sun.

Then again the scene shifted - and the mode of warfare too. Instead of the insipid fighting in the dark between two stationary forces, the action now took on a more fluid hue, a series of running dogfights between the cavalry and infantry of both sides. Sir Nicholas Slanning, unsung hero of Lansdown, briefly stood with his regiment on the northern edge of Pewsham Forest,[*] and invoked a ferocious cavalry charge by the Parliamentary vanguard. His men, almost as unmoving as the nearby oaks, resisted the onslaught, while the rest of the Royalist army took cover in the extensive woodland behind. Fighting continued throughout the southward withdrawal, solidifying once again near Bromham Hall, the peacetime home of Sir Edward Baynton. Slanning ordered his

---

[*] alternatively known as Chippenham Forest at that time

musketeers to hold their positions in the fields on either side of the road, and the earlier action was neatly replayed.

On Sunday, July 9th, the fugitive army entered Devizes. In a desperate effort to hold the Roundhead pursuit, Maurice left Lord Mohun's regiment of foot to hold the ford at Rowde, funnelling the rest of his men down the road from Chippenham into the open market place in the centre of the town.

Royalist strategy seems questionable. Cooping the entire army in a town with few defences, and with a hungry fox baying for blood only miles behind, can hardly seem sensible. But expediency, and a need for rest, had forced Maurice's hand: the town was viewed simply as an oasis for refreshment on the journey to Oxford. Yet it might easily have emerged as a trap or even graveyard for the King's tired army. Open downland, the great expanse of Roundway Hill, lapped the town in the north and east, giving mastery of the field to whomever held its slopes. Maurice, slow to realise its full potential, deployed his men within the town, and only later considered a move towards Roundway's southern slopes. But for Waller, who could sculpt points of advantage from even the most unpromising terrain, it was a godsend, a chance to hammer down the lid on the Royalist coffin. Surveying its impressive rise in the evening light from beyond the brook at Rowde, he decided to occupy its level crest as soon as dawning day permitted.

Yet first he had to force the crossing, a task which he attempted in the fading light of the summer's day. Lord Mohun's rearguard resisted, holding the line of the Summerham brook for half an hour, but losing 60 men in the process. Falling back and joining the rest of the slow moving foot, the Royalists developed a far stronger position across the road from Chippenham, just to the north-west of Devizes' outer buildings.

But these positions were never tested. Having camped for the night on the moorland near Rowde, Waller nimbly side-stepped the Royalist positions, and led his army of 5,500 men around the town's northern outskirts to the southern flanks of Roundway Hill.

Below, imprisoned as much as defended by the town's fragile defences, lay the Royalist army, a tired and dejected mass of men, like penned animals waiting to be slaughtered. Yet the master tactician's early morning drive had achieved something more: the instant snapping of the Royalist route of retreat towards

Portrait of Hopton

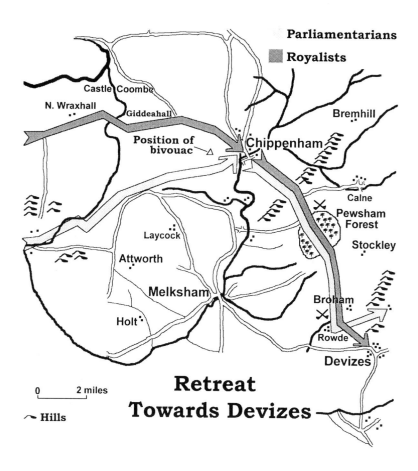

Retreat Towards Devizes

Marlborough and Oxford's distant spires. For most of that day, Waller's scouts roamed without challenge across the Wiltshire Downs, like a pride of hungry lions.

Only Hopton could salvage this situation of near disaster. Fortunately for the Royalists, he had partially recovered, and now ordered the outlying forces to fall back for the defence of the town. It was almost exactly as Waller had hoped, a chance to choose his ground and dictate the pace of the coming action. Maurice and his companions had unwisely allowed themselves to be besieged - and their route of retreat lay blocked.

That afternoon, part of an interminably long day for both sides, Waller was informed that a large ammunition train was approaching, escorted from Oxford by a detachment of dragoons under the command of Ludovic Lindsay, the Earl of Crawford. Instantly he sent Major Francis Dowett with a sizeable force to intercept the Earl's slow progress. At Beckhampton, the Parliamentary major struck, launching a ferocious thrust at the unsuspecting train. Outnumbered and outmanoeuvred, poor Crawford abandoned his charge and fled, leaving 200 soldiers and several containers of ammunition in the hands of the enemy. Dowett was to play a major part in Wiltshire's later war. Stung by Westminster criticism, he was to throw in his lot with the King. Controversial in all that he did and inclined to bouts of insubordination, he was successively stigmatised by both sides, and accused of just about everything!

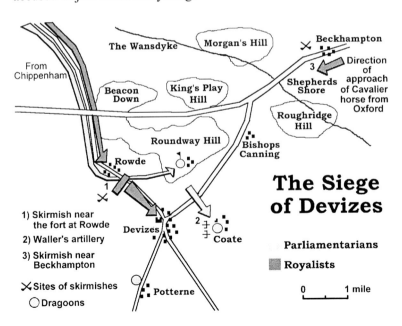

The Wansdyke Morgan's Hill Beckhampton

From Chippenham

3 Direction of approach of Cavalier horse from Oxford

Beacon Down King's Play Hill Shepherds Shore

Roughridge Hill

Roundway Hill Bishops Canning

Rowde

The Siege of Devizes

1) Skirmish near the fort at Rowde
2) Waller's artillery
3) Skirmish near Beckhampton

Devizes Coate

✕ Sites of skirmishes
○ Dragoons

Potterne

Parliamentarians
▨ **Royalists**

0 ___ 1 mile

The distant sound of gunfire alerted the Royalist command. Part of the army, a mixture of both horse and foot, advanced towards the higher ground at Coate. Seeing sections of Waller's army descending the down near Roundway village, and mistaking it for Crawford's men, they advanced in greeting and were nearly destroyed by the Roundhead response. Hurriedly they evacuated their positions and went to earth within the town, leaving Waller and his men to occupy Coate and plan their subsequent move.

But it was to be the Royalists who responded first. Anticipating the closing of the net and aware that there was insufficient accommodation or food in Devizes for the entire army, '...it was unanimously advised', says Clarendon, '...and consented to, that the Lord Marquis and Prince Maurice should that night break through with all the horse to Oxford; and that Sir Ralph Hopton... with the Earl of Marlborough, the Lord Mohun, and other good officers of foot, should stay there with the foot and cannon...till the generals might return with relief from Oxford.'[3]

On Sunday, 9th July, these men slipped out of the town, their hooves muffled and voices hushed, winding their way under cover of darkness through the quietened Roundhead lines.

Storming Devizes, a possible option for Waller, should theoretically have been easy. The town had no defensive walls, and only a series of minor ditches and low earth banks presented any likely obstacles to an enemy approach. Hurriedly constructed barricades at the street ends complemented these fragile works, but they were hardly the materials for a robust defence. Behind, stretched to cover the entire perimeter, were the 2,500 Cornishmen left after the departure of the horse. But Waller chose instead to tease out his opponent, baiting the Royalists with a merciless bombardment from seven guns placed on the ridge at Coate. So began the siege of Devizes, a full scale action between two full size

---

[3] Clarendon, Earl of. 'The History of the Rebellion and Civil War in England'. Vol III, Bk VII, Page 112.

armies, and in no way comparable with Wardour. For the towns-people, forced like badgers to share their sett with a grounded fox, that cruel cannonade from the nearby slopes must have appeared as retribution for their indifference. Throughout the nation, communities were discovering the hazards of neutrality - successive or simultaneous punishment by the armies of either side. For three days, the Roundhead guns thundered, pouring their pitiless shot upon the town's huddled houses, citizen and belligerent alike withering under the almost incessant fire. Poor Sir Jacob Astley nearly lost his genitalia from a chance or well aimed shot.

> *'Monday and Tuesday (10th and 11th) were spent in repulsing the continued storms of the enemy,'* wrote Hopton in his own account of events, *'which both night and day attempted them in several parts with foot, horse and cannon.'* [4]

Waller, despite a more determined Royalist resistance than he had expected, remained optimistic throughout. Soon after his guns had opened, he wrote to Westminster, boasting that he would be providing a full list of captives taken and the details of their property. His dragoons, numbering about 500, were stationed near Potterne on the south side of town to prevent any escape in this direction, while most of his horse kept vigil near the crest of Roundway Hill. That same evening, Providence again declared itself in Parliament's favour, rescuing him from almost certain capture during a sortie from the town. Returning to the farmhouse in Roundway which served as his base, he found that his supper was not yet ready.

> *'In a sudden impatience I resolved not to sup at all,'* he explained in his own account, *'and so took horse again and rode up to the top (of Roundway) where the body of*

---

[4] Hopton, Lord R. 'De Bellum Civile'.

my horse lay. I was not gone above a musket shot, but some of the enemy....rationally supposing I might quarter in that place in regard of the convenient situation of it, between my horse and my foot, came into the house...made a search for me.[5]

Denied their expected prize, they broke the furniture instead.

Wednesday provided a welcome respite. At Hopton's suggestion, a trumpeter was sent to Waller, requesting free passage for the body of Grenville. The Roundhead commander apparently consented, silencing his guns for a few hours in accordance with Hopton's request. Something, however, must have happened during this passive interval for Hopton later spoke sourly of his rival and former friend.

St. John's Church, Devizes

---

[5] 'Recollections of William Waller'. Quoted in Waylen.

'Which, (the request for free passage), though granted, was not so honourably performed, as from Sir Wm. Waller's ancient friendship with him (Hopton) might justly be expected. [6]

Most pressing for the trapped Royalists was the shortage of powder and match. Following the explosion at Marshfield and the defeat of Lord Crawford's force at Beckhampton, only 150lbs weight of match was left and virtually nothing in the way of powder and bullets. Almost in desperation, Captain Pope, a careful man and Comptroller of the Ordnance under the command of the Earl of Marlborough, informed Hopton of the desperate shortage of these three essentials. Sir Ralph, physically injured but retaining all his former agility of mind, saw a chance to improvise. He instructed Pope to gather bed cords from the citizens: these objects, when beaten and boiled in resin, provided more than fifteen hundredweight of passable match! Versatile minds also found a way of providing bullets. Lead was stripped from the roof of St Mary's Church, and a supply of powder was provided by Alderman Richard Pierce, an individual who, for reasons best known to himself, had stockpiled vast quantities of the material over the previous months. For this service to the Royalist cause, he was later proscribed by Parliamentary sequestrator's and obliged to pay for his crime.

This individual generosity, possibly forced, transformed the Royalist stance. In place of the cowed humility of the previous days, the defenders became almost vibrant. The episode was commemorated in the 'Caroloiades', a collection of hackneyed verse written by Edward Howard, one of the sons of the Earl of Berkshire:

'Provided this, with bold joy they defy

---

[6] Hopton, Lord R. 'De Bellum Civile'.

By peals of shot the daring enemy;
And with recruited fury sallies make
Where posted they kill, and prisoners take
Scorning that works their valour should confine
Who durst the place defend without a line.'

Replenishment only just occurred in time. The long delayed Roundhead assault was delivered during the closing hours of Wednesday the 12th. Waller and Dowett jointly led the attack, breaking through the flimsy barricade near St John's Church, and appearing at the head of their cavalry in the streets adjacent. Marks on the building's outer walls record that afternoon's fighting, small pit-like features caused by canister shot. But, unable to hold this miniature bridgehead, Sir William withdrew, leaving several of his unhorsed troops in enemy hands.

He chose instead to demand surrender. The Royalists, spirited by the action, chose to stall, asking for two hours to consider the Parliamentary demand. Waller agreed, even extending the period of truce by a further six hours. It was an almost open confession of his inability to take by force what the enemy seemed unwilling to concede. He had played his most valuable cards too quickly, and his only means of prizing the enemy from the town had been severely blunted. The skilled chooser of terrain and mover of armies was still a cadet in the more subtle arts of negotiation.

Yet time would increasingly dictate the pace of his campaign. For Devizes was now under the national spotlight, and the attention of Oxford and Westminster focused on the Wiltshire struggle. The Royalists had most to lose. The King's standard in the south was carried by Hopton's tired army, the only Cavalier field army south of the Thames. Destruction of this besieged force would be cataclysmic. Already the relieving party was in the process of formation, with Maurice and Hertford at its head. Every hour that Devizes held intact brought that force a little closer. Seen in this context, Waller's extension of the truce was unwise, and hardly the product of sound thinking.

Siege of Devizes

But division in the Parliamentary ranks might be partly to blame. Sir William was the tool, not the craftsman of Roundhead strategy in the south. With larger forces, he might have done more. Watching resentfully from his quarters at Thame was Waller's superior, the Earl of Essex, Lord General of Parliament's armies, and a man increasingly jealous of Waller's recent success. Compared with the Earl's dull lethargy, Sir William's mercurial movements were like golden days of sunshine after weeks of mist. Burgeoning animosity and jealousy of the junior's growing reputation, fuelled by a desire to do nothing to assist Waller to gain yet further credit, slowed the peer's movements still further, and requests for help were largely ignored. So while Waller was losing his battle with time at Devizes, Essex remained immobile at Thame, arguing that the need to hold the Oxford Royalists prevented him from marching to Waller's assistance.

Westminster's M.P.s were fortunately more appreciative of Waller's efforts. On the 12th they voted £10,000 for his immediate use, and simultaneously addressed urgent appeals to the committees of the neighbouring counties to provide him with assistance. But events had overtaken posturing, and no amount of London goodwill and financial assistance would halt the Royalist advance from Oxford or alter the immediate situation in Devizes. Waller's generous truce dragged on into the early hours of the 13th. By then, the relief party had already passed through Marlborough. The siege, into which Waller had entered with such well grounded optimism, was about to be transformed.

But not before another injection of divine involvement. Sometime during that final day of siege, Waller rode south to visit his dragoons at Potterne.

> *'And being to return back'*, he states, *'it suddenly came into my mind to go by another way than that I came; which some of the party and some of my own servants who stayed a little behind, not observing, but taking the*

former way, they were almost all taken by the enemy. I
came back safely.[7]

God might have again rescued his general. Yet during the next few hours, He would become a more impartial observer, watching the unfolding events from a dispassionate distance. That afternoon, Waller's scouts came galloping frantically to the farmhouse headquarters: lines of Royalist cavalry were ascending the ridge of Roundway Down. Waller, it seems, had lost his fight with time.

---

[7] 'Recollections of William Waller'.

10

'His formidable regiment of lobsters'

MAURICE and Hertford, also contesting that race with time, had won. Covering the 44 mile trip to Oxford in one night, they had an audience with the King on the morning of the 11th. Here they received his immediate blessing to launch their crusade of salvation. They, and no other, were to author the Royalist victory that emerged during the afternoon of the 13th on the Downs above Devizes. Yet they were to be assisted by errors of judgment and strategic planning on the part of Parliament, problems of co-ordination that played into Royalist hands.

Only three hours after that brief audience, the horses were again in harness. There had been barely time to refresh the tired animals, and now the hurrying was to begin again. Saddle sore troopers assembled in silence at their muster points, checking their mounts and weapons. Accompanying them on the long journey were Sir John Byron and a body of the King's Lifeguard, 500 or so men, whose normal task was to protect the King's person.

The force that left Oxford on the afternoon of the 11th, more than 1,000 men in total, was headed by dignitaries. With Prince Maurice were Lord Crawford, the fugitive of Beckhampton, Lord George Digby, the Earl of Carnarvon and, of course, Sir John Byron. Lord Henry Wilmot, Lieutenant-General of the King's Horse, had already left Oxford on the 10th, probably ordered south to protect Crawford's ammunition train. Cruising somewhere in North Wiltshire, he was now ordered to unite with the expeditionary force at Marlborough and assume command. Two days later, this united force, formed into three brigades, reached Beckhampton and began their deployment east of Roundway Hill.

Waller, unaware of this determined activity somewhere to his north, was now strategically bankrupt. The physical and mental demands of the siege had drained his men, and his jaded troops waited listlessly on the grassy slopes outside Devizes, wishing only for the chance to sleep or for a new found sense of purpose. Thoughts of home were ever present and the long summer days and nights without sleep or action were more destructive of morale than even the most unfavourable military engagement. For many, the war already seemed limitless and elastic, like a horizon in constant recession. When the Royalist cavalry eventually appeared in the vale beyond, their arrival consequently evoked mixed reactions: the fear of fighting mingling with a more welcome sense of immediate involvement.

Waller's thoughts are hardly recorded. For part of that morning, the 13th, his guns had ranged on the tower of St John's, a Royalist observation point. But he had probably already decided to lift the siege, and his futile bombardment was little more than a cover behind which to conceal the planned withdrawal of his troops. Soon after midday, the Parliamentary army was observed evacuating Coate and the fields to the north. The siege of Devizes was over.

Sometime during those hours of frenzied activity, two cannon shots were heard from the far side of Roundway Down. This was the pre-arranged signal, a message to the besieged of the town that relief was imminent. The Earl of Marlborough answered with the castle's ordnance, their sudden and unexpected voices unnerving the lines of Roundhead soldiers clambering up the southern slopes of Roundway Down. Then all was silence again - the almost proverbial silence that precedes the storm.

But the Royalist commanders, despite the distant herald of relief, were wrapped in indecision. Some of those present in the council of command advocated extreme caution, suspecting that Waller's regression might be a ruse to draw the Royalists from the town. They had not, after all, received any written confirmation of Wilmot's arrival. Hopton, initially keen to order an immediate advance to the Down, conceded the wisdom of this caution and so decided to await further events.

Waller, however, had no doubts. Breathless scouts came riding in, bringing him full details of the enemy movements. Those they passed in the Parliamentary lines placed differing interpretations on the messages they carried, and a thousand inquisitive faces searched the furrowed brows of the hurrying horsemen for confirmation of their thoughts. Strategically, they were now at a disadvantage, caught between two enemy forces simultaneously. To the northeast were Wilmot's horsemen, the undefeated flower of the Royalist army. Behind, in the sunlit town, were the Cornishmen, straining at the leash to avenge themselves on their tormentors. Waller's only chance of victory lay in attacking each Royalist force in turn, eliminating the two parts before they could launch a concerted assault. Numerically, he had the means: with 2,000 horse and 2,500 foot, he could outnumber each of his separated adversaries. He also held the high ground, that long ridge of Roundway Hill which overlooked the road from the east by which the Oxford army would be most likely to advance.

But Roundway Hill was just one of four prominent features in the coming battle's landscape. Across Roughridge and Morgan's Hill, the two most easterly members of the quartet, ran the Wansdyke, an ancient man made ditch and bank. Still evident in the countryside today, this narrow line is punctuated at Shepherd's Shore by today's busy A361. The long deceased Bath old road ran further north, passing between Roundway Hill and outlying King's Play Hill on its unobstructed way to the west. It was promising terrain, certainly for the army which first mastered its topography and gained the commanding points. Flat-topped and with gentle vale-like ground between, these separated hills would permit the deployment of forces even larger than those now about to meet in conflict. Any one of these hills might equally have been chosen:

Roundway's only claim to predominance was its proximity to nearby Devizes.

It is not entirely clear which of the two forces deployed first. Wilmot, recognising as much as his adversary that Royalist victory might well hinge upon the role played that day by the Cornishmen, urgently dispatched a fleet-footed messenger to the town, requesting Hopton to fall immediately on the rear of the Parliamentary army. It seems however, that this sole ambassador fell into enemy hands. The Royalist infantry consequently remained in town and the hoped for co-operation was delayed. He then moved his cavalry south-westward towards Roughridge Hill, a point from which he might view Hopton's advance from Devizes. Captain Richard Atkyns, one of those travelling with Wilmot that day, suggests that the signal gun was fired from Roughridge, and that the Parliamentary ranks had already formed in battle order on the eastern slopes of Roundway Hill.

Slopes of Roundway Down

'We lost no time, but marched towards the enemy, who stood towards the top of the hill...upon one of the hills we discharged our cannon, to give notice to our foot that we were coming to their relief.'[1]

Recognising the dangers of confronting an enemy which consisted entirely of mounted troops, and the equally dangerous threat to his rear, Waller had deployed his army in the conventional pattern, with his foot in the centre and his cavalry on the flanks. Sir Arthur Heselrige and his famous 'Lobsters', the curiously armoured Cuirassiers, formed the right flank, placing themselves either on the south-east slopes of the hill, or on the gentler land at its base. The infantry, five regiments, lay across the ridge.The left flank cavalry, commanded by Waller himself, ranged north of the hill as far as the old Bath road. Filling the gaps between horse and foot were the seven guns, still hot from their prolonged bombardment of the town of Devizes.

Tested on many previous occasions, this deployment was the formula for successful defence, a solid compact body of horse and foot that could be instantly fluid if the need arose. Massed infantry in the centre, opaque lines of tall pikes and supporting muskets, could withstand most frontal assaults while the horse on the wings could wrap themselves around the enemy flanks and cut the route of retreat. But as a weapon of attack, this military style was limited. Designed for setpiece battles between two confrontational armies, it left the rear exposed, open to sudden attack from behind. In adopting this orthodoxy, Waller was drowning in self-deception. For Roundway Down was to be no two dimensional setpiece action. Like a snake in a basket, the entire Royalist infantry lay enclosed and coiled in Devizes, temporarily stunned, but ready to strike when the moment arrived. Waller, too experienced to expect anything less, could do little to prevent it, and his positions on Roundway Hill were adopted in some vague hope that the

---

[1] Atkyns, R. 'The Vindication'. Page 23.

serpent in his rear would fail to spring. Urgency then forced the pace of his decision. He chose to deal with the threat on his east before the Cornishmen in the town could take their revenge. His purely defensive stance was suddenly transformed, Clarendon, although no tactician himself, was critical of Waller's sudden decision to abandon those structured positions on the hill.

'Here Sir William Waller, out of pure gaiety, departed from an advantage he could not again recover; for, being in excellent order of battle...and gratifying his enemy with the same contempt which had so often brought inconvenience upon them...he marched with his whole body of horse, from his foot, to charge the enemy, appointing Sir Arthur Heselrige with his cuirassiers apart to make the first impression.'[2]

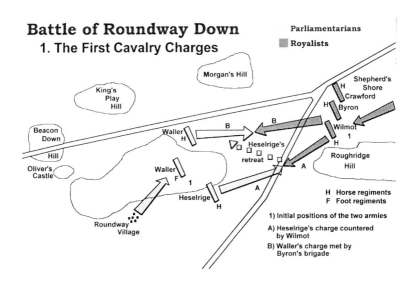

Battle of Roundway Down
1. The First Cavalry Charges

Parliamentarians
Royalists

Morgan's Hill
King's Play Hill
Shepherd's Shore
Crawford
Byron
Beacon Down
Waller H
B
B
Wilmot
1
Hill
Heselrige's retreat
H
Oliver's Castle
Waller F 1
A
Roughridge Hill
Heselrige H
A
H Horse regiments
F Foot regiments
Roundway Village
1) Initial positions of the two armies
A) Heselrige's charge countered by Wilmot
B) Waller's charge met by Byron's brigade

---

[2] Clarendon, Earl of. 'The History of the Rebellion and Civil War in England'. Vol III, Bk VII, Page 118.

Wilmot, still stationary on the edge of Roughridge Hill, had positioned his brigades in stepped formation, each unit overlapping the one behind to present a cohesive and unbroken front. His own brigade, forming the front and left flank of the Royalist force, would be most exposed to the enemy attack. Both commanders had screened their forces with a Forlorn Hope, a body of musketeers, and the day's battle began with a brief skirmish and volley of musket shot before the heavily armed cuirassiers moved into action. In ranks six deep, the 'Lobsters' surged forward, spurring their horses into a furious charge across the open ground between the two armies.

Wilmot's men were also in movement, matching the sudden rush of Parliament's elite with a swiftly executed counter-charge. Surprised perhaps at the Royalist courage, the 'Lobsters' stopped briefly to fire their carbines. Then, drawing their pistols, they lurched savagely forward into the less densely packed ranks of the Royalist horse. But Wilmot had something of an advantage. Advancing only three deep, his longer lines overlapped the Parliamentarians. His men were therefore able to turn inwards and threatened to enclose their enemy. Within minutes that first Roundhead charge had been repulsed and the Parliamentary battering ram was dented.

Sir John Byron, observing the clash from the front of his own brigade, reports that the Parliamentarians then charged again, but with no greater success:

> *'Sir Arthur Heselrige seconded these (the Forlorn Hope) with his formidable regiment of lobsters, I mean his cuirassiers, whom the lieutenant-general undermined with his brigade, and forced them to retreat; not so, but that they rallied themselves again and charged the second time, but with worse success...so then...they all ran away*

that could, and from that time, Sir Arthur Heselrige appeared no more in battle.[3]

Poor Sir Arthur appears to have been wounded, a convincing reason for withdrawing from the fight. Captain Richard Atkyns claims responsibility:

'Twas my fortune in a direct line to charge their general of horse, which I supposed to be so by his place. He discharged his carbine first, but at a distance not to hurt us, and afterwards one of his two pistols before I came up to him, and missed with both. I then immediately struck in to him, and touched him before I discharged mine...And I'm sure I hit him, for he staggered, and presently wheeled off from his party and ran...I came up to him, and discharged the other pistol at him, and I'm sure I hit his head, for I touched it before I gave fire, and it amazed him at that present, but he was too well armed all over for a pistol bullet to do him any hurt, having a coat of mail over his arms and a headpiece.[4]

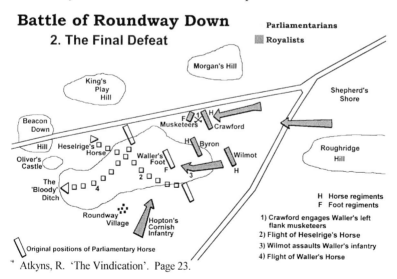

Battle of Roundway Down
2. The Final Defeat

Parliamentarians

Royalists

Morgan's Hill

King's Play Hill

Shepherd's Shore

Beacon Down

Hill / Heselrige's Horse

Oliver's Castle

The 'Bloody' Ditch

F Musketeers

H Crawford

H Byron

Wilmot

Waller's Foot

2 F

3

H

Roughridge Hill

Roundway Village

Hopton's Cornish Infantry

Original positions of Parliamentary Horse

H Horse regiments
F Foot regiments

1) Crawford engages Waller's left flank musketeers
2) Flight of Heselrige's Horse
3) Wilmot assaults Waller's infantry
4) Flight of Waller's Horse

[4] Atkyns, R. 'The Vindication'. Page 23.

But Sir Arthur took revenge, cutting the nose of Atkyn's horse, '*...that you might put your finger in the wound*', and cutting away part of the bridle. The Parliamentarian, pursued by several other Royalist glory-hunters, was the target of several more close range shots, but '*...twas but a flee-biting to him*'. Charles, informed of this hand to hand combat and the miraculous survival of the Roundhead knight, was ruefully heard to comment: '*...had he been victualled as well as fortified, he might have endured a siege of seven years.*'[5]

At some time during this confused fighting, the Royalists captured four of the Parliamentary guns, dragging them back towards their own lines. But although these were promptly recaptured and pulled back to safety, Heselrige's '*impenetrable regiment*' (Clarendon), had almost ceased to exist.

Waller clearly delayed his own entry into the battle until this moment, choosing not to commit his left wing until he had seen the results of the fighting on his right. Heselrige's broken 'Lobsters' had retreated northwards, passing across the front of Waller's waiting ranks. This, or disbelief at the scale of the rout, might have slowed his reactions and prevented him from moving to his colleague's support. But now his own cohorts were at last in motion, the brigade's advance sharpened by two cannon, and his left flank protected by a detachment of musketeers.

His advance merely triggered a corresponding move by Byron, and the resulting clash of horse was to be a mirror image of what had happened on Parliament's right. Byron again takes up the tale:

'As I marched towards them up the hill, their cannon played upon me at a very near distance, but with very small loss, killing two in Colonel Sandy's regiment; the musketeers all this while played upon our flank...By this

---

[5] Byron, Sir John. 'Relation to the Secretary of the last Western action between the Lord Wilmot and Sir William Waller'. Journal of the Society for Army Historical Research. Vol 36, Page 131.

time were come very near to Waller's brigade, and the command I gave my men was, that not a man should discharge his pistol till the enemy had spent all his shot, which was punctually observed, so that first they gave us a volley of their carbines, then of their pistols and then we fell in with them, and gave them ours in the teeth. [6]

His account makes no claim to runaway victory or the superiority of Royalist arms. Instead he talks almost impartially of brave enemy resistance and spirited fighting. But the Parliamentarians had spent their ammunition and most of their energy in the early moments of the attack, and Waller's cavalry wall began to crumble. Gradually the Parliamentarians were driven back up the hill, their humiliation disbelievingly observed by the rest of the now passive field. It was to be one of the most rapid and complete routs of the war, a point made by Clarendon: *'In half an hour'*, he states, *'the entire body of the horse were so totally routed and dispersed that there was not one of them to be seen upon that large spacious down.'* [7]

One of the agents of that rout was the Earl of Carnarvon. Unofficially present on the field of Roundway, he apparently volunteered to serve in Byron's regiment. The latter, in deference to his peerage and proven military qualities, placed him at the head of his charging regiment, and generously attributes much of the credit to this dashing youth. Crawford chose to stake his claim in the closing minutes, sending his unused brigade thundering up the hill in support of Byron. For a short while, his men were engaged by the body of Roundhead musketeers on Waller's left, but the speed of movement and the thunder of hooves soon left the

---

[6] Byron, Sir John. 'Relation to the Secretary of the last Western action between the Lord Wilmot and Sir William Waller'. Journal of the Society for Army Historical Research. Vol 36, Page131.

[7] Clarendon, Earl of. 'The History of the Rebellion and Civil War in England'. Vol III, Bk VII, Page 118.

Roundhead foot passively watching from the sidelines, like spectators at a football match. All of Waller's cavalry, their escape route to the south blocked by Wilmot's waiting men, were now galloping westward in flight, each man infected by the panic of his neighbour.

Nature also seemed anxious to take some of the credit for victory. The land beyond was deceptive, for the gentle rise of Roundway Hill ended abruptly at its western limits in a steep drop of 100 metres. Horses and riders, unable to rein in time, cascaded downwards to their deaths, perhaps more than 100 in total. Ironically Waller, the skilled chooser of terrain and sculptor of topographical advantage, had unwittingly positioned his men on the lips of a natural trap.

The men of Cornwall, desperately attempting to interpret the play of events on Roundway from distant Devizes, witnessed that unparalleled catastrophe. *'We could see the enemy's whole body of horse face about and run with speed,'* says Colonel Slingsby, *'and our horse in close body firing in their rear, till they had chased them down the hill in a steep place, where never horse went down nor up before.'* [8] Only then did the slow advance begin, goaded as much by curiosity as a desire to become involved.

Lord Wilmot's Brigade	Sir John Byron's Brigade	Earl of Crawford's Brigade
Lord Wilmot's Regt.	Sir John Byron's Regt.	Earl of Crawford's Regt.
Lord Digby's Regt.	Sir Henry Sandys' Regt.	
Sir John Digby's Regt.	Thomas Morgan's Regt.	

Plus 300 dragoons under the command of Major Paul Smith.

---

[8] Hopton, Sir R. 'De Bellum Civile'. Page 98.

The Roundhead foot, with the exception of the rudderless detachment on Waller's left, had remained inactive throughout the fight, witnessing the decommissioning of the cavalry, but without the power to intervene. This, after all, was destined as a cavalry battle, a contest between the mounted warriors of both sides, and there was consequently no conceivable role for the foot. So while the horsemen of both sides swirled in tightly packed confusion, firing their pistols at close range in a fight for survival and victory, the infantry could do little more than observe. Throughout that brief half-hour, they remained in disciplined lines, colours and pikes erect, and with their thoughts and emotions unrecorded.

But their time was soon to come. While Byron set out in pursuit of the cavalry, Wilmot, with little else to do, savagely turned on Waller's infantry, hurling his jubilant horsemen at their stationary lines, and capturing four guns in the process. As resilient as the summer breeze that blew across the hill, the pikemen stood their ground, parrying the waves of horse that struck incessantly. For a brief but indelible moment, it seemed that the untired ranks of Roundhead infantry might yet inflict irreparable damage on the Cavalier horse, and a Roundhead victory was suddenly possible.

Hopton's Cornishmen arrived in time. With their arrival, that brief hope of changing fortunes faded. And with it went the resolution of Waller's stubborn foot soldiers. The captured guns had now been turned, and were disloyally firing on their former owners. Unable to cope with Wilmot's frontal attack and an impending assault on their flank, the Roundhead cohorts broke, their solidity liquifying in seconds. Men streamed northwards, anxious to escape the inevitable punishment. Waller's army, the veterans of Lansdown and his earlier battles, had ceased to exist.

Byron, returning from the pursuit of the cavalry, jubilantly reports the details:

> *'They began first gently to march off, their officers marching before them, amongst which (as I have been told since) Sir W.W. himself was, and Popham. With that,*

I advanced towards them with those troops I had rallied, and shot at them with the cannon I had formerly taken...Our horses fell in amongst them and killed six hundred of them, and hurt many more, and took eight hundred prisoners and all their colours, and this was the success of their great conqueror. [9]

No amount of polemics from London could alter that unpalatable fact or conceal the truth. Waller did not even try. *'My dismal defeat'*, he wrote in his Memoirs, *'the most heavy stroke of any that did befall me...I had nearly sunk under my affliction.'* [10] Parliament's field army of the south had evaporated, destroyed in a summer's instance on the slopes of a Wiltshire hill. Perhaps as many as 1,800 Roundhead prisoners were taken that day. Waller escaped to Bristol, rallying some of the horse on the way. Many of his dejected men took brief refuge in Chippenham, cruelly killing a townsman, William Iles, who unwisely crossed their path. Clarendon crows comfortably, placing Roundway amongst the most celebrated Royalist victories:

'This glorious day, for it was a day of triumph, redeemed the King's whole affairs, that all clouds that shadowed them seemed to be dispelled and a bright light of success to shine.' [11]

That sunshine was to burn even brighter. News soon reached Oxford of a simultaneous Royalist success at Adwalton Moor in Yorkshire. The entire county had been snatched for the King. *'The*

---

[9] Byron, Sir John. 'Relation to the Secretary of the last Western action between the Lord Wilmot and Sir William Waller'. Journal of the Society for Army Historical Research. Vol 36, Page 131.

[10] 'Recollections of William Waller'.

[11] Clarendon, Earl of. 'The History of the Rebellion and Civil War in England'. Vol III, Bk VII, Page 119.

county was clear to the very gates of Hull,' wrote Slingsby, *'and no enemy to oppose.'*[1]

God, it seemed, had changed sides. And sometime during those moments of euphoria, Charles again extended his hand of forgiveness to his rebellious Wiltshire subjects. *'Distressed and poisoned people of Wiltshire'*, he declared, *'a forgiving and virtuous heart awaits all those who will now lay down their arms against their lawful King'*. But for those who continued to obstruct his ways and choke his path with smothering weeds, the wrath of God and his anointed would be awful to behold. The heavy shadow of persecution would fall upon their halls and hearths.

---

[1] H. Slingsby. 'Original memoirs written during the Great Civil War'.

11

'A town most fit for assault'

CHARLES had never chosen to submerge his reign within a forest of political uncertainty. For almost a year he had been forced to battle his way through choking woodland. Now at last, it seemed, he had emerged at the other side, and ahead, on a sunlit and treeless plain, lay his crown, his throne and his dignity.

The propagandists who accompanied him that summer serenaded his successes, ridiculed his enemies and exalted his friends. Essex and Waller, the two arch-demons of the wood, lay trampled underfoot. *'They call his Majesty's forces Woodheads,'* crowed Mercurius Aulicus, *'and since their hand is in, we desire they may think of some word that may put them in mind of Basing, Roundway and Chalgrove.'*[1]

Against Waller, they were particularly vituperative. A poem by the Royalist poet, Sir John Denham, is one of the most stinging:

> *'But now without lying, you may paint him flying,*
> *At Bristol they say you may find him.*
> *Great William the Con- so fast did he run,*
> *That he left half his name behind him!'*[2]

- and Roundway, in Royalist circles, became mockingly known as the 'Battle of Run-away'!

---

[1] Mercurius Aulicus. 1643.

[2] 'The Second Western Wonder'. Printed in London 1643.

Yet the Royalists were far too tired to follow up their success. Abandoning Devizes in the flush of victory, the King's army withdrew to Oxford. Atkyns was among those affected by physical exhaustion and lack of sleep.

> *'My horse had cast two shoes and I was forced to set them at Lambourn,'* he explains, *'when leaning on a post I was so sleepy that I fell down like a log of wood...I fell off my horse twice upon the Downs, before I came to Farringdon, where I reeled upon my horse so extremely that the people took me as dead drunk.'*[3]

But rest and food at Oxford would soon restore their fighting edge. For the King's enemies, however, there seemed little hope of resurgence. Waller was quick to blame Essex for failing to come to his assistance. Essex was equally quick to exonerate himself, reminding the Houses of the smallness of his army and the vital need to defend London. While mud and recriminations flew at Westminster, the Royalist war machine began to turn its hungry eyes towards the remaining Parliamentary positions in the south, hoping to net Waller in the process. But the Roundhead general had escaped to Gloucester and now lay beyond Rupert's avenging trawl.

Bristol ranked first in priority. Second only to London in wealth and the value of its trade, the port's capture would open the western seaways to Royalist shipping and allow unbroken access to Charles' sympathizers on the continent. On July 18th, only five days after the victory at Roundway, Rupert left Oxford at the head of thirteen regiments of foot and an impressive array of horse. Accompanying him was Bernard de Gomme, an accomplished military engineer, and a train of artillery under the Frenchman de la Roche. A purely national war had now been widened, encompassing foreigners in its wake. Soon it would swallow

---

[3] Atkyns, R. 'The Vindication'. Page 22.

Irishmen, Papists from the Emerald Isle, and a host of continental adventurers. And Westminster, too, would import large numbers of foreigners, engaging such men without scruple wherever the need arose.

The Royalist force, approaching Bristol from the north, was to attack in conjunction with Hertford's western army arriving from the direction of Devizes. The capture of Bristol seemed an almost Herculean task, something which the Royalists might never have attempted before their run of recent victories. Enclosed almost entirely by the Rivers Frome and Avon, and by an outer defence line with five forts, each self-contained and connected by five foot deep dry ditches, the city seemed impregnable. But the Royalists were prepared to attempt the impossible and hurl themselves at some of England's most robust defences. On the 23rd, the two Cavalier armies took up positions north and south of Bristol, and began their detailed reconnaissance. Below lay their target, humming with the routines of daily life. On Rupert's right, near his position outside the Brandon Hill Fort, were moored the city's ships, their masts rising as high as the adjacent church towers. In front, more tangible than the flimsy backcloth behind, stretched the city's walls. Like eagles on a rocky ridge about to swoop on prey, they searched for the any chink in the enemy's armour and the key that would let them in.

The following morning, his standard fluttering from the slight prominence of Clifton Hill, Rupert called on the garrison to surrender. His thirteen regiments of foot had been deployed in three brigades or tertia, each under the command of an officer of proven experience. Lord Grandison, slightly wounded at Roundway, and Colonel John Belasyse were positioned to attack from the north while Colonel Thomas Wentworth threatened from the west. Facing Redcliffe, on the south side of the Avon, lay the western Army, Hopton's loyal Cornishmen, also formed into three separate brigades. After consultation with the six brigade commanders, the prince ordered a concerted attack the next day, a simultaneous drive by the entire Royalist foot to break the city's nerve.

Success that day was probably never in doubt. In place of the poorly organised and unconcerted efforts that had dulled the weapons of assault at Cirencester and Marlborough, were instruments of precision, sharpened to cutting perfection by Rupert and his generals during days of careful planning. Synchronisation for the assault was to be achieved by the firing of two demi-cannon placed on the hills north of the city. To avoid confusion, every man in the assaulting army was to wear green, a twig or branch sufficing in the absence of green clothing, and the password 'Oxford' hovered on the lips of every Royalist soldier. Each commander was to concentrate his efforts upon the ditch immediately in his front, regarding the earth wall beyond as his particular zone of action. To combat this unity of purpose, Nathaniel Fiennes, the city's unpredictable Parliamentary governor, had 100 guns, 300 horse, 1,500 foot and the unquantifiable support of the town's more partisan inhabitants. Throughout the night, the defenders were kept awake, plagued by the noise and movement beyond the walls, and the flickering of campfires on the hills above. Deliberate and incessant, these activities were cruelly designed to unnerve the inhabitants and crack their powers of mental resistance.

The Cornishmen in the south, for reasons of their own, chose to 'jump the gun' and launch a nocturnal assault. Soon after 3 a.m. they attacked, throwing their might against the Redcliffe and Temple gates. Rupert, now obliged to work to the Cornishmen's forced timetable, ordered Lord Grandison's gunners to deliver the signal, and a premature attack was launched. In 19 hours it was all over. Colonel Henry Washington's men punctured the defensive cordon between Windmill Hill and Brandon Hill forts, and the small breach was then exploited by Wentworth's and Belasyse's brigades. Ironically, the impatient Cornishmen, who had triggered this early assault, failed to enter, held at bay by Redcliffe's determined defenders. Three of the regimental commanders were killed. Colonel Brutus Buck, the senior commander, was the first to fall. Nicholas Slanning, just 25 years of age, who *'had always despised bullets'*, died of a fractured thigh on the very day that his wife gave birth to a son. Colonel John Trevanion, of a similar age and described by Clarendon as the *'life and soul of the Cornish regiments'*, died only minutes later. This triple tragedy, the killing of veterans of Lansdown and the siege of Devizes, tarnished for ever the glory of that brilliant day.

That evening, Fiennes asked for terms of surrender. At 10 p.m. Bristol passed into Royalist occupation. For the final three hours the fighting had been internal, raging in fury along Bristol's ancient streets. Colonel Henry Lunsford, died during that later fighting while leading his men in an attack on the old town. Other senior Royalist commanders had died outside the walls: Lord Grandison, brigade commander, *'killed in the head of his regiment with a musket ball in the forehead'*, actually died several weeks later. Colonel John Belasyse, attacking near the Windmill Hill fort, was injured by his own sword. Leading his men in the assault on the Roundhead positions, he advanced with weapon in hand. A chance musket ball struck the blade, *'with such force that it bowed like a bow, and remaining still in his hand was driven upon his forehead, that he fell to the ground'*.

The city's fall rocked the gossamer foundations of Parliament's fragile hold in the west. Wiltshire men had fought for Waller at Roundway, fighting for a cause for which they did not much care. Shattered on those grassy slopes, most had returned to their peacetime occupations. When the Royalists, fuelled by their capture of Bristol, turned towards Wiltshire's northern borders, they were to find little to oppose their progress.

Malmesbury changed hands for the fifth time on July 21st. Laid bare by the defeat at Roundway, the town was taken by Royalist forces on their way to Bristol. Mercurius Aulicus gives only a brief description of what might have happened: *'notice being given to some of his Majesty's commanders quartered thereabouts where the guards were weakest, and the town most fit for assault, they fell upon it at night, and having forced an easy passage through the careless guards, made themselves masters of the place...some of the soldiers being killed and the most part taken, the rest providing for themselves, by some close conveyance, under the cover of the night.* [4]

With Malmesbury's loss, Royalist sentiments in Wiltshire quickly resurfaced. The Cavalier gentry, muted and inarticulate during the period of Parliamentary success, slowly re-emerged and called on their neighbours to work for the King. Amongst these new arrivals at the military front was Sir James Long of Draycott Cerne, who now recruited a regiment of horse at his own expense. Parliament, unwilling to agitate the county's political waters too violently, had, unwisely perhaps, left these malcontents alone. Roundhead horse had occasionally grazed on the lawns of Compton House, the home of the Penruddockes, and Hungerford's troopers had reined briefly before the gates of Long's old home. For armchair Royalism had never been a crime, and so remained the path to personal survival.

It would now be the turn of Westminster's supporters to sense the watching eye. Parliamentarianism would survive in men's minds only and in the urban cores of Wiltshire's larger towns. But Cavalier garrisons in Marlborough and Devizes would remain vigilant, searching for sudden sparks that might light the fire of local conflict. Alone in Wiltshire, Ludlow held Wardour, a small burning torch in the darkening night.

Wardour was of limited military value; and its retention would be of little strategic advantage. Sir Henry Ludlow, aware of this obvious fact, tried to persuade his son to abandon the castle, even obtaining from Westminster an order for Wardour's immediate destruction. But Edmund saw things differently. Retention was symbolic, and nothing would induce him to abandon his charge.

---

[4] Mercurius Aulicus. 1643.

His tenacity would do more to raise his reputation than any victory in battle could ever do.

It came at a time when Wiltshire had been effectively abandoned by its former Parliamentary leaders. Sir Edward Hungerford, whose last service to the county had taken place at Roundway, was now campaigning in Somerset. Edward Baynton, his rival for the leadership, was held in distrust, following an attempted duel with a fellow M.P. and almost continuous friction with John Pym and the Parliamentary leadership at Westminster. In August, he was to be arrested for treason, either just before or immediately after writing a letter to Sir Edward Hyde. In this he asks for the King's pardon, and his treachery is beyond any doubt.

> *'...let me entreat you to present my humble service to my Lord Marquis of Hertford, with this request to you both, that his Lordship with your assistance would procure my pardon from the King, which if you can obtain, I will presently come home to my house in Wiltshire...I have written to Sir Lewis Dyves and Mr. Robert Long, who, if you please to speak with them, will be able to assist you with some reasons for this shute.'*

Almost simultaneously Sir John Evelyn was arrested, infected presumably by the same desire to save his skin.

The siege of Wardour did not commence in earnest until the winter of that year. Throughout the summer, Ludlow was to play the heroic adventurer, issuing from his lair on brief mischief making expeditions. But he was unable to prevent the plunder of Salisbury's citizens. This had become an almost daily event, whichever side ruled the city's streets. Many claims for compensation survive, most from the long period of Cavalier domination that would stretch uncomfortably into the coming year. The King's soldiers seem to have had a strong penchant for women's clothing. The theft of petticoats was particularly appealing. John Ffussell, a cotton worker, complained of the loss of *'a cloak, a coat, and other wearing apparel, one petticoat of my wife's and waistcoat with all our best linen'*, while Thomas Bridman lost *'a petticoat, two pairs of boots, a saddle, a yard and a half of satin with other household stuff and money'* - at least £15. Royalist soldiers were later seen dancing in the streets, dressed in these ladies' clothing.

Their superiors were involved in more weighty matters, and had little time or wish to mete out punishment for this kittenish light-heartedness. But towards the enemy, they were less forgiving, and a period of merciless witch-hunting would now commence. This would require a framework of law and a magistracy prepared to hunt. Hastily constructed in December 1643 and legally unsound, the resulting Commission of Assize was to fall with a crash before its intended victims could even be summoned. The rhetoric of its opening was to be far more poisonous than its bite:

> *'There is an inconsiderable number of men now gotten together (who are mad as I think), that have not only gone about to frustrate and make void the King's Broad Seal, by which authority we sit here...And therefore they ought to be enquired after, and be presented and indicted here, together with all those that adhere to them, as many as you can find.'*[5]

Three names were mentioned for immediate trial: Pembroke, Robert Nicholas and Sir Edward Baynton, all to be coloured with the charge of high treason. But the jury, sensing the illegality of the proceedings, refused to regard these men as wrongdoers and the trial collapsed before it began.

Ludlow might well have been a future candidate for committal - and probably with good reason. Waging a one-man war against impossible odds, he probed incessantly at the Cavalier nerve. On one of his outings, he was very nearly captured. Probably intending to mix with the morning's market folk at Salisbury and

---

[5] Public Records Office, Wiltshire.

Portrait of Edmund Ludlow

personally head count the enemy, he set out from Wardour at the head of just six men. At Sutton Mandeville, he found six well groomed horses outside the village inn. Suspecting that they might be Cavalier mounts, he went in, his primed carbine his only companion.

The door slammed shut behind him. Two Cavalier troopers faced him with loaded pistols, and his Memoirs might never have been written. But his own men burst in and a brief fight followed. Three of the Royalists escaped, one cheekily making off on Ludlow's horse! His appetite for adventure now dulled, Ludlow returned to Wardour, taking his captives with him.

But his feeble antics were hardly noticed by the Royalist commanders in the west. Ludlow's tenure of Wardour was to be extended by events that took place outside Wiltshire. Seen in the context of activities during the summer and autumn of 1643, his brave posturing in western Wiltshire was an irrelevance, something which the King's men chose to ignore. They were more interested in bigger prey in neighbouring counties, and military operations in Wiltshire came to a virtual standstill. Within the county, there was to be a long period of inactivity, unrocked by the wild dash of hurrying men on country roads or the steely clash or arms on village greens. For a while, at least, the whirl of national politics receded and the fogs of parochialism descended once more. Seeing no further than the boundaries of their communities, men and women would be able to concentrate again on the coming harvest and the challenges of the season.

12

'Like a grove of pines in a day of wind and tempest'

THE capture of Bristol unleashed a spate of Royalist energy that sent tremors of disquiet through the scattered Parliamentary garrisons that existed in the valley of the River Severn. This valley remained the single most important playing field of war, the route for access to Wales and the north. Its towns and castles, almost without exception, feature in the war's annals, some changing colour more frequently than the seasons. Supreme amongst the tenuous toeholds of Roundhead strength in the west midlands was Gloucester, held since the start of war by Colonel Edward Massey and 1,400 men. On August 1st 1643 King Charles visited Bristol, and there plans were laid to conquer Gloucester. Seven days later the Royalist army reached Berkeley, and from here deployed northward to threaten the city. Near Brockworth, a small detachment of the Cavalier army under Lord George Chandos was savaged by a Parliamentary scouting party that might have misjudged the enemy's strength. In the skirmish which followed, a young Roundhead, having used up all his musket balls, apparently loaded his weapon with a pebble and killed a Royalist officer.

On the 10th, the siege began. Charles had good reason to be confident. When fully mustered, his force might have numbered as many as 30,000 men, and the city's defences were nowhere as formidable as those at Bristol. Moreover, his army had full command of the Severn and its local daughter streams, and the besiegers were able to divert the flow and deprive the town of its water supply.

> *'We were forced to content ourselves with pump and Severn water,'* one of the defenders later wrote, *'and to grind our corn with horse mills. Their pioneers plied their works in their trenches, the musketeers on both sides playing hard; we lost only a boy and a girl through their indiscretion gazing over the walls.'*[1]

Every conceivable military and psychological weapon was to be employed. Enormous mortars, wide-mouthed beasts capable of propelling missiles weighing more than forty kilograms, were dragged into action by the besiegers during the opening hours. Fearsome in appearance, however, they were frequently ineffective in operation.

> *'That night the enemy shot several granadoes out of their mortar pieces,'* states one account of the siege, *'they all broke, but did no harm; we have since received intelligence that their biggest mortar piece broke at the first discharging of it; they say the biggest in England.'*[2]

Almost simultaneously, in a frantic effort to reduce morale, besieging soldiers began to taunt the guards on the walls. *'Your God Waller has forsaken you,'* they called, *'and Essex is beaten like a dog.'*[3]

In fact, this siege was to become one of the war's most eventful, exhibiting all the dramatic characteristics of siege warfare: sporadic

---

[1] Dorney, J. 'Brief and Exact Relations of the Most Material and Remarkable Passages that happened in the last well formed siege land before the City of Gloucester'. Reprinted in Fosbrooke, T-D. 'An Original History of the City of Gloucester' 1819.

[2] Ibid.

[3] Washbourn, J. 'Bibholtheia Gloucestrensus' 1825.

sorties by the defenders in search of a specific objective, bombardment of the walls by besieging guns, frantic repairs to blistered defences by the city's women and girls, insidious attempts to undermine both the walls and morale of the besieged, and the unrecorded suffering of the innocent. Yet ultimately, it was to no avail. The King was forced to withdraw, and the euphoria of early summer began to dissipate.

News of the fall of Bristol had prompted a rush of pamphlets. One, appearing on the capital's bookstalls during that final week of August, aimed at the waverers rather than the unswerving supporters of the cause. The pen had spat with poisoned rhetoric:

> *'What is the matter, noble citizens, that your hearts are down, do you think the day is lost? Do you think England is lost because Bristol is lost?...Strive to set yourselves in order, for order is the strength of an army, and of a city, but disorder is the confusion of both...strive therefore to find them (malignants) out, give them the Covenant, if they refuse to enter into Covenant with you, let them not live in the city with you...secure them and banish them...cast them out, spare none...*[4]

Gloucester's predicament had caused fresh concern in London. On the 23rd, an ordinance authorised the London military commanders to mobilise six regiments of foot and 1,500 horse, specifically to rescue Gloucester from catastrophe. But this alliance between the politicians and military was rooted in barren ground for there was no money with which to pay the freshly raised troops. Appeals were therefore made to the City, the cause's wealthy paymasters. They responded immediately and the following day members of the London trained bands assembled on Hampstead Heath.

---

[4] Money, W. 'The Battles of Newbury and the Siege of Donnington Castle'.

Two days later, Essex began his advance westwards, adopting a route that would take him close to Oxford and the nerve centre of the Royalist war effort. On September 1st the Parliamentary army crossed the Cherwell and entered the wild Cotswold country. Suddenly it seemed that the course of the war would depend on what happened in the next few days.

News of the Roundheads' approach reached the actors at Gloucester. Massey, anxious to be informed of progress, sent two men to wait on Wainlode Hill, ordering them to light a beacon as soon as the relieving army was sighted, and placed a light at the top of the Cathedral's tower as a sign that the city still held.

On the night of the 4th, despite strong winds and fiercely driven rain, the beacon fire on Wainlode Hill shone brightly: Essex and the Parliamentary army had been seen on the road from Stow. The following morning, buffeted by the elements, the Roundhead force climbed Prestbury Hill and looked down on the blighted rooftops of Gloucester. Few of those present were ever likely to forget the scene below. Parliament's colours still fluttered above the city's battered walls and a maze of empty trenches broke the level ground to the east. For the besieging guns had gone, dragged away by the dejected lines of Royalist soldiers that could be seen merging with the distant mist. Charles, unable to dent the besieger's metal will, had ordered a withdrawal.

Yet it was to be two more days before Essex could enter the city in triumph. Strengthening westerly winds slowed the descent from Prestbury Hill. On the 6th, the weary army entered Cheltenham, driving away an enemy detachment that had been quartered there. On Thursday 7th, Parliament's army at last entered Gloucester, greeted by a message pinned on the south gate which read: *'A city assailed by men but saved by God'*. Providence, not Essex, had been given the credit for the city's deliverance. Massey had just three barrels of powder left when the Royalist guns at last fell silent.

Essex's advance to the distant west, however, had uncovered London. Charles, falling back to Painswick with his army intact, took full advantage of this fleeting opportunity. The campaign that followed was consequently never planned, having emerged as the result of sudden circumstance. Instead of returning to Oxford as his more cautious commanders advised, the King headed north towards Pershore, hoping to entice the enemy still further from London.

Essex was fortunately too wise to take the bait. Noticing that the King's northward movement had again unblocked the path to London, he decided instead to return to the capital by a more southerly route than the one he had followed on the outward journey. But to deceive the King, he first headed north to Tewksbury on the 10th, hoping to convince the Royalists that he was intending to fall on Worcester.

This began a territorial game of chess, each trying to outwit the other by carefully staged moves. Five days of Parliamentary subterfuge followed. On the night of the 15th, Essex at last dropped his mantle of deception. Taking advantage of the dark, he suddenly swung south on the first leg of his march to London. Charles, sitting indecisively beside the Severn, had been wrong-footed.

The chess game now became a race. The Royalists, fifty miles to the north, found themselves engaged in a race towards London. Soon the two armies were marching south-east on roughly parallel tracks, the King's men at least two days behind their quarry.

They were to clash briefly on the way. The Royalist army, moving swiftly through Stow, arrived at Alvescot on the 17th, only ten miles north of the Parliamentary camp at Swindon. Newbury, conveniently placed on the main road between London and Bristol, was Essex's intended destination. From here his army would have a clear run to London through largely friendly territory. Preventing Essex from reaching the capital would require a manoeuvre of brilliance and the good will of Heaven.

The King, however, chose to rely on more earthly help. Rupert, the dashing prince, was just the person to execute a near miraculous move. On the 18th, the young man left the bulk of the

Royalist army at Alvescot and swung south to intercept the Roundhead army as it crossed the open downland of Aldbourne Chase. Colonel John Hurry, one of the war's most celebrated turncoats, at the head of 1,000 men, was detached to hit the enemy column in the rear while Rupert himself led the main body of the cavalry in an attack on Essex's mobile left flank.

Hurry's attack, delivered in close formation on the five cavalry regiments comprising the Parliamentary rear, caused considerable confusion. Rupert, however, fared less well and soon Sir Philip Stapleton, commanding the Earl's vanguard, had turned back to assist the stricken centre regiments.

He struck the Royalist pack in the rear. Charge was met by counter-charge as the two sides clashed in conventional cavalry combat. Men were unhorsed, pistols discharged at close quarters and regimental order lost in a struggle for survival or mastery. The Queen's regiment, commanded by stately Lord Henry Jermyn, bore the brunt of Stapleton's savagery and was almost surrounded. The commander himself managed to escape, but the Marquis de Vieuville, one of the foreign noblemen of the Queen's court, was killed as he fought his way to freedom. Rupert, revelling in this spirited sort of action, was in constant danger, and only narrowly avoided capture after his horse was shot in the head.

It is difficult to unravel the threads of Aldbourne. Rather than a setpiece action, it was a schoolboy brawl, a sort of spontaneous free-for-all that happened without planning. But perhaps this action on the open downland near Marlborough was inevitable. Notions of superiority filled the minds of the horse soldiers of both sides, convincing them that they were better than the infantry arm with which they were obliged to co-operate. Socially this is largely true: the cavalry consisted primarily of gentry and their retainers, the social elite of pre-war England. Militarily this claim to superiority is far more doubtful. At Edgehill it had been the infantry that had shown constraint and greater staying power, and subsequent clashes had done little to dispel this unpalatable fact. But cavalry vanity flowed more deeply than this surface rivalry with the foot: the mounted bodies of both sides wished also to prove themselves as superior to the opposing horse. Few opportunities had presented themselves recently for testing this conviction: Aldbourne had become the jousting ground for which these men had so long sought.

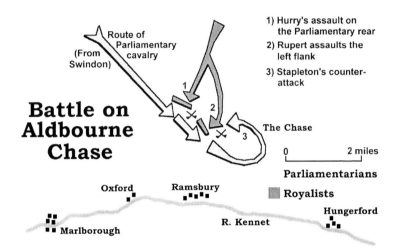

Battle on Aldbourne Chase

Route of Parliamentary cavalry
(From Swindon)

1) Hurry's assault on the Parliamentary rear
2) Rupert assaults the left flank
3) Stapleton's counter-attack

The Chase

0   2 miles

Parliamentarians

Royalists

Oxford

Ramsbury

Hungerford

Marlborough

R. Kennet

The verdict of Aldbourne seems generally to favour Parliament, eroding the view that the Royalist horse were indomitable. Sir Philip Stapleton had shown his skills as a commander and his men had rivalled the dash and style shown by Rupert's men at Edgehill. From now on, until the professionalism and training of the New Model Army swung the advantage in favour of Parliament, the cavalry of both sides seemed generally well matched.

But the battle was a victory for neither side. Although the Roundhead cavalry had successfully driven off a frantic enemy attack, Rupert had just as effectively slowed the Roundhead advance, and Essex consequently only reached Hungerford that night, still nine miles from Newbury.

Heavy rains the following day were to be even more effective in slowing the Roundhead retreat, and it was to be the Cavaliers who reached Newbury first. The Parliamentary army, seeking only the Kennet valley's direct route to London, found their way blocked at Wash Common, just one mile south of the town. This was to bring on the war's second major battle, an action that would be coloured by the consequences of missed opportunities and too hasty planning.

Failure to occupy Round Hill in strength, a gentle prominence that commanded the field, was Rupert's first mistake. Essex, slower moving but quicker thinking, drove the small Royalist detachment from the hill and, by establishing a battery, stole the field of action. But beyond, deployed between Round Hill and the Kennet's banks, lay the Royalist cavalry, solid packs of mounted men that held the road to London. The King's infantry had not yet arrived, but Essex realised that an attack across this narrow neck of rain sodden ground would be bound to fail. Throughout the remaining hours of daylight the field commanders of both sides considered their restricted range of options.

Charles retired to rest in Newbury at midnight, confident that he could now deal Essex's army a lethal blow. His rest might have been untroubled. For Essex, however, searching for the key to victory in tiny Bigg's Cottage, his Enborne H.Q., the flickering lights burned endlessly. Riding at the zenith of his reputation, but dogged by suspicions about the true depth of his loyalties, Essex knew that defeat on the morrow would deliver him into the hands of his critics. To the Lord General of Parliament's armies and his subordinate commanders, huddled around the little table in the parlour, Round Hill was clearly the fulcrum upon which all conceivable strategies might hinge. At some point during those hours of darkness, Skippon's infantry regiment was sent forward to secure the hill's heights and two further regiments were later advanced in support. The entire army slept that night in the open, most bivouacking on the yellowing grass of Skinner's Green, less than one mile from the enemy's quietened ranks. Dawn's grey light exposed their huddled shapes, men in their thousands on the dew sparkled ground, and Parliament's colours flying solidly on the summit of Round Hill.

Lord Essex's strategy largely evolved from what he observed that morning, the 20th. The elite of the Royalist horse, perhaps 4,000 men under the personal command of Rupert, had now drawn up on Wash Common. Essex's immediate response was to reinforce Philip Stapleton, who had only 2,000 men with which to confront this Royalist strength. But the heightening daylight also revealed the sturdiness of the Royalist right, where four entire brigades of infantry manned the eastern edge of Skinner's Green from Round Hill to the winding Kennet. The remaining infantry were consequently sent northwards to secure the river's banks, leaving only Holborne's three regiments to anchor Stapleton's position on Wash Common. The six regiments of the London trained bands, unwilling to fight so far from home, formed the reserve, drawn up in mass behind the Parliamentary centre. 28,000 men stood on the field, roughly equal numbers on either side, and an ominous silence reigned.

Both commanders thought that they had been disadvantaged. Essex, visiting his troops on a morale-raising quest, was forthright, claiming that the Royalists were better positioned. They had, he admitted: '...the hill, the town, hedges, lane and river'. But at almost the same minute, Sir John Byron, a Royalist brigade commander, was criticising the Prince for not occupying the Round Hill in time, '...though we had day enough to have done it'.

Parliament's two guns on the Round Hill sounded the call to arms, their sudden reports sending breakfasting rabbits scuttling for cover. Minutes later, the Royalist artillery on Wash Common responded. The resulting duel is said to have been one of the most prolonged and savage of the entire war. But separated by more than 300 metres from their targets, these guns were merely part of the war of angry words.

Rupert, like an impatient hunting dog on the leash, was ready to tear his Roundhead quarry to pieces. Resplendent as ever at the head of his well formed lines, he saw battle as a frivolous sport, structured only by the laws of the chase with personal glory as its single goal. Separating him from Stapleton's smaller force was almost ideal cavalry country, sloping grassland split by the occasional hedge or unkept enclosure. Soon after 7 a.m. a Royalist skirmish line of musketeers advanced across Wash Common and engaged the Roundhead cavalry. Minutes later, Rupert's troops charged through the musketeers' open line against the raised pikes of Holborn's brigade. These men, locking pikes in an instantly impenetrable wall, held the assault and deflected the Royalist aggression southward against Stapleton's waiting horse.

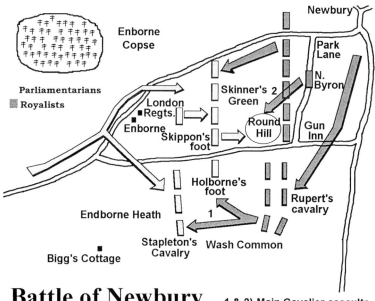

Battle of Newbury   1 & 2) Main Cavalier assaults

Aldbourne was avenged in the next few minutes. Stapleton's men were swept away, little stronger than corn before the reaper, and the brigade was to play no further part in the action. In the centre of the field, Sir Nicholas Byron, one of a prolific family of Royalist supporters and uncle of Sir John, led his infantry towards the northern slopes of Round Hill. Parliament's two guns were promptly swung to face this new threat and the assailants were forced to take cover behind a bank at the south end of today's Dark Lane. Sir John, called to their assistance, scouted the hedges along the hill's northern slopes in search of enemy weakness and found a gap wide enough for one horse to pass through at a time. Lucius Carey, Viscount Falkland, the King's Secretary of State, was riding with Byron's men. In the act of passing through the narrow gap, both he and his horse were killed. His death, probably the most memorable feature of the battle, is commemorated by a memorial near the road to Andover.

Sir John Byron and his men, having broken down the flanking hedge, now stormed angrily up the hill, thrusting at Skippon's infantry with sword and carbine. The defenders, according to Byron's own report: *'entertained us with a great salvo of musket shot, and discharged their two drakes upon us laden with case shot'*. The punishment was devastating, and the proud Royalists were forced to withdraw, leaving many of their comrades dead on the hill's northern slope.

Revenge, however, followed swiftly. Sir Thomas Aston's fresh regiment of horse combined with Sir John's in a further charge and the double fury of their ascent shook the defenders from the summit and back towards a high hedge that lay on the western rise. Temporarily trapped by this product of peacetime farming, Skippon's men, according to Byron: *'...poured in another volley of shot upon us, when Sir Thomas Aston's horse was killed under him, and withal kept us off with their pikes'*. Skippon, watching his tormentors regroup, and surveying the now noticeable gaps in his own lines, fell back to a narrow lane and called on the Londoners of the reserve to assist.

The cruellest killing of the day was now to occur. The Royalist horsemen were faced by an unbroken line of lowered pikes. When finally the Cavaliers withdrew, more than 100 horsemen lay dead at the foot of Parliament's unflinching ranks. This prolonged dialogue between horse and foot had again contradicted the established pattern of warfare and a long held axiom that cavalry normally excelled. Military conventions were overthrown on the little hill; ill-disciplined infantry had weathered the blasts of well mounted cavalry.

The sequel was even more impressive. Skippon, determined to hold the hill at any cost, posted two of the London regiments near the summit. The Blue regiment, placed on the right, was suddenly assailed by Rupert's horsemen. The trained bands stood, *'...undaunted like a grove of pines in a day of winds and tempests...they kept their footing sure'*. Faced by such stubborn resistance, Rupert's attack faltered and his personal pride ebbed.

The day's conflict faded soon after 7 p.m. Nothing momentous or decisive had happened on the battle's northern front. Fighting throughout the field seemed to end by common consent, both sides disengaging before the first hints of darkness fell across the field. It had been a cocktail of missed opportunities and mixed success, one of the war's many indecisive and haphazard battles. Neither side had been forced from the field and the Royalist army still blocked the road to London.

But only for a little while longer. In the hours of darkness, Charles held council. Influenced by a *'foolish and knavish suggestion of want of powder'*, he decided to quit the field. Some of his advisers, amongst them Rupert, argued for remaining at arms on the field and resuming the battle the next day. They were overruled by the faint-hearted King. At midnight the Royalists quietly fell back through Newbury, unwitnessed by the enemy who lay all night on the field. Early the next morning a single shot was fired into the Royalist positions of the night before, but the last of the King's tired men had already gone. Charles's withdrawal had turned stalemate into Roundhead victory and the road to London lay open.

Recriminations were bound to follow in the Royalist ranks. The cavalry perhaps were beyond reproach, but the infantry, with the exception of Sir Nicholas Byron's brigade, had done too little and became the object of criticism in the days to come. *'Had not our foot'*, Sir John later wrote, *'played the poltroons extremely that day, we in all probability had set a period to the war, our horse having behaved themselves with as much gallantry as could be.'* He might well have been correct. Nothing but Essex's army stood between the King and his capital and the probable end of war. But perhaps the single biggest flaw in the Royalist war machine was the King himself. With Charles at the helm, the ship of state would increasingly flounder. Faced by this certainty, many of her crew, in order to save their skins, would abandon ship and swim to foreign shores. Newbury had shown that Parliament was unbeatable.

13

'Surrendered for want of a handkerchief'

LACK of clear strategy and a hazy vision of the future might explain why the King failed to capitalise on his success in Wiltshire. Roundway Down and the threat to London had drained the county of most of its active Parliamentarians, and it is probable that, apart from those serving Ludlow at Wardour, not a single company of men remained in arms for Parliament, and the towns without exception lay open to the Royalist advance.

Royalist disinterest in the county at this stage of the war is hard to explain. The policy of expansion towards the west that had taken Cavalier armies crashing through the earth walls of Marlborough and the gates of Bristol had been largely diverted on new crusades in Dorset and Hampshire, and the Royalist presence in Wiltshire was almost self-extinguished. Devizes, Marlborough and Salisbury, Wiltshire's three main towns, were scarcely visited, and Ludlow in Wardour was only periodically challenged by the Sir Francis Doddington, the county's Royalist commandant.

But although Royalist planning had faltered, Parliamentary strategy for the defence of the county was weakened by personal squabbles and a lack of military muscle. Essex, lauded as victor of Newbury, was applauded when he returned to London on September 29th. Three days later his six London regiments, stalwarts of the Newbury field, were disbanded. The men had been recruited for a specific campaign, and any obligation to continue in arms had now ended. Their departure eroded Essex's strength so dangerously that he felt compelled to abandon Reading. On 3rd

October 1643 the Royalists re-occupied the town and installed Sir Jacob Astley as governor.

Parliament's cause was endangered still further by unnecessary feuding between Waller and Essex, the two men on whom success depended. Waller, perhaps the better general, had long resented his subordinate position and made little effort to disguise his disdain for the Earl. Consequently he worked almost in isolation, openly rebuking his senior, and causing division within the high command. The London press were quick to point out the likely long-term consequences of this unwarranted disunity: *'Can the plough go'*, wrote a pamphleteer, *'where there are no men to hold?'*

The loss of Reading seems to have provided a well needed glue, cementing the two men in an uneasy alliance. On 7th October, an agreement was reached by which Waller consented to take orders from the Earl, but in return was given command of a new army to be raised for service in the west. But mere rhetoric or wishful words were insufficient to physically mould the new force which the Westminster leaders envisaged. Short-term contracts, the sort of arrangement that had allowed the Londoners to lay down their arms, had long bedeviled the recruitment efforts of both sides. For Parliament, relying almost entirely on voluntary enlistment, it was a particular weakness. In an attempt to overcome this, Westminster passed an ordinance in September 1643, permitting the recruiting generals to impress, taking any person between the ages of 18 and 50, with the exception of clergy, scholars, trained band members, widows' sons and the servants of peers still attending the Upper House.

This valuable legislation enabled Waller to secure 5,000 soldiers with which to commence his undefined campaign. The nucleus of the army was formed from the three regiments of horse which had served with Waller at Roundway Down. Waller's own regiment, the oldest of the three, had been amongst those routed at Edgehill. Sir Arthur Heselrige's 'Lobsters', formed only weeks before the Lansdown campaign, had re-emerged, phoenix like, in all its quaint splendour from its destruction at Roundway, and the minor regiment of Col. Robert Burrell was now reconstituted under the command of the able Dutchman, Jonas Vandruske. A fourth regiment, the London horse of Col. Richard Turner, served intermittently with Waller in the campaigns that followed.

The infantry regiments were all new creations and largely the result of the act of impressment that challenged all the notions of freedom and voluntary enlistment that had underpinned participation in the war so far. On 12th October Waller reviewed the assembled army at Hounslow Heath, 7,000 men in total.

Almost coincidentally, the King remodelled his western army. But unlike the woolly semantics which atrophied the Parliamentary decision making, Royalist strategy now emerged more clearly than at any previous time. Hopton, fully recovered from his injuries, was appointed to the command and given specific instructions to clear Wiltshire and Hampshire, and then strike towards London through untouched Surrey. But unfortunately this belated clarity of thought failed to produce an army of sufficient size for the tasks required. On November 4th his force, mustered at Amesbury, consisted of only 2,000 infantry and fewer than 1,600 horse, the latter arranged in twelve miniature regiments.

It was to be some time, however, before these rival creations pitted their wits or strength in direct combat with each other. When the two sides did eventually meet, it was well beyond Wiltshire's eastern borders, and the county was to enjoy another lengthy respite. In the neighbouring counties, most of the campaigning was local, initiated by local men with purely limited objectives. It was to include a struggle for control of Winchester, suddenly and unexpectedly seized from under the noses of Waller's roving forces.

Further west Wareham was seized and Royalist forces attempted to take Poole, Parliament's main bastion in southern Dorset. By the time that Hopton felt able to assist these local initiatives, his infantry strength had mushroomed to nearer 3,000, augmented by recently imported Irishmen and part of the Bristol garrison. Amongst this infantry force was a smattering of Wiltshire volunteers, many of whom had served in the Marquis of Hertford's regiment. This army, forming partly within Wiltshire's now peaceful borders, was destined for service outside the county. Days later, it spilled eastwards into Hampshire, causing panic at Westminster and even further afield. *'There are about 2,000 foot and 2,000 horse of the King's forces,'* wrote Sir Samuel Luke, a prolific letter writer and commander of the Parliamentary garrison of Newport Pagnell, *'...and 'tis thought that they intend either for Chichester or Southampton.'*[1]

Sir Samuel was not entirely correct. On 18th November Hopton's fast moving force appeared near Farnham on the Surrey border in what appeared to be a drive on London.

On Wiltshire's western borders, Ludlow felt able to take full advantage of this autumn reprieve. He and his men fished without hindrance in Wardour's lakes, and their sorties to nearby villages in search of provisions were jaunty relaxed affairs, untroubled by the Royalist forces sent by the King to pen the Roundheads in. Not until December 1643 did the siege begin in earnest, and even then it would long remain a light-hearted affair, with little of the trauma of a vigorous siege.

It is also anecdotal, full of tales of treachery, many described by Edmund Ludlow himself in his 'Memoirs'. Soon after the formal siege of Wardour began, probably in January 1644, the enemy employed a boy to serve as a spy and saboteur.

> *'He was not above twelve years of age,'* writes Ludlow, *'and yet, as I was afterwards informed, had already attempted to poison his grandfather. This boy, he (a Captain White of Dorsetshire) sent to the castle to desire of me to be admitted to turn the spit, or perform any other servile employment; to which I consented, his youth freeing him, as I thought, from any suspicion.'*[2]

---

[1] 'The Letter Book of Sir Samuel Luke'.

[2] Ludlow, Sir E. 'Memoirs'. Page 59-60.

But Ludlow's guards were less trusting. They forced the lad to tell the truth, threatening him with instant execution unless he confessed. The boy then admitted the purpose of his errand: to poison the well and the beer and to blow up the ammunition - for which he was to receive half a crown! He had already been at work. The day previously, a wall gun, fired from the battlements at an adventurous party of the enemy, burst asunder. But he had fortunately not had time to attend to the beer or the well.

Waller's western army

Foot
The Westminster Regt.
The London Green Auxiliaries
The London Yellow Auxiliaries
Sir William Waller's Regt.
Sir Arthur Heselrige's Regt.
Col. Andrew Potley's Regt.

Total: 5,000 men

Horse
Sir William Waller's Regt.
Sir Arthur Heselrige's Regt.
Col. Jonas Vandruske's Regt.
Col. Richard Turner's Regt.

Total: 2,000 men

Hopton's western army

Foot
Sir Ralph Hopton's Regt.
Prince Maurice's Regt.
Lord Hertford's Regt.
Col. Arthur Griffin's Regt.
Col. Allen Aspley's Regt.

Total: 2,000 men

Horse
Sir Horatio Carey's Regt.
Sir John Covert's Regt.
Earl of Crawford's Regt.
Sir Nicholas Crisp's Regt.
Sir Edward Dering's Regt.
Sir James Hamilton's Regt.
Sir Edward Ford's Regt.
Col. Richard Spencer's Regt.
Lord Hertford's Regt.
Ralph Hopton's Regt.
Sir Edward Stawell's Regt.
Sir George Vaughan's Regt.

Total: 1,600 men

The Royalists now built a breastwork to command the castle's main gateway. Probably no more than 200 besieging troops lay in the makeshift camps in the castle's spacious parklands, and possibly fewer than 50 at any one time were engaged in pressing the siege. A Captain Christopher Bowyer commanded the detachment in this new breastwork. Impatient for a victory (or foolishly convinced of his own immortality), he advanced at the front of a storming party and was promptly shot in the heel. Lying unattended for the rest of the day in full view of the castle's defenders, his wound gangrened and he died two days later, the first fatality of the siege.

A Colonel Barnes was now sent to take command. A large pond flanked the castle's western side, hampering the movements of both defenders and besiegers. Higher ground to the east, however, commanded Wardour's other walls. A timber fort was built on this rise, and musketeers were placed in the adjacent outhouses.

Wardour Castle

Ludlow countered every Royalist movement. One evening he sent 40 men, half his entire garrison, down a vault that led from the castle to these outbuildings, ordering his men to remain in the underground passage until he gave the word for attack. But one of the Parliamentarians accidentally discharged his musket and the Royalist guard escaped. Frequent scuffles took place at the vault's exit in the days to come.

Bitter winter days were softened by the first touches of Spring. At last the castle well thawed, and it was no longer necessary to venture by night to collect blocks of ice from the park's great pond. Ludlow had devised an effective roster during that never ending winter, moving his men around in an effort to convince the watching Royalists that his force was much larger. In mid-February a Royalist messenger, seeking to discover the terms on which Ludlow would be prepared to surrender, was permitted to enter. Sir Edmund offered to deliver the castle if Essex had not relieved him within six months. Negotiations were promptly broken off.

There followed another tale of treachery. A soldier sent from the castle on an unspecified errand met a local, possibly a Royalist trooper, who offered to signal news of the arrival of relief forces by standing beneath the castle walls with a white cap on his head and blowing his nose noisily into a large handkerchief. But no sign was subsequently seen of him. Instead a new Royalist battery made itself menacingly visible, raised in the earthworks opposite the castle's gateway. A chance shot cut the chain of the portcullis and the structure crashed to the ground. The defenders hastily erected a barricade to fill the opening. The only exit (and entrance) was now through a window!

The Royalists tried to solve this shortage of openings by blowing a hole through the wall, and experienced miners from the Mendips were employed to tunnel towards the defences. To provide a protective roof below which the miners could work in safety, the besiegers brought up two dozen oak planks. But vigilant sentinels on the castle's walls soon forced the workmen back.

'We heard a noise of digging,' reported Ludlow, *'but for sometime could not perceive where. At length we discovered the place, and endeavoured to remove them, by throwing down hot water and melted lead, though to little purpose. At last with hand grenades we obliged them to quit their work and to leave their tools behind them, with their provisions for three or four days, and though we had no way out of the castle but by a narrow window, yet we brought in their materials and provisions.* [3]

Days later Sir Edmund received a visit from a distant relative, a Captain Henry Williams, a Royalist officer. Obviously sent by the besiegers, this man tried to reason the Parliamentarian into an honourable surrender. But Ludlow was in no mood for discussing surrender. He had recently addressed urgent appeals to the Parliamentary garrisons of Poole and Southampton, offering to send them the castle's plate and a large amount of money in return for their prompt assistance.

But no relieving force arrived and the siege was about to enter its bitterest and most crucial phase. The heady resilience of the formerly well fed garrison was gradually replaced by defeatism and hunger, something from which even Ludlow was not immune. He was seen at night, pacing his chamber, a single candle flickering at the tower window. Sir Francis Doddington arrived to take personal responsibility for the negotiations and the Royalist investment was intensified.

Early in March 1644 , after a week or so of hectic mining and counter-mining, the white capped informant suddenly reappeared, blowing his nose on his sleeve *'for want of a handkerchief'*. Initially taken as indicating relief, its real meaning became clear in the days following: a mine beneath the castle's walls was almost complete and the man's drama was nothing more than a warning of

---

[3] Ludlow, Sir E. 'Memoirs'. Vol I, Page 67.

impending disaster. Ludlow's reign was drawing to a close and his survival lay in the hands of others. Massing his men to storm the building, Doddington sent in his final summons, to which he received an equally forceful reply on the 13th.

> '...I shall never seek by-paths....to attain the haven of peace and happiness. Yet shall I not be so presumptuous upon the mercies of the Almighty, to draw down his justice upon my head, for the guilt of so many men's blood, as are now with me, by an obstinate resolution to withstand all opposers without hopes of relief. If you shall think fit therefore...to permit that a messenger have free egress and regress into our armies, by whom if I understand our condition to be so helpless, as by you I am informed it is, I shall then ease you of a chargeable and dangerous summer siege, by proposing such terms, as to any indifferent man, shall seem most reasonable. If so be you shall continue to lend a deaf ear to this motion, I have herein laboured to discharge a good conscience, and do assign myself that for all the blood that hath or shall be spilt...there shall be a strict account required from you at the dreadful day of judgement.'[4]

Five days later, Ludlow gave in. Only a half carcass of a cow remained hanging in the cellars, and the emptying of the larder had softened his will to resist. And the castle's outer walls had just gone crashing to the ground.

> '...upon the Thursday morning,' he wrote, 'being very weary, I lay down and slept till between ten or eleven of the clock, at which time one of my great guns firing upon the enemy, shook the match which they had left burning

---

[4] Ludlow, Sir E. 'Memoirs'. Appendix II. Ed - by C.H. Firth (1894). Page 454-455.

for the springing of the mine into the powder, so that the mine springing I was lifted up with it from the floor.[5]

Obliged to leave his shattered chamber, he climbed a nearby tower and threw stones at the enemy. But this was hollow defiance, as meaningless as the tantrums of a scolded child, for he had already been persuaded by his personal minister to ask for terms. While waiting for a reply, Ludlow narrowly avoided injury or worse when a musket ball penetrated his hat. That afternoon, the 18th, his men laid down their arms, relinquishing Parliament's last physical hold on Wiltshire. Mercurius Aulicus, crowing over this fact, poured unfair scorn on Ludlow.

'Master Ludlow left off preaching...for when he saw the mine deprive him of his fortifications, he delivered up himself and all the garrison without so much as promise of quarter.[6]

It seems to have been one of the war's less dignified surrenders. Ludlow and his 75 men, however, were taken in chains to Oxford. Accusations of vandalism followed in their wake. Mercurius Rusticus claimed that Ludlow and his men had caused £100,000 worth of damage to the furniture and the park. But Lord Arundell, the owner of Wardour, and now attending the King's court, showed Ludlow unwarranted kindness and made no attempt to exact revenge. Years later, Ludlow was able to repay his generosity by intervening on Arundell's behalf in the Commons at a time when the fabrics of Royalism lay in tatters.

And in March 1644, when Wardour surrendered, more favourable times for Parliament seemed around the corner. Both sides had fought themselves to a virtual standstill, victory in one area offset by defeat elsewhere. On January 25th, however,

[5] Ludlow, Sir E. 'Memoirs'. Vol I, Page 72.

[6] Ludlow, Sir E. 'Memoirs'. Appendix II, Page 455.

Cheshire Roundheads had thrashed the Royalists at Nantwich, suddenly destabilising the King's previously sound ownership of Cheshire and Lancashire. Almost simultaneously, a Scottish army had invaded England, converting the flat two dimensional struggle into something far more complex and vigorous. Slowly but firmly, it pushed south against the strong Royalist presence in Northumbria and Durham. On 28th February, after involvement in a number of running engagements, the Scots crossed the Tyne, and the relentless drive towards York began. Northern England, solid, safe, reliable, and held for the King by the energetic Marquis of Newcastle, was suddenly seen to be vulnerable. Victory in the war seemed likely to go to whoever won in the north, a point which the Marquis of Newcastle made in a letter to the King: *'If your Majesty beats the Scots,'* he declared, *'your game is absolutely won'*.

What happened in southern England's chalky downland and clay vales seemed less important, almost irrelevant beside the great flow of events in the north. Yet even here a decisive Parliamentary victory was about to occur. Throughout the winter, Hopton, carrier of the King's torch in the south, had roamed almost unchallenged. In February he passed through Wiltshire from the west, his arrival causing flights of speculation about his intentions.

> *'If they remove to Ringwood or Salisbury as is supposed,'* one diarist remarked in alarm, *'it must be through want; that part being so poor, and all the country store eaten up, that they (the country) have it not for themselves, much less for such cormorants.'*[7]

On 22nd March, nearly 2,800 Royalist horse and 3,000 foot assembled at Winchester, dispelling lingering doubts about the Cavaliers' true designs. Hopton's reckless intrusion into south-east England was a deliberate thrust at Parliament's soft belly and a personal challenge to a former friend. Reacting with all the outrage

---

[7] 'Letter to the Wiltshire Committee'. Wiltshire Public Records Office.

of a wounded bull, Waller set out in pursuit. Balfour was sent with most of the Roundhead horse to occupy Alresford, the town that lay astride the road to London. And on the 29th, he faced his rival at Cheriton, near Petersfield, in a little corner of England that had so far been almost free of war.

Much of the early fighting took place in the woods to the east and the still existing 'bloody lane'. Acts of heroism and insanity were to become fashionable, but as rash and as pointless as any in the war. Colonel Henry Bard, *'with more youthful courage than soldier like discretion'* led his regiment in a suicide bid against the Parliamentary centre. Not a man of his command returned to tell the tale. Sir Edward Stawell, a man of similar mould, and his brigade were no luckier. Infected by the same lust for self-destruction, other Royalist regiments followed Stawell's example, thundering formlessly against the Parliamentary lines. Sir John Smith, Sergeant-Major-General of Hopton's army, was killed by a Lobster's carbine when his horse reared. *'With this wound he falls,'* lamented Colonel Walter Slingsby, *'and with him the fortunes of the day and the courage of our horse.*[8]

The Royalist infantry were no more successful. But by 3 p.m., after more than six hours of fighting, a Parliamentary pincer movement was developing and the Royalist survivors struggled to resist its clasp.

Yet even then belated acts of heroism took place, pulled like rabbits out of the Royalist hat. Lord John Stuart led the Queen's Regiment on a sudden counter-attack. He fell dead at the feet of the enemy infantry. Then, and only then, did the epidemic of defeat sweep through Hopton's ranks: men pulled off their regal colours and hid them in their breeches.

---

[8] Hopton, Sir R. 'De Bellum Civile'.

166

And the verdict? Clarendon hardly conceals his contempt for the actions of the cavalry. *'The King's horse never behaved so ill - and left their principal officer to shift for themselves.*[9]

Parliament saw it as a deliverance and sweet revenge: *'We acknowledge the great goodness of God'*, the letter of congratulation from Westminster read, *'we are very sensible of the great advantage that will come to the kingdom by a careful and diligent improvement of this success against the enemy for the recovery of the west.'*

Just three days after defeating the Royalists at Cheriton, Waller's army entered Salisbury, frightening away the few vocal Royalists residents in the Close. The see-saw had swung again.

---

[9] Clarendon, Earl of. 'The History of the Rebellion and Civil War in England'. Vol IV, Bk VIII, Page 460.

14

'Prest all of a heap like sheep'

IT was to be Edward Massey, controller of Roundhead fortunes in *'that unfortunately obstinate town'* of Gloucester, however, who eventually carried Parliament's banners back into Wiltshire. Hamstrung by lack of pay for his troops and the refusal of the London regiments to serve too far from home, Sir William Waller's post-Cheriton energy was to be largely expended on fruitless requests to the London committees to forward the arrears in pay, a total of about £1,000 for the London brigade alone, and in efforts to obtain the active co-operation of the Roundheads of Lyme and Poole. Any new Roundhead advance was likely to be forcefully opposed.

The Royalist presence in Wiltshire had expanded in the months since Newbury. Sir George Vaughan, the county's high sheriff, and his small regiment kept a watchful eye over Salisbury, and Goring frequently visited. A townsman has left his own report of the behaviour of Goring's troopers during one of these policing patrols in March 1644.

> *'The soldiers drank hard at day, and at night, having cut holes in their hats and placed lighted candles in them, to run about the streets dancing and roaring.'* [1]

Worse was to follow! The devil himself was said to have joined in! John Vicars, a chronicler of events, describes an evening's drinking session.

---

[1] Vicars, J. 'A Looking Glass for Malignants'.

168

'Divers of Goring's godless soldiers being together drinking and carousing in the "Katherine's Wheel"...one of them starts up and swore desperately he would not pledge such a health (to the King) nor he did not know whether there was a God or a Devil, but that if there were, and he could only see him, he swore he would pledge his health. Whereupon there was immediately a most monstrous filthy stink and suffocating stench all over the room, as it were of brimstone, together with a most dreadful and hideous hissing noise...and then there appeared in sight of them all a most horrid and ugly creature...[2]

It apparently crashed noisily through a window and was lost in the street below. Vicars was not alone in believing that, throughout the war, the Devil assisted the King.

But Charles could also rely upon more earthly support. Two miles east of the city a garrison had recently been installed at Longford Castle, the home of Lord Coleraine, the King's close friend and a generous contributor to the Royalist coffers. Malmesbury was firmly held by Colonel Howard's regiment and two or three troops of horse had retaken possession of Marlborough. In the county's far west William Arundell, brother of the Catholic lord of Wardour, had placed 100 men in his home at Woodhouse, arming and equipping this garrison at his own expense. Clearly not short of money, he had purchased the service of 500 Irish Papists and positioned them at Maiden Bradley, Sir Edward Seymour's family home, an action which caused Mercurius Aulicus to wail in protest:

'Master Arundel of Maiden Bradley hath lent Master Edward Seymour five hundred men, but not one Protestant among them all.'

---

[2] Vicars, J. 'A Looking Glass for Malignants'.

But Chippenham and Devizes, the latter the seat of the county's Royalist commissioners, were largely untroubled and only intermittently garrisoned during that period of Royalist ascendancy. Royalist enthusiasm in the county was excessive. Sir Edward Dering, commander of the Marlborough garrison until his personal submission to Parliament in February, had seized a Master Reynolds, the constable of Everley, who had confessed to having collected money for Parliament. During the man's brief interrogation, in which he declared that he could not simultaneously serve God and Mamon, Dering is alleged to have struck him with his cane and had his hands bound tightly with match. And reports reached London that the men of Marlborough were being forced to take an oath of allegiance to King and Church, a 'Popish oath' which was denounced in the capital's broadsheets. These reports were probably fanciful embroidery and without any real substance. Sunday worshippers, it was stated, were stripped of their clothing whilst in church and given a choice: take the offered oath or receive a bullet in the breast.

The Royalist Commission of Impressment, issued in the Spring of 1644, was unpleasantly real. Addressed to the constables of the county's hundreds, it read:

> *'Whereas by virtue of his Majesty's Commission, under the great seal of England to us and other directed, for the impressing of six hundred and sixty seven able men within the said county of Wilts...These are therefore to will and require you, and in his Majesty's name straightly to charge and command you that presently upon sight hereof, you impress within your said Hundred (number stated) able men, and to bring them to us his Majesty's commissioners at the Devizes...Hereof fail not at your peril.'*

> *First...'you shall make choice of such as are of able bodies'*

> *Secondly... 'they shall be of quality fit to be common soldiers'*
>
> *Thirdly... 'they shall be fit for their age'*
>
> *Fourthly... 'they shall be single men rather than married men'*
>
> *Fifthly... 'being single men, are not housekeepers'*
>
> *Sixthly... 'not being housekeepers, are out of service rather than such as are in service'*
>
> *Seventhly... 'such as are mechanics, tradesmen or others, rather than husbandmen, but no marines'*
>
> *Eighthly... 'you shall take care that they be conveniently apparelled either of their own or by the assistance of the parish where they are impressed'[3]*

Reports of the King's strength in Wiltshire were probably exaggerated. At the beginning of April, Sir Samuel Luke, commanding the Roundhead garrison at the midlands town of Newport Pagnell, informed Westminster that:

> *'The King is quartered in the Earl of Pembroke's house there, (in Ramsbury), and that the King and Lord Hopton have 5,000 horse and 5,000 foot, which are quartered in Ramsbury.'[4]*

This coincided with a rapidly spread rumour that Charles had set up his battle standard at Marlborough and had been heard to say that he *'would be either a King or no King'*.

The Parliamentary campaign which now unfolded was consequently purely defensive. Painfully aware that his diminished force could be no numerical match for the Royalist army that was reported to be massing at Marlborough, Waller set out from Wilton on April 5th, intending to do nothing more than re-establish

---

[3] Waylen, J. 'History of the Devizes'.

[4] The Letter Book of Sir Samuel Luke.

Parliamentary domination on the Hampshire-Dorset border. Limited to the capture of Christchurch, his subsequent push failed to dislodge the strong Royalist presence in West Dorset or materially assist the beleaguered garrison of Lyme.

Massey complemented Waller in every respect. Together the two men might have moved mountains. Adventurous in place of Waller's intuitive caution, Massey displayed restless energy and undoubted loyalty. Inspiring his troops with that same steadfastness, he relished any opportunity to exploit the enemy's weakness and searched tirelessly for the chance to relieve the pressure on Gloucester. But to do this successfully, he demanded an independence of command and the autonomy to operate without reference to the Earl of Essex and Westminster. Permitted to act as he saw fit, he began to forge his own strategy.

His ability to assist Waller was, for a long time, circumscribed by the energies of the Severnside Cavaliers. Sir William Vavasour, the King's commander on the lower Severn, exerted constant pressure on Gloucester. Charles, however, frustrated at Vavasour's lack of success, appointed Colonel Charles Mynne, a man with a reputation for greater aggression, in his place. His arrival sparked Massey into immediate action. In early May, he pounced on the Royalist garrisons at Westbury and Newham, and days later he was leading his forces into the Wye valley, where the nerve centre of Royalism increasingly lay. But he was to remain in Herefordshire for just a few days. On the 20th Parliament's forces evacuated Ross and retired towards Gloucester. More attractive targets lay to the south of the Severn, amongst them Malmesbury, just inside Wiltshire's northern border.

Tetbury, the home of a small Royalist garrison, fell with hardly a shot fired. Nearby 13th century Beverstone Castle, held for the King by a Colonel Ogilvey, was less compliant. Massey, in unwarranted optimism, ordered an assault on the main gate in an attempt to overpower the guard and break the drawbridge chains. Losing a dozen men in just five minutes, the Parliamentarian was forced to search for less costly methods. Placing two drakes within pistol shot of the gate to act as cover, he sent a party of 50 musketeers to fix a petard to the gate.

It failed to explode. Unreliable and hastily placed within full view of the enemy on the battlements, the fuse of this primitive incendiary device went out. Again the musketeers went in under covering fire from the drakes, this time to retrieve the valuable petard for future use. Minutes later, Massey was seen to be in full retreat, pulling back his men in the direction of Tetbury. But his true intentions were masked by deceit. Far too tenacious to voluntarily abandon his catch, the Parliamentary fox had merely withdrawn to await more favourable circumstances.

The opportunity soon arose. Ogilvey had a lady friend in Chavernage, just one mile from the castle's outer walls. Signalling her husband's welcome absences by a candle placed at an upper window, she would periodically invite her Royalist lover to her bedchamber. That night the candle flickered brightly: both her husband and the Roundhead soldiers had gone. Ogilvey set out, taking just six men as a bodyguard. He never reached the lady's arms. The small party were ambushed and sent in chains to Gloucester. Forged orders were sent to the lieutenant left in charge of Beverstone to surrender the castle. At 2 a.m the castle was again surrounded and sixty unguarded horses left grazing outside were captured. Under a flag of truce the surrender demand was then delivered. The young lieutenant, never questioning the authenticity of the document, immediately complied.

Massey was now free to pick a quarrel with the Cavaliers in Malmesbury. The town's Royalists had long expected an attack, but Colonel Henry Howard, son of the Earl of Berkshire and the town's governor, was sanguine about his chances of survival. Late on the 24th, during a violent thunderstorm, Massey drew up his forces near the Westport and delivered a threatening summons. Colonel Howard's reply was courteous but firm: *'I have received your summons, and without any unsavoury language do return you this answer: that we will maintain this town for the King and Parliament now sitting at Oxford, in defence of those rights which that pretended Parliament at Westminster have abused and robbed our nation of*.[5]

Massey, recalling Waller's earlier success, prepared to force the Abbey Bar, the route of that memorable success.

'Thereupon our foot and artillery were brought up...and within two hours drawn into the suburbs and lower part of the town,' states a contemporary account of the action. 'The foot broke their way through the houses till they came almost up to the works, and the only place of entrance into the town, which is built upon the level of a rock.[6]

Expecting a fierce resistance at this point, Massey placed his ordnance near St Mary's Church, positioning his guns to face down the Abbey Road towards the Bar. At some point during the preparations, belief that the Royalists were about to sortie caused some of the Parliamentarians to run. *'This unexpected accident struck those men that at other times would brave it in the face of an enemy'*, states the same report, *'with such distraction and fear, that they all fled, and left their cannon in the open street.'*[7]

Enough, fortunately, remained and Massey prepared to launch these men simultaneously at the three weakest points of the town's defences.

The assault, however, was never launched. The height of the walls on either side of the Abbey Road forced Massey to think again. He chose instead to mass his forces at the break of day on the 25th and throw his entire weight at the Bar.

[5] 'A full and true relation of the several remarkable and victorious proceedings of the ever renowned Colonel Massey'. Reprinted in Bibliotheca Gloucestrensis, Page 325-326.

[6] Corbet, J. 'Historical Relation of the Military Government of Gloucester'.

[7] Ibid.

'The forlorn hope advanced,' the account continues, *'seconded with a good reserve, all put on together, came up to the turnpike, and threw in granadoes, the enemy made many shots at random, in the disadvantage of a rainy night, and their muskets lying wet on the works. So that our men came all in a crowd to the narrow passage, and thronged in, and not a man slain or wounded in the storm.*[8]

Massey had promised to reward the first man into the town. Two horsemen promptly jumped the Bar, cut off the arm of a Royalist soldier who tried to stop them, and shot another in the head. Three balls penetrated Colonel Howard's clothing, but miraculously he was uninjured.

The fighting in the Abbey Row was over in minutes. Thrown back from the barricades by the force of the Parliamentary surge, the Royalists soon fled, dropping their weapons in the ditches on the way. Amongst the 100 or so prisoners taken that day were two sons of the Earl of Suffolk and most of the Beverstone garrison, men who had taken refuge in Malmesbury the previous day in the mistaken impression that they would be safe.

Malmesbury's capture had neither been approved or ordered by Parliament's high command. But on receiving this welcome news, Westminster voted *'that the town of Malmesbury and the castle of Beverstone, as to the government of them, shall be left wholly at the disposal of Colonel Massey'*. The latter promptly appointed Colonel Nicholas Devereux and his regiment to garrison Malmesbury and placed Colonel Thomas Stephens in command of Beverstone.

This was just the start of the Parliamentary triumph. Outside Chippenham, Massey captured a convoy of carts and an entire troop of horse. His men prodded the cargo with the points of swords and unintentionally punctured some well-hidden barrels.

---

[8] Corbet, J. 'Historical Relation of the Military Government of Gloucester'.

Sack and wine trickled down the sides onto the dusty road, and the reward for a day's hard work was lost. But the capture of George Lowe in Chippenham just minutes later was seen as a partial compensation. One of Calne's two M.P.s, this man had recently abandoned his seat at Westminster and joined the King's rival body in Oxford.

In the days which followed, a cavalry outpost was placed at Charlton Park, garrisons were placed at nearby Rowden House, the peacetime home of Sir Edward Hungerford, and at Lacock Abbey. Mr. Sherington Talbot, the abbey's owner, a closet Royalist, was sent as captive to London, a rather harsh treatment for one who had played almost no active part. Chalfield, the 15th century moated manor house owned by Lady Anne Eyre, was also seized and held without incident throughout the summer. Devizes, too, received a fleeting visit. A Royalist troop of horse, part of George Vaughan's widely spread regiment, departed only minutes before the Parliamentary troops arrived. Hoping to capitalise on the Royalist confusion, Massey occupied the town and issued demands for money with which to pay Devereux's troops, and instructions to the local constables to help him destroy the town's Royalist fortifications.

> *'You are hereby required and commanded to summon all the able bodied men for work about your hundred, with such spades, shovels, pickaxes, and other tools as they have, for the present demolishing and throwing down all such works and fortifications as are now standing about the Devizes.'* [9]

Days later, Edmund Ludlow, recently released from imprisonment in Oxford in exchange for three Royalist colonels, made a brief appearance at Marlborough. On June 23rd, the day of the midsummer fair, he fell on the Royalist impressment gang with

---

[9] Commons Journals. Vol III, Page 511.

his small troop of horse, only hours before Hopton himself arrived to take command of the unwilling recruits. 180 grateful men, freed from the Royalist ranks, joined Ludlow's force, swelling his troop to nearly 300. Perfect Diurnal, the Parliamentary newsheet, crows over this personal humiliation of Sir Ralph.

> *'Sir Ralph Hopton, that sun which first arose in the west, is now in a cloud; and for all his great services done to the Cavaliers, is left to the wide world as an obscure outcast, with some few broken remnants of horse which now and then make a shift to plunder and rob in Wiltshire.'*[10]

Bolstered by numbers, Ludlow made his own visit to Devizes in an attempt to augment his force still further. But Massey's high handed demands had almost alienated the townspeople and Ludlow felt compelled to withdraw.

The county's west, however, offered more promise and he now advanced to the assistance of Henry Wansey, a Warminster watchmaker, who, almost single-handedly, had taken on the Royalists of the county's west. This strange man was the head of a divided family, his seven sons fighting in the armies of both sides. His little daughter, present at one of his councils of war during the early summer, claimed that she was given blood to drink! It was, in fact, port wine! In mid-June, he had taken peaceful possession of Woodhouse, a mansion near Longleat. Doddington, at something of a loose end since the surrender of Wardour, had promptly laid siege, scattering his men widely through the house's huge park. Ludlow saw his chance for revenge. With his 300 troops, Ludlow occupied Warminster and prepared to confront Doddington.

On July 7th, his scouts, perhaps no more than 40 in number, collided with an equal number of Royalists on the heath above Warminster Common. He was subsequently attacked by a larger

---

[10] Perfect Diurnal

Royalist force and chased from the town towards Salisbury. Ludlow, with fewer than 50 men remaining at his side, felt unwilling to contest the ground with Doddington's larger force. But Alexander Popham, commanding one of the troops of horse, persuaded his commander to stand and confront the Royalist horsemen. Drawing his men from the road into the safety of the woods, Popham prepared an ambush while Ludlow withdrew into a field to don his armour.

Within minutes, however, Popham was in flight, the entire Roundhead force hurtling past Ludlow on the road to Salisbury. One of Ludlow's troopers was thrown from his horse and sent sprawling in the dust. His gallant commander, despite the nearness of the Royalist horsemen, helped the unfortunate soldier to mount behind him. But the load was too heavy for Ludlow's tiring horse and the man was obliged to dismount. Fortunately another trooper had managed to catch the trooper's own horse and both men were narrowly able to avoid capture.

Passing through Salisbury in an effort to reach the safer haven of Southampton, Ludlow fought a brief delaying action at Mutton Bridge, near Whiteparish, forcing the Royalists to discontinue their pursuit. Popham, with just six men remaining in his troop, took hurried leave of Ludlow and rode hell-for-leather to sanctuary at Poole. Edmund, with the shaky remnants of his command, arrived in Southampton that evening, riders and horses equally bathed in sweat.

'In this long pursuit', wrote Sir Edward Walker, 'he (Sir Francis Doddington) slew about 100, took as many more prisoners, besides 100 new pairs of pistols, and about 40 muskets, and released divers countrymen the rebels had taken; and so dispersed this growing body, as that of 300, not 40 got in to Southampton.'[11]

---

[11] Walker, Sir E. 'Historical Discourses'. Page 39.

Mercurius Aulicus finishes its report of the action with a triumphant comment about Popham's distress: *'Alexander Popham, hardly pressed.....had he not worn a better head-piece than his own, his brains had been dashed out.'*[12]

Doddington had inflicted his second punishment on Ludlow and was free to return to besiege Wansey in Woodhouse. Provided with two cannon from the armoury of Bristol, he quickly breached the wall and forced the defenders to surrender. Twenty Parliamentarians were killed in the assault, the remaining 80 were taken captive and assembled in lines for conveyance to prison in Bristol.

But one of the war's more horrific scenes took place first. In retaliation for the recent execution in Dorset of some Irish troops, Doddington hung twelve of the prisoners from the bough of a large oak tree that grew in front of the house. The rope suspending one of the chosen victims broke and he fell uninjured to the ground. Rising to his feet, he asked to be allowed to fight for his life, offering to take on two Royalist soldiers at a time. His brave offer was turned down. All twelve, clothiers by trade, were buried nearby. The little hillock is still known today as the 'Clothiers Grave'.

Doddington is accused of many similar atrocities. Bulstrode Whitelocke, writing in his 'Memorials', speaks of the man's personal crimes, one incident in particular being described in detail. Riding one day near Taunton, Doddington met a priest on the road, *'Well, priest, whom art thou for?'* He is said to have asked. *'For God and his Gospel'*[13], was the vague reply. Taking out his pistol, the Royalist shot him. Men were no longer seen as impartial: neutrality was a synonym for siding with the enemy.

Massey's incursion into Wiltshire probably accelerated the summer reorganisation that took place in the west. On July 1st a Parliamentary ordinance established 'The Western Association', a

---

[12] Mercurius Aulicus. July 1644

[13] Whitelocke, Bulstrode. 'Memorials of the English Affairs'.

grouping of the counties of Wiltshire, Somerset, Dorset, Devon and Cornwall for defence purposes, and the appointment of committees in each county to sequestrate estates and property and levy fresh taxes. Another ordinance, passed a fortnight later, gave the Wiltshire committee the power to raise troops. Part of the preamble to this ordinance states:

> 'Whereas the said county of Wilts and the inhabitants thereof, for the space of almost two years now last past, have laid under the intolerable pressures, taxes, impositions, and plunderings, of the enemy's forces by means whereof they are now in a very sad condition; for remedy whereof there is a great and urgent necessity that such a competent number of horse, foot, and arms should be forthwith raised, as may defend and preserve the said county, and maintain the garrison of Malmesbury.'[14]

One of the first commissions issued, apparently by Waller on behalf of the Wiltshire committee, was to Edmund Ludlow, still smarting in Southampton after his defeat at Warminster. On July 30th he was appointed to the command of a regiment of horse and given sole responsibility for its recruitment. Massey was made commander-in-chief of the proposed Wiltshire forces, an office in which he was only nominally subordinate to Waller, at that time the commander of Parliament's western army. Westminster's military efforts in the area were to be confounded by this duplication of responsibilities and the discord between the two men could easily have been avoided. Massey's autonomy was not removed until the Spring of the following year: in May 1645, although serving as commander-in-chief of the forces of the Western Association, Massey found himself under the command of Thomas Fairfax, the newly appointed commander of the New Model Army.

---

[14] Lords Journals. Vol VI, 612 and 637.

The summer of 1644, however, was mainly to be concerned with events elsewhere. On June 29th, Waller was mauled at Cropredy Bridge in the midlands. Although militarily inconclusive, this battle, in which the Parliamentarians lost all their guns and many of their standards, was a personal humiliation for Waller. But on July 2nd 1644 Parliament's disgrace was lifted by victory at Marston Moor, a battle in which the King's northern army was wiped out. Cavalier reputations were broken that day. With Charles and Rupert were more than 21,000 men and the cream of the Royalist high command. Stretched out along a two mile front to the south of York, the King's army had seemed invincible, almost God-sent in the golden light of the summer evening. Yet five hours later, it lay dashed to pieces and several generals were amongst the nocturnal fugitives. *'The runaways...were so many, so breathless, so speechless, and so full of fears, that I should not have taken them for men'*, states one of the Royalist officers. The 'Immortals' of the cavalier army, the Marquis of Newcastle's legendary Whitecoats, were the last to crumble, fighting on with pike and musket until just 30 men remained. The marquis, who had expended so much energy in the service of his monarch, lost heart completely. Not prepared to endure the 'laughter of the court', he abandoned the cause and took ship for the Continent. In the battle's wake, his northern garrisons began to capitulate and soon active Royalism in the north of England was all but extinguished. Parliament and its Scottish allies had worked in tandem to secure that victory, and the combined weight of the victors could now move south to consolidate their success.

Yet one man seemed intent on wrecking that new found teamwork. The Earl of Essex, proud, unbending and jealous of potential rivals, was prepared to work with no-one. His refusal to assist Waller in the midlands had led to the latter's near defeat at Cropredy Bridge. Had the two generals combined forces before the engagement, this midlands action might well have been as devastating for the Royalists as Marston Moor. Essex was later to

AN
ORDINANCE
OF THE
LORDS and COMMONS
Affembled in PARLIAMENT;

For the fpeedy raifing and maintaining
of a competent number of Horfe and Foot for
the defence and prefervation of the County
of *Wilts*, and the Garrifon of
Malmsbury.

With the names of the Committees appointed to
put in execution the feverall Ordinances of this
prefent Parliament, and that they fhall have
power to fet and let the Lands, Tenements and Hereditaments of all
Malignants, Delinquents, and
Papifts Eftates in that faid
County.

Die Lunæ 15. Iulii 1644.
Rdered by the Lords in Parliament affembled, that
this Ordinance fhall bee forthwith printed and
publifhed.

Ioh. Browne Cler. Parliamentorum.

London printed for *Iohn Wright*, in the old Bayley.
July 17. 1644.

Ordinance of Lords and Commons

compound his error in a personal bid for glory against the King's western forces. Advancing into Cornwall, his army was ensnared on September 2nd beside the Fowey and subjected to punishing attack. Concerned for his own safety, Essex took ship for Plymouth, leaving Philip Skippon to negotiate the terms of surrender. Essex was quick to justify his escape. His value as a commander might well be debatable, but his political worth as a hostage was considerable.

'I thought fit to look to myself', he wrote, 'it being a greater terror to me to be a slave to their contempts than a thousand deaths.'

Few of the 6,000 who surrendered at Lostwithiel ever lived to see the capital again. Robbed of clothing and dignity as they journeyed homeward, and with untreated injuries, they died by the wayside, their carcasses lining the route of retreat for months to come. Richard Symonds, who witnessed their departure from Cornwall, describes their distress: *'...prest all of a heap like sheep, none of them except some few of the officers that did look any of us in the face'.*[15]

But the King's hold on Wiltshire was not sufficiently strong to exploit this distant event and news of Marston Moor had saddened even the stoutest hearts. Few of the shire's Royalist activists had remained within the county and Devereux's activities in the north had destabilised the previously solid regal footing in the rest of the county. Almost in desperation, Royalist parties roamed the countryside, attempting to force enthusiasm into those they met. But amongst the M.P.s of Westminster and the merchant traders of London the repercussions of defeat in Cornwall weighed just as heavily. From the heat of their fresh anxiety and frustration at the failures of their generals would be forged a new army and a determination to win.

---

[15] R. Symonds. 'Diary' (Camden Society 1859).

15

'The courteous Avon and its straggling streams'

GARRISON building was now fashionable. The fluid war of movement of the last twelve months, in which rival armies tramped vast distances in pursuit of set objectives, had congealed into a series of local struggles with a region's manor houses and castles as the building blocks of success.

This had been the practice in the midlands since the war's start. Roundhead and cavalier, neighbours in times of peace, had jostled for supremacy from behind stout walls. Able to defy enemy attack, these garrisons could dominate the surrounding countryside and do more to win territory for their chosen cause than any half day battle in a mud-strewn field. Vast areas of the Welsh borderlands were held for the King this way: Royalist forces in castles such as Flint, Ludlow and Raglan imposing an unquestioned control from the Usk to the Dee.

That lesson had now been learned in Wiltshire. Until this moment, none of the towns had been continuously garrisoned, and both sides had relied on the success of passing armies to snatch a sudden advantage. The failure of the Royalists to occupy these places in strength had unwisely left the county in contention, but Massey's success at Malmesbury began an autumn race to seize the county's strong points, and so gain by stealth what it had been impossible to achieve by force.

Chalfield was the first to change hands. Taken by the Parliamentarians in May, it was held without incident until the approach of the King's army caused a hurried evacuation on 5th

September 1644. Charles, returning to Oxford from the west found an empty house to greet his arrival. He promptly placed a troop of horse and two companies of foot as Chalfield's new garrison and continued on his way to Oxford. Just 48 hours later, it was back in Roundhead hands, and there it remained until the end of the war. Massey, according to his own account, made a sudden dash south to rescue the house from Cavalier clutches. His letter to London provides only the briefest of details:

> *'They, in turn, understanding of my advance thither, quitted it also and retreated to Bath and Bristol and so put me upon my march to this place yesterday evening.'*

He remained in Chalfield for less than a day. But he left a substantial garrison in occupation.

Great Chalfield Manor

Devereux at Malmesbury was another competent soldier, but hardly the man to wage a one man war. Ludlow fortunately was again at hand, returning to Salisbury with 80 men at the beginning of September from self-imposed exile in Southampton. But a viper's nest of sullen Royalists lay within the Close, and Ludlow trod warily. Choosing only to punish the city for some earlier misdemeanours, he decided on the briefest of flag-waving visits.

'...which town, having triumphed upon our defeat,' writes Ludlow in his memoirs, *'I thought most proper to supply us with what we wanted. And to that end having procured a list of the disaffected in the town, I required them, without delay, to collect amongst themselves five hundred pounds for the recruiting and paying of my troop, who had not received any pay since they came out.'[1]*

The townsmen, Royalist and Parliamentarian alike, prevailed upon him to take £200. Laden with this wealth, he retired to London to complete the recruitment of his new regiment.

His withdrawal from Wiltshire, however, was brief. In mid-September, itching for revenge, he was back in the county, testing his regimental strength against Stourton House, Lord Stourton's mansion near Mere. A tiny garrison had recently been installed to watch and report on Roundhead movements along the Somerset border. Gates and a low wall provided their only defence, and an attack was probably expected. Ludlow's men approached at night, silhouetted by flaming faggots and flickering torches. Burning down the flimsy gates, they hurled their torches through the windows of a ground floor room. Flushed from their nests by choking smoke, the Royalist garrison slipped out through the back door and disappeared like rats into the night.

Ludlow was in mischievous mood. Leaving Stourton House in ruins, he took his troops through yellowing fields to Witham, Ralph

---

[1] Ludlow, Sir E. 'Memoirs'. Vol I, Page 95. Ed. by C.W. Firth, 1894.

Hopton's family home, just five miles from Stourton's smouldering ashes. Here Ludlow was just as successful: 100 cattle were taken from the park as part of the prize, and the money obtained from their sale was used to pay his troops.

But Longford Castle, two miles from Salisbury, remained untroubled for more than a year. Away from the zone of fighting, Colonel Griffin's small garrison was to enjoy an almost idyllic lifestyle, fishing in the Avon's rushing waters, and taking game from the castle's extensive park. A contemporary report speaks almost rapturously:

> *'And then the courteous Avon draws up all its straggling companies of streams to defend the gardens and grounds of the manor, and gliding gently down in a straight line to the mouth of Neale, while he salutes at Bodenham Mill, he makes this fat water both an outguard and a Nilotic improver to this manor.'*[2]

The area was to be only briefly visited during the autumn by the armies of both sides. On 9th September, Waller, marching belatedly to the assistance of the Earl of Essex, reached Salisbury. He found a city devoid of troops, Royalist or Parliamentarian. But with only 800 horse at his back, he made no effort to formally garrison the place. Strategically valueless and without defences, apart from the low walls of the Cathedral Close, Salisbury was to remain an 'open house' throughout the war, a place of rest for weary generals and tired soldiers. In November, Colonel Wansey, now one of Ludlow's troop commanders, reined up at the gates of Longford with three troops of horse, causing Griffin to write hurriedly to Lord Digby in Oxford, and one of the first references to impressment appears:

> *'My Lord, it was his Majesty's pleasure to assign me some hundred for the raising of men for this garrison...I*

---

[2] Pelate, H, The Rev. 'The Longford Mss'. Archives of Longford Castle.

*am not able to get near the number of men which is
assigned me. Therefore I must humbly crave that I may
have order to prefer men in these hundreds which lied far
from the enemy and near to the garrison which lies most
convenient for me.*[3]

But Wansey, with only a handful of men, could do little more
than scratch at the earthen defences, and chose instead to place a
garrison in Sir John Evelyn's house at West Dean, four miles from
Longford, and a point from where events in Salisbury might be
closely observed.

The destruction of Essex's army at Lostwithiel had sent the
Parliamentary high command reeling, and nothing could have
prevented Charles from striking at London if he had chosen to do
so. The Earl with 3,000 men was sulking at Portsmouth,
Manchester's army of the Eastern Association had progressed no
further south than Watford, and Waller had dissipated his force in
garrisoning the south coast. Clearly unable to hold the King's
advance from the west on his own, Waller, complaining bitterly of
Manchester's lack of support, wisely withdrew to Andover, and the
threat of a major clash in the Avon valley receded.

'You must not expect', (Waller wrote to the
Commons) *'to hear we have done any service; the best we
can hope for is to trouble and retard the enemy's march
and make them keep close together. Should we engage
the horse before your foot come up, and they miscarry,
your foot would be all lost, and the King could go which
way he pleased.'*

More than a month later, on October 15th, the Royalist army,
with Charles at its head, visited Salisbury and Longford, leaving
the cannon captured at Lostwithiel to bolster the castle's defences.

---

[3] Unpublished letter - Archives of Longford Castle.

'His Majesty leaving Somersetshire in so good condition,' explains that month's edition of Mercurius Aulicus, *'advanced into Wiltshire...and came into Salisbury on Tuesday last, whence the rebels made such haste that they left good store of their friends behind them in the town which his Majesty's forces seized on.'*

A delay in Wiltshire, however, would clearly be unwise. Parliamentary strategy was in tatters, but Westminster's three field armies might miraculously unite. Charles, informed that the Earl of Manchester was advancing towards Oxford with orders to block the Royalist route, hurriedly withdrew. Remaining in Salisbury for just three nights to regroup his army in Clarendon Park, and leaving a token garrison in Wilton, he set out on the 18th for Andover, conscious that Waller lay across his path. Sir William, now with 3,000 horse and dragoons, had placed his men in battle order south of the town. Throughout the hours of a fog-soaked morning, the Parliamentary ranks waited, listening for the sounds of horses and marching feet on the road from the west.

By noon, however, the Parliamentarians were in full retreat, drawn back to the town without a fight. Impressed by the size and cohesion of Charles' force, Waller had chosen to withdraw his men, and leave only a rearguard to block the King's advance. Mercurius Aulicus again takes up the tale:

'...somewhat short of Andover a forlorn hope being sent out, met with another of the rebels very near their main body; both charged and kept their ground, till two bodies of his Majesty's horse (probably Goring's brigade) came up and marched into the field where the rebels stood; at sight whereof the rebels' forces began to fly out at the other end of Andover town; yet made not so good speed but that his Majesty's horse overtook them and slashed them soundly....pursuing them through Andover a

good way beyond, till the dark night stopped further pursuit. [4]

Described by this biased account as a rout of Waller's army, it was really little more than an embarrassment. Probably no more than two dozen men were killed in total and the fighting , watched by bemused townsmen, certainly lasted less than two hours. It was, however, like a tonic of spring water to the Royalist forces, infusing the King's colonels with notions of invincibility. For instead of retiring along the direct path to Oxford, the Royalists now decided to march to the assistance of the besieged garrisons of Basing and Donnington and throw all remaining caution to the wind.

The second Battle of Newbury, fought in meadows north of the town, might therefore never have happened. It was not the King's intention to seek battle with his enemy or contest the road to London. Over-confidence encouraged him to reach for the heavens and attempt the impossible.

On the 21st his army advanced to Kingsclere. The following day, in still unbridled optimism, Charles despatched James Compton, the Earl of Northampton, with 500 foot and 800 horse to unite with Oxford forces under Colonel Henry Gage in an expedition to salvage Banbury. Exposing his chest to three Roundhead daggers simultaneously, Charles had chosen to rely for deliverance on God and his angels. Still hoping that he could avoid battle altogether, he was merely searching for a position from which he could both protect Oxford and simultaneously savage the road to London.

Continuing to respond to events which had not been of his creation, he drew up his army on the 25th along the northern side of the River Kennet, his right flank protected by the river and the left by the course of the smaller Lambourn. The centre of the King's position, and effectively the front line, rested upon Shaw

---

[4] Mercurius Aulicus.

House, while the army's rear was covered by the defences of Donnington Castle, of which only the keep now exists. Lord Astley, faithful maintainer of the King's cause and one of the wisest heads at the King's evening table, was given command of the centre's three brigades; Maurice commanded the rearguard drawn up in Speen, and Goring's four brigades of cavalry lay close to the Lambourn's southern banks.

Donnington Castle

At Basingstoke, some twenty miles to the south, Parliament's three armies had recently united. The two earls, Essex and Manchester, would now be required to work in harmony, something which the two men's long standing jealousies would probably prevent. Recognising the dangers, the Committee of Both Kingdoms placed the combined army's command in the hands of a committee of eight, the earls being just two of the members. Most prominent amongst the others were Cromwell, Waller and Heselrige, practical men with experience of field commands.

191

On the 21st, the day that the Royalists reached Kingsclere, the Parliamentary army, almost 18,000 strong, entered Swallowfield, intending to secure Reading and the lower Thames Valley before turning to challenge the King. From here the bulk of the army swung west, brushing briefly with a Royalist screen near Thatcham, and then settling in strength on the 25th behind Clay Hill, close to the confluence of the Lambourn and its parent.

This skilful deployment had taken place despite the new command structure, and not because of it. The committee system, scattering the responsibility for decision making over several shoulders, was bound to be cumbersome. Every decision and planned movement had first to be endorsed by London. Worse still, Lord Essex was struck by illness and was confined to bed in Reading, leaving the less able Manchester as the senior commander in the field. Beneath him, jealousies between the section commanders had almost become formalised, part of the rituals of the High Command, and the army was in clear danger of crumbling to dust. Cromwell, commander of the Eastern Association's cavalry, was convinced of his own merits and seemed determined to act autonomously if the chance arose. Balfour and Skippon, generals of the horse and foot in Essex's army, resented Manchester's usurpation, while Harrington and the City brigade were only prepared to accept orders from the councillors in London.

It is therefore remarkable that this ill-coordinated war machine assumed the offensive at all. That afternoon, the 25th, the Parliamentary soldiers took possession of the grassy top of Clay Hill and gazed down at the King's straggling positions below. Three brigades of Cavalier infantry, 5,000-6,000 men, manned the grounds of Shaw House, drawn up behind a line of ancient earthworks which served as ready made defences. Goring's horse, proud, well disciplined, and with a sense of their own grandeur, strutted like peacocks in the meadows of the Lambourn, seemingly oblivious of unfolding events. More conscious of their supporting role, Prince Maurice's regiment lay in wait to the west of Speen.

The King spent the night in Shaw House, dangerously close to the enemy positions. But the significance of the coming day had already dawned - the drawn out war might be about to end. *'This day will bring us judgement on my crown,'* Charles wrote that evening, *'and upon your shoulders lies the burden. See to your King and secure your peace with God.'* Alternatively his crown and his dignity might lie trampled underfoot in the blood stained mud of the Kennet valley. But for the inhabitants of Newbury, there was less finality. War had knocked at their doors a year before and nothing had been settled then.

Some, no doubt, witnessed the first tentative movements of the Parliamentary army on the morning of the 26th. Manchester's foot probed the Royalist positions on the dew laden lawns of the great house. Colourless, fluid and as silent as the grave in the half-light, they might have been the armies of the dead. Then the dialogue of distant guns began, Parliament's guns on Clay Hill roaring in anger, and being answered in turn by the batteries of Donnington Castle. Here lay the real terrors of war for soldiers and civilians alike: the deafening discharge of foul-mouthed guns, the whine of shot, and the uncertainty that followed before the missile landed. For men accustomed only to the bellow of cattle, the sound of the lathe or the familiar roar of rushing water, the noise of battle was both devilish and terrifying. Hearts beat louder, blood pulsed faster, pikes were gripped in whitening hands, and the drifting shades became men again.

Yet the King's lines at Shaw House were far too dense to be taken by frontal assault. Parliament's scouts were already at work, searching for hidden chinks in Charles's impenetrable armour. It clearly lay somewhere behind - within the scattered regiments of horse and foot that constituted the Royalist second line.

The strategy that emerged from the battlefield conference that now took place was instant, forged from the materials of unfolding events. Waller was probably the author - it bears all the imprints of his quick thinking mind rather than the slow methodology of the more ponderous Manchester. A decision was made to send just part of the army on a wide detour to the north, penetrating behind the Royalist positions in an attempt to find a crossing of the Lambourn and so fall on the King's rear. In its conception and execution, it demonstrates that Parliament had at last accepted that calculated risks would have to be taken if stalemate were to be avoided.

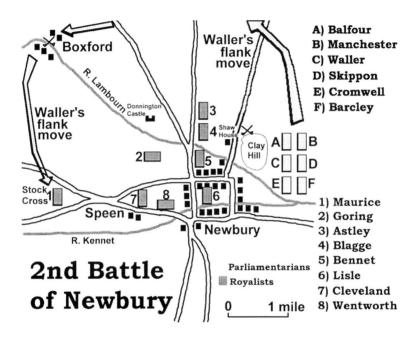

The King had assembled only 9,000 men on the field that day, only half the size of Westminster's combined forces. Waller set out after dark at the head of 12,000, pushing his way through Hermitage, Chieveley and North Heath before bivouacking for the remainder of the night. Left behind on the slopes of Clay Hill was the remainder of Parliament's army, on its own equal in strength to the entire Cavalier command. The first pale streaks of dawn coaxed his army into motion again and the Lambourn banks were reached just as the first of the King's men began to stir.

Waller's movements were not detected until more than four hours later! Sometime during late morning, lookouts on the parapets of Donnington Castle spotted his columns in the meadows to the west and the fortress's guns fired in hurried warning. Maurice's men had worked like moles during the night, throwing up mounds and ditches on the Kennet's northern banks. When the Parliamentary forces fanned out along the ridge west of Speen, with Skippon's infantry in the centre and the cavalry on the flanks, they found that Maurice was ready and waiting.

But fighting had already roared into life at Shaw. Manchester's initial role was meant to be diversionary, a skirmishing tease launched in the early morning to hold the enemy's attention while Waller pounced on the enemy rear. The sound of Skippon's guns behind the Royalist lines was to serve as a signal for greater effort, an attack with his entire strength as part of a concerted action by both wings of the Parliamentary army, and a giant pincer would then be set in motion. But caught in a furious Royalist counter-attack, Manchester's modest strike that morning soon developed into something more, igniting almost spontaneously along the entire eastern front, and the report of Skippon's cannon was consequently never heard.

Waller enjoyed some early success. The regiments of the Earl of Essex, the men defeated at Lostwithiel, saw a sudden chance for revenge. A single word of encouragement had been enough to send them hurtling towards the Royalist trenches. An hour later they were in possession of Speen...and eight guns snatched from them at Lostwithiel. But further advance was impeded by the maze of hedges east of the village and the Parliamentary steamroller was halted in its tracks.

Balfour's supporting cavalry advance was impressive by any standard! His men thundered across the open land that lay between Speen and the Kennet, throwing aside the thinly spread ranks of Maurice's cavalry that lay in their path. Thomas Wentworth, Earl of Cleveland's brigade, seconding the prince's unfortunate men, fared no better, and their commander himself was captured. Only the firm stand of the Royalist third line, the Queen's regiment and Lifeguard, held the Parliamentary advance and saved the King's rear from total collapse.

Adept minds in the Royalist councils saw a possible advantage in this apparently unfavourable position. For the Parliamentary army was now dangerously divided while the King's army remained intact and simultaneous Parliamentary hammering from two directions had merely served to make it more compact. Its full weight could now be brought to bear on the weaker half of the Parliamentary army. And just beyond, still waiting on the Lambourn's pastures, Goring's brigade remained unused, able and willing to punch where it was most needed.

Cromwell could have dealt with Goring's latent threat. Yet instead of thundering into action on Waller's northern flank, he held his men back beyond the range of Donnington's guns. This uncharacteristic tardiness has been explained away by his apologists: he was positioned upon unfavourable ground with intersecting hedges, and an advance would subject his men to withering fire from the Donnington artillery. Such excuses are hardly credible, for there were known to be only four demi-culverins in the castle and these had a limited range and doubtful accuracy. Caught in the open, Cromwell's horsemen must have provided only a fleeting target and would have soon become mixed with Goring's men on the flat meadows beside the river. When Cromwell did eventually lead his men to battle, Goring, supported by Sir Humphrey Bennet's regiment, easily held back their long awaited advance.

Waller's cleverly forged weapon became blunted on the rock of stubborn enemy resistance. Thomas Blagge's musketeers, positioned north of Shaw House, had moved to Maurice's assistance. Against these stubborn and immovable men, Skippon's infantry could make no progress. The outcome of the battle would probably be decided on the deeply rutted lawns to the east of Shaw House.

But here the Parliamentary assault was to be no sharper. The full attack was not launched until after 4 p.m., more than two hours after the western push had begun. Advancing in two columns, Manchester's men were greeted by a hail of musket and cannon fire from the lawns of the house and were soon driven back in confusion. Unable to chip at the King's solid ranks or find an alternative route to victory, Parliament's generals recalled their troops before the daylight faded.

So ended the second fight at Newbury, no more decisive than the first. Both sides had lost about 500 men, but had gained hardly a single strategic advantage to compensate. Men, drained of blood and souls for someone else's cause, had gone to meet their Maker, their bodies discarded like casual litter in a country park. Others called for their mothers, and weakened hands clutched all night at the damp earth that might soon become their graves. As in the earlier conflict, both sides remained hovering on the field, numbed by the day's activities into a state of vague uncertainty. The King's soldiers were the first to recover. Seeing little to be gained from remaining on a blood-stained field, they stole away under the blanket of the autumn night through the open gap between Shaw House and Donnington Castle.

The chance of ending the war stole away with them. If Manchester had deployed his army in a closed circle, this nocturnal bolt would never have been possible and the entire Royalist army would have been captured. The war would have been ended in one final and decisive stroke. Bad generalship and poor co-ordination were again to blame and the struggle would continue.

16

'The grasping talons of these greedy vultures'

NEWS of victory or disaster inevitably travelled more slowly than the men involved. Newbury's tale failed to reach Wiltshire until early November, days after the King and Prince of Wales had been seen galloping through Marlborough at the head of just twenty men! Those who witnessed this strange event might have chosen to speculate, and defeat of the King seemed the most plausible explanation.

But such theories were rapidly blown to bits. On 12th November 1644, the King returned to the Wiltshire town with an impressive show of strength and openly declared his intention of establishing a garrison here. Sir Samuel Luke was one of the first to broadcast this event.

'Last night the King went into Marlborough with about 600 horse,' he states in his letter book, *'and there came into the town divers cartloads of provisions which they had warned the country to bring in.'*[1]

On the 19th, a London paper publicly warned:

'The King intends to make trial what new strength he can raise in Wiltshire, and increase his numbers by the losses and ruin of that county. Some are of the opinion that he hath an intent to fall on Malmesbury, but I cannot be so readily induced to believe it; the ways this winter

---

[1] The Letter Books of Sir Samuel Luke.

season are so very foul and heavy from Marlborough to Malmesbury.'

Charles, however, remained in Marlborough for just five days, lodging at the Seymour's house beside the Mount. He left behind two cannon, drawn from the battery of Donnington, and strict instructions to prepare the town's defences. On the 17th, he returned to Oxford, dining at the Bear in Hungerford on the way.

Further Royalist activity was to follow. The church at Highworth was suddenly manned, an inappropriate building for defence, but suitably positioned to guard the county's north-east corner. And Sir Charles Lloyd, an Oxford courtier and skilled engineer, was sent to Devizes to revive the town's fortifications and take command of the intended garrison.

'We see they intend to reduce the West into the state of the netherlands,' complained the Parliamentary Scout on 20th December 1644, *'and have a garrison at every five miles, and not to fight so often in the open field.'*[2]

Lloyd seems to have had no qualms about the methods used to secure his aims. Michael Paradise, the constable of Wick, was just one of many who fell victim to his ways. Unable to provide the required men to work on the fortifications, he was promptly arrested and virtually charged with treason. Attempting to resist, the poor man was staked out on the green at Devizes and left to consider the error of his ways! At Marlborough too, countrymen were forced to act as labourers for the town's defences.

'A woman or maid durst not now stir out of doors upon any occasion,' moaned the True Informer, *'for fear of falling into the grasping talons of these greedy*

---

[2] Parliamentary Scout, Westminster News Sheet. December 1644.

vultures. They sweep away and drain all manner of provisions, leaving nothing but the bare walls. [3]

Parliament, without the drive or resources, could do little to match this Cavalier energy. Garrisons still held the line of the Avon at Rowden, Lacock and Great Chalfield, but Wiltshire beyond was the domain of the Devil, part of the King's western regime that extended almost unbroken from Oxford to Cornwall. Only Evelyn's house at West Dean and a recently installed garrison at Pinhill House near Calne held for Parliament. Patrolling this vast area, three quarters of the entire county, were detachments of Lloyd's Devizes garrison and the newly formed horse regiment of Sir James Long, the county's Royalist sheriff.

The loss of Pinhill was soon to follow. Named after a grove of pines that lined a nearby summit, this moated house fell to a sudden assault on December 28th, the result of a predatory raid by a group of Goring's Western Horse and men from the Devizes garrison.

'...at first summons, the rebels denied to surrender,' reports Mercurius Aulicus, *'...till they saw his Majesty's forces begin to fall on, and then they presently submitted themselves prisoners at mercy, and accordingly had their lives given them...When the Scoutmaster General (who was sent to take possession) entered the house, the rebels begged they might not be stripped naked, he bid them look out and they might see his Majesty's soldiers all new clothes, so as they would not take the rebels' clothes if offered to them.* [4]

59 prisoners, part of Massey's Gloucester regiment, were taken that day. The house, a brief stage set in a long sad play, was then made untenable. Sir Charles Lloyd unilaterally ordered the

---

[3] The True Informer, Westminster News Sheet. December 1644.

[4] Mercurius Aulicus.

neutralisation of Pinhill, despite Prince Rupert's demands that the place be garrisoned.

> *'Blake's house I have made uninhabitable and have drained the moat'*, he wrote to the Prince on January 8th by way of explanation, *'I could not burn it because it would have incensed the country against me.'*

The Royalists were not so fortunate in their designs upon Salisbury. In the first week of November, Cavaliers under the command of Colonel Sir Francis Cook attempted to fortify the cathedral Close, where the King's religion still flourished, like Christianity in the catacombs of Rome. Ludlow at that time was assisting in the siege of Basing, but still boasts of the indirect part he played in scotching this Royalist plan.

> *'Some of the enemies under the conduct of Col. Cooke came to Salisbury and were fortifying the Close for the King, of which Major Wansey having advice, marched thither with the forces which I had sent into Wiltshire, and falling upon them, caused them to retire in haste; but finding the gates fortified against him, he set fire to them, and seizing upon all their horse, took the colonel and four score more prisoners*[5]

According to the Scottish Dove in its own account of this incident on December 8th, the first recorded fighting in Salisbury, only four Parliamentary soldiers were injured. With Wansey at the gates of the Close that day were Major Duet or Dowett, soon to become one of the war's more controversial heroes, and the Hampshire officer, Colonel Norton. Other Parliamentary soldiers chose to set out on a rampage of revenge, administering private punishment on Royalist sympathizers. Finding Henry Penruddocke, younger brother of the family head, in his house at West Lavington, a group of unnamed troopers burst in and:

---

[5] Ludlow, Sir E. 'Memoirs'. Original edition, Vol I, Page 135.

'...pulled him by the hair, knocked him down, and broke two pistols over his head, without so much as tendering him quarter...one of the troopers, who was a collier, swore that he should die for his father's sake, and putting a pistol to his belly, shot him. [6]

The ladies of the family were forced to watch. Penruddocke had played almost no part in the war so far and his murder might have been an act of personal vengeance rather than a political killing. The perpetrators of the crime were never brought to justice.

Less than a month later, a running battle took place in Salisbury's snow lined streets, a light affair by the standards of most of the war's skirmishes, but pronounced enough to be known thereafter as the Battle of Salisbury. Leading the Parliamentary troops on this occasion was Ludlow himself, newly returned to Wiltshire from a campaign in Somerset. Probably intending to deal with the Royalist garrison at Longford before crossing into Hampshire, he set about fortifying and garrisoning the cathedral's tall belfry, the detached medieval structure swept away in a wave of zealous architectural renewal at the end of the eighteenth century.

But news reached him of a cavalier advance from the north towards Amesbury. He immediately sent sixty men under a Captain Sadler to discover the truth of this report, advancing more slowly with the rest of his regiment from their base at Netherhampton. On the road to Amesbury he was met by one of Sadler's breathless scouts, and a mile further on found Sadler in silent and impotent surveillance of the Royalist troops.

Clearly outnumbered by Colonel Sir James Long's command, Sadler had probably been wise in his decision not to engage. But his men seemed to disagree and he was later censored by his own men for his apparent cowardice. Ludlow, with the whole of

---

[6] Waylen, S. 'History of Marlborough'.

Wiltshire's destiny lying on his shoulders , had no choice at all. Dividing his regiments into two columns and taking personal command of one, he charged the enemy, collecting thirty prisoners in his opening sweep. But Major Marshall, leading the other column in pursuit of the enemy towards Amesbury, was suddenly confronted by a much larger Royalist force and the supporting prong of Ludlow's assault was brought to a halt.

Murder of Penruddocke

That night the Cavaliers took their revenge. Ludlow, anticipating a visit, remained vigilant behind the Close's walls, his men posted as sentries at intervals in the city's streets to bring immediate warning of the Royalist approach, or guarding the prisoners in the belfry. Others, ordered to keep their horses bridled and ready for action at a moment's notice, rested in closely wrapped cloaks on the chilled ground and chatted over the dying embers of evening braziers, talking, no doubt, of daughters, sons and tear stained sweethearts in the villages of the west.

Then came the sound of rapid hoof beat in Castle Street, menacingly amplified in the cold night air. Ludlow with just six men rode to investigate. Encountering the enemy squadrons in the market place, he galloped back to the Close to gather reinforcements. But, despite his orders, few of his men were actually ready. *'Some, contrary to orders,'* he explains in his memoirs, *'were gone to bed, and others, taking advantage of the night, had stolen away; so that those remaining were not much above thirty horse'.*[7]

Edmund was consequently forced to rely on a cloak of deception, hoping that the darkness of the night would smother his shortage of numbers. Ordering a cornet with just ten men to charge the enemy in the market square, Ludlow remained to gather up the rest. Minutes later, he led them furiously into the square. Hoping to mislead the enemy into believing that yet more Parliamentarians were following in Ludlow's rear, he left a solitary trumpeter in the Close to sound the advance!

What followed might be exaggerated heroism or just a distortion of the truth. The cornet was already 'pickeering' with the enemy when Ludlow and his tiny force arrived. Entering the market place in single file, Ludlow, apparently now at the head of only five or six men, assaulted the Royalist left flank and within minutes had miraculously cleared the square of the intruders!

More than a hundred Royalists, infected by a sudden epidemic of ill-founded fear, dashed up Winchester Street and escaped through the town's most easterly gate. Another two hundred passed into Endless Street, searching for salvation in the country snows beyond. But Endless Street had no exit and was walled at its furthest end. Prevented from escaping, the fugitives spun to face their tormentors' fury, carbines levelled and swords raised in a gesture of self-defence. The true size of the Roundhead force would be discovered in the minutes which followed.

---

[7] Ludlow, Sir E. 'Memoirs'. Original edition, Vol I, Page 137.

A personal bout of heroism followed. Lt. Colonel Middleton, a keen Papist, leaped an intervening ditch and single-handedly rode to engage the Parliamentary force. A shot brought him crashing to the ground, unwounded but horseless and with his pride lying scattered in the crystal snow. Others, steeled by his individual example, followed, and soon it was to be the Roundheads' turn to flee.

Ludlow tried to re-group in the Close. But the enemy were soon hammering at the Close's North Gate, and only flight through Harnham would save the Roundhead band. In the purple light of a winter dawn, Ludlow's men pulled back over Harnham Bridge, one of the troopers with a cavalier sword still embedded in his arm! Stenton, Ludlow's servant, was caught on the bridge and dealt a severe blow which fractured his skull. The rudderless survivors of this brief melee rode hurriedly for their lives over snow capped Harnham Hill. But somewhere near Odstock, they missed the Fordingbridge road and so chose to scatter for personal safety in the whitened fields beyond. Abandoned by the last of his companions, Ludlow turned at bay in a frost bound field to face the hungry hounds.

Here fell the last of the victims of Salisbury's small battle. A solitary Royalist approached and called on Ludlow to surrender. A single ball from Ludlow's carbine sent the man crashing to the ground and Ludlow was free to go. With only his horse for company, Ludlow made his way to Southampton, the base of his previous excursion into Wiltshire. Here he heard that Lieutenant-Colonel Read and the tiny garrison left to hold the belfry had been forced to surrender. The Cavaliers had coerced a collier to leave his cart, laden with smouldering charcoal, at the door. Smoke had done the rest, burning the ancient wood and flushing the Roundhead vermin from their lofty nest. West Dean, the remaining Parliamentary stronghold in the south, seems to have been evacuated a few days later as a direct consequence of those events beneath the spire. Parliament's brief hold on South Wiltshire had been extinguished, a fact which Mercurius Aulicus was quick to broadcast.

Harnham Bridge, Salisbury

'...He (Sir Marmaduke Langdale) *took in all five captains, besides divers other officers, fourscore prisoners, 150 horses and arms, some powder and match, and three colours. M. Ludlow himself escaped very narrowly, though very much hurt, his whole regiment absolutely routed. Those few which escaped fled into Dean House, but the Lord Goring sending some horse after them, found the fugitives gone thence, and the garrison also quitted, the rebels labouring to reach Southampton.* [8]

---

[8] Mercurius Aulicus.

Ludlow had attempted to hold Salisbury against forces far larger than he could possibly have imagined. Langdale's cavalry, working in co-operation with Sir James Long, was part of General Goring's western force. Ordered on a crusade of liberty from Somerset towards Sussex, it had been passing through South Wiltshire on the way. This swollen Royalist presence would be a new phenomenon, injecting sudden heart into the closet Royalists of the area, and even the allegiance of Salisbury's flimsier Roundheads began to wobble. On January 22nd 1645 Goring himself visited Salisbury, proclaiming the virtues of Royalism to those few that witnessed his arrival. His visit, however, was to be brief: he had been given fresh instructions to develop the siege of Taunton. But garrisons prospered in Wilton, Longford and Goldborne *, and Royalist hopes remained alight.

A month later both Lacock Abbey and Rowden House were in the monarch's hands. Hopton, keeping an interest in Wiltshire affairs from his base in Bath, had long nurtured a personal desire to establish garrisons at these two points. Presumably unaware that both had fallen into Parliamentary hands, he sent Colonel Jordan Boville in the first week of February with a troop of horse to take possession of Lacock's monastic walls. Finding the abbey doors shut, Boville rode to Devizes to consult with Sir James Long and Sir Charles Lloyd about how best to extract Lacock from Parliament's light clutches.

Parliament's faint-heartedness assisted. Hearing of the Royalist intentions, the Lacock Roundheads evacuated the property and joined their colleagues at Rowden. Here they awaited the inevitable Cavalier visit from behind far stouter walls. Later that day, a troop of Royalist horse clattered into Chippenham, surprised the tiny detachment of Parliamentary cavalry that had recently installed itself and captured Colonel Ludford, Rowden's governor, and eight troopers.

---

* The actual site of Goldborne is still conjectural.

This was exactly the sort of Royalist activity that Parliament most feared. Rowden, *'a large, well-built, gothic house, square, with a court within...and a moat about it'*, according to Aubrey, was physically robust and seemed almost impregnable. But the garrison within, a detachment of Devereux's stretched Malmesbury regiment, perhaps 200 men, lacked the resources or manpower to hold for long and their defence of Rowden could only be short lived. On February 15th the two Royalist knights drew up before the house at the head of 500 men and demanded surrender. A volley of musket fire was the only response.

The Royalists required a speedy capitulation. Memories of Wardour, months of inactivity which had drained resources and the patience of the besiegers, haunted the two commanders. Hasty messages were sent to Bath for the loan of heavy guns and additional manpower.

The response from both sides was immediate and predictable. 400 dragoons under the command of Sir Bernard Astley arrived from Cirencester and Sir Francis Doddington rode in at the head of a train of artillery and additional troops. But two days later, Colonel Stephens, governor of Beverstone and 'mock sheriff' of Gloucestershire, responding to request for help, arrived with 120 horse in an attempt to relieve the men inside.

The Royalists were unprepared for his visit. Punching without warning at the regal lines and scattering the besiegers like rabbits before the plough, his well drilled troopers quickly swept up to the house, bringing with them much needed supplies of food and ammunition. Doors and gates slammed shut behind them and it seemed that Stephens and his men had deliberately chosen to join the besieged.

One hour later, however, they tried to leave. But the Cavaliers had taken the opportunity to block the gateway with mounds of earth. In the park lay 3,000 men, and escape seemed quite impossible. Stephens, employing his men as excavators and still bubbling with the euphoria of earlier success, sallied from the house in an attempt to force an exit. Parties of musketeers at the windows and gate covered these operations, firing at the Royalist forward screen to draw the enemy fire. But within minutes the entire party had been forced back into the house by the sheer size of the besieging army.

Two days of heavy bombardment followed. Stephens, a practical if vain man, saw that any further resistance was hopeless and tactfully surrendered.

> '...they submitted themselves prisoners,' reported Mercurius Aulicus, 'being betwixt 3 and 400 horse and foot...with 317 common soldiers, 120 horses and almost 400 arms. Not any one rebel was plundered to the value of a penny...and when it was pressed to them, that some of his Majesty's soldiers had been stripped naked when by them taken prisoners; an impudent ungrateful rebel answered; that the cavaliers often had no power to plunder for God would not suffer it.* [9]

The house was destroyed to prevent its further employment against the King, and Boville was given command of the new Royalist garrison established at Lacock.

> 'The hand of God,' boasted Mercurius Aulicus in the same issue, 'appeared evidently for his Majesty. For why else did the King now command so many towns and armies?' [10]

---

[9] Mercurius Aulicus.

[10] Ibid.

17

'Blessed be the Lord for this success'

THE hand of God might clearly have helped. But Goring and Langdale had trodden on favourable ground, their task made easier by the King's earlier visit. Charles' personal appearance in the county during the autumn of 1644 had rallied men to his cause. Fortification of Devizes and Marlborough had followed in his wake, and Royalist eyes could begin to look hungrily towards the county's south. Yet the solid fact remained: Wiltshire had been won for the King, not by Wiltshire men, but by men of stature from outside the county.

Parliament, by contrast, had few local men on whom they could rely. In March 1645, Ludlow chose to resign his commission, angered by recent swipes at his authority.

> '...yet they (the county commissioners) ...combined against me and procured me to be laid aside, under colour that they stood not in need of more than four troops for the service of the county, of which they offered me the command; yet...I chose rather to desist and wait for a better opportunity.'[1]

He had paid the price for his allegiance to Waller. Throughout the period of bitter personal squabbling between Essex and Sir William, Ludlow had stood four square behind the latter, even refusing to accept a commission to serve under the Earl. Now the peer's men had presumably secured their revenge, poisoning the opinions of the county's commissioners and relegating Ludlow to Parliament's back row. This deprived Wiltshire's Parliamentarians

[1] Ludlow, Sir E. 'Memoirs'. Original edition, Vol I, Page 147.

of his mercurial personality at the very time when he might have been most effective. Almost as disastrously, some of his most able lieutenants were about to desert. Wansey, a lesser copy of his former colonel's fighting spirit, had apparently fallen out with his energetic chief. Increasingly suspect in his actions, he was eventually to join the King. Dowett, less honourable and driven only by the desire for personal glory, would go the same way.

Until the advent of the New Model army, it would be left to individuals from outside the county to fight Wiltshire's tiny war. Massey's clever snatch of Malmesbury and the Avon valley had been launched without Westminster's full approval and the Commons made little effort to supply him with men or weapons with which to hold his conquests. Parliament's interests clearly lay further afield and the narrow springtime bridgehead had swiftly crumbled. Only Malmesbury remained.

Continuing in the same vein of utter disinterest in Wiltshire, Westminster ordered Waller, wintering in Farnham, to advance to the relief of Taunton and the Dorset outposts. Across his pathway to the west lay Southern Wiltshire and the silenced Parliamentarians of Salisbury. Here at least lay a chance to reverse the fortunes of the winter's fighting. For Goring had now departed and the Christian God would surely now be firmly on the side of Parliament's crusaders.

Waller was unfortunately to be delayed in Surrey until mid-February, paralysed by near mutiny in his ranks and personal squabbles amongst the army's leadership. Only a hurried collection of funds in London and punishment of the ring leaders softened their stubborn limbs and allowed the advance to commence at last. Cromwell and his cavalry were fortunately ordered to join Waller, raising the army to about 6,000 horse and foot. Skirmishing briefly on 9th March at Andover, this hesitant Parliamentary force spilled into Wiltshire and clashed unwittingly with Royalist patrols near Devizes.

But the campaign in Wiltshire which followed was never intended and was purely the result of circumstance and unplanned events. Proposing only to rest his army for the night before continuing his advance to Somerset, Waller quartered his forces at Amesbury and Durrington. Sometime on the 10th, however, he received reports that Sir James Long and his cavalry were about to quit Devizes, leaving Lloyd with only a regiment of foot to hold the town against a sudden attack.

Waller had received no instructions to try his hand against Devizes and had been forbidden to delay unnecessarily before its walls. Only Mercurius Britannicus seemed aware of the town's vulnerability, mocking the enemy defence efforts in its January issue: *'Hopton is fortifying amain at the Devizes, but all the "devices" in the world will never keep him from the reach of Parliament'*. But this was a quiet voice, heard only by the London intelligentsia. Waging its ideological paper war, it was largely ignored by Parliament's military planners. Wiltshire was the domain of the Devil and its inhabitants had been consigned to Hell. But despite these orders, Waller chose now to sail with the winds of opportunity. At midnight his entire force were on the move, crossing the blackened Wiltshire fields in an attempt to surprise the town and its defenders.

Waller's army during the Wiltshire campaign

Foot	*Horse*
Arthur Heselrige's regt.	Arthur Heselrige's regt.
James Holborne's regt.	John Fitz-James's regt.
Samuel Jones's regt.	Edward Cooke's regt.
Ralph Weldon's regt.	Michael Livesey's regt.
William Waller's regt.	Richard Norton's regt.
	George Thompson's regt.
	Jonas Vandruske's regt.
	William Waller's regt.

In addition, Oliver Cromwell's horse augmented Waller's cavalry.

212

But his strategy left a lot to chance. About one mile north of Amesbury, the Parliamentary army was halted and four horsemen were selected from every troop to serve as a forlorn hope. These then rode at speed towards Devizes, leaving the main body, now drawn up in three brigades to follow at a more respectable pace through Shrewton and Market Lavington.

Early the following morning, some sleepy Royalist sentinels at Southbroom were seized where they stood. The rest, however, succeeded in withdrawing towards Devizes and raising the alarm. When Waller's army first saw the indistinct shape of St John's mist shrouded church, 400 hundred Royalist defenders were waiting fully armed at the town's barricades, searching into the late winter mist for visible signs of the Parliamentary advance.

But no attempt to storm the town was taken. Impressed indelibly against the northern sky from where he stood were the slopes of Roundway Hill and the bitter memories of that summer siege and battle were no easier to erase than the hill itself. He was content instead to remain at a respectful distance from the town, holding his men near Potterne, and curiously leaving the town's northern and southern exits unblocked.

It was probably deliberate. Like a shrewd huntsman wishing to take his quarry in the open field, he was allowing the Royalist fox to bolt, and Waller's strategy might be seen in the context of one who had no designs upon Devizes, but only on its prized defender. That night Cromwell's and Waller's brigades quartered at Potterne and Market Lavington to hold the town's attention, while Hardress Waller's brigade made ready to advance on a lone expedition in the direction of Melksham, Long's expected route of escape.

On the 12th, Sir William Waller 'demonstrated' towards Devizes, probing casually at the town's southern defences in an attempt to force the vermin from his nest. Lloyd's men had stood at arms all night, and the sudden aggression probably came as a relief. For now at last the Parliamentary attack had started, lines of cavalry moving slowly forward in an open show of force. These were the famous 'Ironsides', the disciplined cavalry of the Eastern Association tutored by Oliver Cromwell, and now making their debut in Wiltshire's tiny war. Approaching to within carbine shot, the Roundhead horsemen discharged just single volleys before retiring, wave upon wave of ordered soldiers, intending only to worry the enemy and hasten Long's departure.

This show of muscle had the desired effect. Flushed from the woodwork, Long departed through the town's north gate and headed towards Melksham and Bath. Crossing the Avon at Monkton, he turned south and unwittingly rode towards an ambush, for Hardress had made rapid progress. Travelling through Steeple Ashton and Trowbridge, he patrolled the road between Bradford and Melksham, stationing his main detachment at Holt to await his quarry.

Sir James's path was soon blocked by enemy horsemen. Their discomfort could have been avoided by the adoption of an alternative route to Bath. The track north through Broughton Gifford would have been far more direct, but lay under the eye of the Chalfield garrison. Lieutenant-Colonel Marmaduke Pudsey and his Chalfield troops had unknowingly played a passive but instrumental role, like beaters at a hunt forcing the prey back into the jaws of the cunning hunters.

Halting only briefly to turn their mounts, the Royalists reined south and galloped towards Westbury with no clear haven in mind. Near Steeple Ashton they were deflected eastwards by detachments of Hardress Waller's brigade, and a few were captured during their moments of bewilderment. The quicker thinking turned back towards Devizes, clattering like bats out of hell through the single street of Seend as though Parliament's entire army were hot on their heel.

Again they were deflected. Confused by the movement of troops west of Devizes, they headed instead towards Potterne where Cromwell's troopers were drawn up to receive them. Two entire troops were taken here with hardly a shot fired. The rest were halted at Market Lavington by William Waller and the remaining section of Parliament's army. Sir James Long and his entire regiment were in Parliament's hands. It was a prize more valuable than the capture of Devizes could ever have been. Only six men were felled in this day of heated hunting, two Parliamentary troopers dropped by casual shots and four Royalists. Lloyd, the cautious but capable commander of the Devizes garrison, had been deprived of his mobile arm.

For Waller, it was hard-earned revenge and the humiliation of Roundway was expunged. It was again to lift his reputation in the judgement of contemporaries. He wasted no time in despatching a report of the action to Westminster.

> '...of 400 horse there escaped not 30', he proudly wrote that day, 'the colonel and most of the officers, with 300 soldiers taken prisoners, with about 340 horses and good store of arms. Blessed be the Lord for this success, which I hope will be the earnest of a further mercy.'

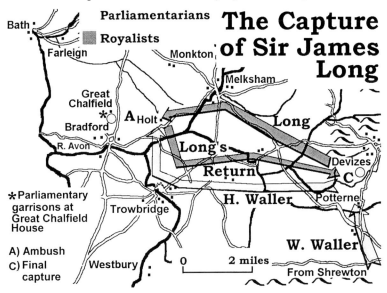

He paid full credit to his subordinates, painfully explaining in detail the parts that they had played in Long's capture. Sir James, resourceful but precipitate, was to spend only a short time in captivity, exchanged in late Spring for Colonel Stephens, the Parliamentary officer taken at Rowden. During his brief custody, his wife Dorothy wrote to his captors, offering to find out the terms on which he would submit to Parliament. But proud and rather vain, Sir James rebuffed her efforts. Weeks later, he was again in the saddle, attempting to revive a dying war.

Waller would have only a small part to play in this future fighting. Briefly leaving the stage to assist the Parliamentary effort in Somerset and Dorset, he re-entered Wiltshire on 20th March, after halting for the night at Marshfield on the county's northern border. Like a spider returning to tease an entangled fly, he again pounced on Devizes, sending a party of horse on a mischief making expedition towards the town. This detachment was engaged on route by Royalist horse under a Captain Jones, and forced to withdraw to Calne.

Calne was about to taste war for the first time, serving as the venue for a light skirmish of no lasting significance. Waller occupied the town that afternoon to await a detachment of musketeers and a battery of artillery hastily borrowed from Malmesbury. But Jones and his troopers were to visit the town too, intent on embarrassing the Parliamentary general and exploiting that earlier success. For two or three hours, the two sides parried blows near the town's southern end. Jones, without either the resources or will to do much more, wisely withdrew before night fell.

Stung by this impertinence, Waller looked for a vulnerable scapegoat and chose to punish Lacock for Jones' misdeeds. Remaining in Calne just long enough to unite with the Malmesbury contingent, he set off at the head of 5,000 men to visit Boville's small garrison. But while on route, however, he received reports that Goring was pursuing Cromwell through Dorset, and he consequently felt obliged to go to his subordinate's rescue, leaving

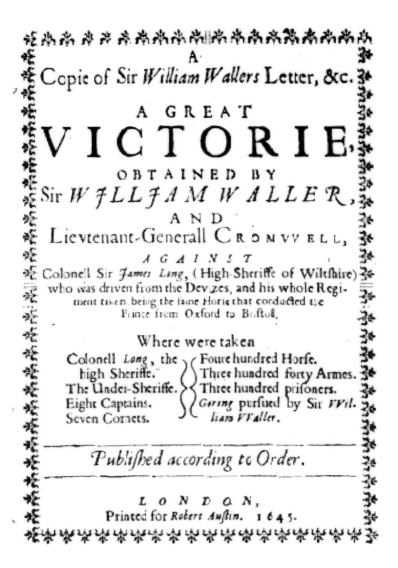

A

Copie of Sir *William Wallers* Letter, &c.

A GREAT

VICTORIE,

OBTAINED BY

Sir *WILLIAM WALLER*,

AND

Lievtenant-Generall CROMWELL,

AGAINST

Colonell Sir *James Long*, (High-Sheriffe of Wiltshire)
who was driven from the Devizes, and his whole Regiment taken, being the same Horse that condacted the Prince from Oxford to Bristol,

Where were taken

Colonell *Long*, the
high Sheriffe.
The Under-Sheriffe.
Eight Captains.
Seven Cornets.

Foure hundred Horse.
Three hundred forty Armes.
Three hundred prisoners.
Being pursued by Sir *William Waller*.

Published according to Order.

LONDON,
Printed for *Robert Austin*. 1 6 4 5.

Frontispiece to the account of the capture of Sir James Long

Southampton
March 14. 1644.

our faithfull and affectionate
Servant.

---

*Here followeth a Copy of Sir William
Wallers owne Letter.*

S I R,

COlonell Cooke and Captaine Butler have
written at large unto you, and therefore I
shall onely confirme it, that with Gods gracious
assistance we have routed the best Regiment the
King had in the West, of foure hundred Horse,
there escaped not thirty, the Colonell, Sir James
Long, eight Captaines, and seven Cornets were
taken, and most of the other Officers, with about
three hundred prisoners. This fell out in Wiltshire, between Troughbridge and Stepston. We
are now marching towards honest Holborne,
with whom (by the grace of God) we will joyn,
or stick half way

March 13. 164.

William Waller.

A list of what was taken.

Col.Sir *James Long*   400. Horse
   the high Sheriffe 340.Armes
The Under Sheriff 300.Prisoners.
8.Captaines   *Goring* pursued by
7.Cornets   Sir *W.Waller.*

F I N I S.

Contemporary account of the capture

Lacock to enjoy a long reprieve.

Waller's route south would take him through Rowde, Potterne and Market Lavington, provocatively close to Devizes. At Cane Hill he was again attacked by the irrepressible Jones. Like a well-aimed dagger, the dashing captain, with less than 200 men in his train, aimed at the Parliamentary heart. Only Sir William's superior numbers deflected the blow and sent the Royalists scampering back to Devizes. Short-lived but bloody, Cane Hill became imprinted in Waller's mind as his second revenge. Hoping to exploit his sudden advantage, he sent his men in pursuit, his lathering horses only yards behind the fear struck Cavaliers.

Penetrating the town's outer defences turned out to be remarkably easy. Parliament's horse swept into the market place and reined before the castle's outer gates. Their quarry, unfortunately, had disappeared, scurrying over the defences to the safety of the fortress. But where men could pass, horses could not: nearly 200 were left outside, a valuable prize for all the Parliamentary effort expended. Jones was personally to pay an even greater price. Returning to the inn where he lodged, he was pistolled by one of the captives taken in the earlier skirmish. How the man acquired the weapon remains a mystery. The fate of the assassin is also not recorded.

The castle's doors remained stubbornly shut. Like a sinner at the gates of Heaven, Waller could only observe and wish. During his long career as a military commander in Parliament's cause, few places could have been so irksome or frustrating as Devizes and its castle. Yet Cromwell a few months later was to take the citadel with comparative ease. But by then the course of war had changed and Royalist defeat was almost certain. Waller chose to withdraw. His infantry lagged some distance behind. Without their support, he was powerless to impose.

The next day, the 26th, found him at Downton, from where he wrote to William Lenthall, the Speaker of the Commons. Reporting the details of Cane Hill, he informed the Speaker of his intention of moving, *'as far as weary legs can carry us'* in support of

Shooting of Captain Jones

Cromwell. The two generals were to jostle with Goring for most of the next fortnight. Their presence, however, failed to prevent the Cavalier general from irrupting across the border and defeating Wansey's patrolling troops near West Knoyle. In the wild encounter, Wansey's personal banner was carried off.

By 9th April, Waller and Cromwell were back in Wiltshire, quartering at Salisbury, and expecting to be followed by Goring. That night Sir William again wrote to London, this time begging for reinforcements with which to see off the enemy threat: *'Send us with all speed such assistance to Salisbury as may enable us to keep the field and repel the enemy...at least to secure and countenance us so, that we be not put to the shame and hazard of a retreat; which will lose the Parliament many friends in these parts, who will think themselves abandoned on our departure from them.'*[2]

Cromwell also shared in this unfolding pessimism. Having been humbled by Goring's movements in the neighbouring counties, both generals feared a rapid Royalist sweep to the east and a jab at London's soft south. Uncharacteristically nervous, he wrote to Colonel Edward Whalley: *'I desire you to be with all my troops and Colonel Fiennes his troops also at Wilton at a rendezvous by break of day tomorrow morning, for we hear the enemy hath a design upon our quarters.'*[3]

But Parliament was about to recast the drama, and the time had come for Waller to leave the stage. The Self-Denying Ordinance, the result of weeks of bitter debate and the cause of much personal

---

[2] Carlyle's. 'Cromwell's Letters'. XXIV.

[3] Sandford D. 'Studies and Illustrations of the Great Rebellion'. Page 616.

recrimination, was to bar members of either House from holding a military command. Essex and Waller were among those flung aside. By a quirk of irrational reasoning, Cromwell was actually to survive. If he had not, the future's course might have been very different.

18

'Poor silly creatures'

MILITARY defeat in Cornwall and muddled Roundhead thinking at Newbury had ignited the autumn's violent debate. But it had long been smouldering and defeat was merely a catalyst. Religious and political in origin, the acrimonious dialogue that now took place in both Lords and Commons would assume an increasingly personal slant, and gradually the real issues of the day became submerged in bouts of mud slinging and character assassination.

At the very epicentre of this debilitating earthquake stood Oliver Cromwell, the Member for Huntingdon, and self-enlightened visionary. The religious argument was bound to be contentious. Episcopacy, the rule by bishops, had been undoubtedly overthrown, but Parliament's adherents were divided about what to put in its place. Presbyterianism, the belief in an ordered but bishopless church hierarchy, held sway at Westminster and in the camps of Parliament's Scottish allies. An increasingly vocal minority, however, had begun to challenge this cosy arrangement, arguing for the autonomy of local congregations to conduct their own affairs without the constraints of a dictatorship from the centre. These Independents, led in the Commons by Henry Vane and Oliver St John, were soon to find that Cromwell was to be their most vociferous spokesman.

But Independency had political and military overtones as well as religious. In the autumn debates, issues of state and the conduct of the war became paramount. Cromwell and his associates looked for scapegoats on which to heap the responsibilities for defeat. Supreme amongst the chosen objects for ridicule was the Earl of Manchester, perhaps unjustifiably blamed for the debacle at Newbury. Whether responsible or not, he was personally targeted by the scornful Cromwell. In the heated debates on the floors of both Chambers, insults took the place of rhetoric and passion was substituted for cool-headed reasoning. Unwisely perhaps, Cromwell added a social dimension, apparently declaring that, *'there never would be a good time in England till we had done with Lords'*. This declaration of class warfare served only to inflame moods still further and cause the Lords to rally to Manchester's support.

The Scots, too, enlisted in the ranks of the Earl's supporters. Cromwell had long argued against the alliance with Scotland and had recently condemned proposals to invite the Scots to assist in taking Oxford. His articulate support for the Independents angered the Scottish Presbyterians who felt that, while Cromwell remained as a barrier, a uniform religion across the realm could never be applied. The Scots now began to angle for Cromwell's destruction and elected Lawrence Crawford, major-general in Manchester's army as their champion of debate. Slandering of Cromwell was about to become fashionable.

The Presbyterian scholar, Robert Baillie, fired the opening salvo: *'We must crave reason of that darling of the sectaries,'* he pounced, *'and obtaining his removal from the army, which himself by his over rashness, has procured, to break the power of that potent faction.'*

This personal attack on Cromwell began at the very moment when the lower house began to debate the reasons for continuing military failures. On November 9th 1644, Cromwell pointed the blame at politicians. *'Members,'* he exclaimed, *'of both houses had good places and commands, and by influence in Parliament or in the army, meant to keep them by lingering on the war.'*

The solution was to remove those with vested political interests from exercising high command and replace them with soldiers of proven skill. The later bitter conflict between the politicians and the military would be moulded from the heated passions that were aroused.

That same day, Zouch Tate, the Member for Nottingham, formally moved the Self-Denying Ordinance. It called for the immediate resignation from their commands of all members of both houses. This measure would not only remove Essex, Manchester, Waller and Cromwell, but would similarly force the resignation of many of the counties' Parliamentary leaders. The incompetent would be thrown out with the competent, after which it would be possible to restructure the high command of Parliament's armies on the basis of merit.

Support for the ordinance, however, was to be largely negative. Both sides, the pro and anti-Cromwell groups, felt able to back a measure which would deprive the other of military command. It passed the Commons with little opposition. But their lordships were not so amenable. Seeing the proposal as nothing less than an attack on the Earls of Essex and Manchester, they refused to discuss it, sowing seeds of dissension at the very time when unity was most needed and successfully delaying its final approval until April 1645.

Re-organisation of the army came next. Success in battle required the forging of a sharper weapon - a professional army capable of delivering victory. In December 1644, Cromwell had addressed the Commons: *'It is now time to speak, or for ever hold the tongue. The important occasion now is no less than to save a nation out of a bleeding, nay, almost dying condition...I do conceive that if the Army be not put into another method and the War more rigorously prosecuted, the people can bear the War no longer, and will force you to a dishonourable peace'*. Most present in the Commons chamber that day seemed to agree. On January 6th 1645, plans were laid for the creation of a new force of 22,000 men with Sir Thomas Fairfax as commander-in-chief. But the New Model Army was the child of political and social motives as well as military. Determined to stamp out all remaining aristocratic influence in the army, the Commons decreed that its regiments were to be commanded by officers of calibre and sound judgement - and men of the right persuasion.

Yet it would be more than three months before the New Army took the field and a keener fighting edge was felt. In the interval, Royalist arms again triumphed in Wiltshire. On May 9th, at the very moment when the New Model's boots first sounded on Wiltshire's highways, Chippenham was briefly visited by the Cavaliers of Devizes. At the head of this Royalist detachment of 200 dragoons rode Sir James Long, just released from custody, and justifiably anxious to exact revenge. Parliament's resistance was brief. Chippenham served as an outpost for Malmesbury and was only lightly manned. Within minutes its guardians were fleeing for their lives, galloping hell-for-leather along the dusty road through Corston towards Malmesbury, the Royalists in close pursuit. Forced to a halt by the guns of Malmesbury, Long was compensated by the theft of 100 cattle from nearby Cole Park and the satisfaction of the chase.

The New Model's first clash followed soon afterwards. On the 12th, a detachment probed hesitatingly towards Devizes from their forward base at Amesbury and skirmished near Lavington. Routed within minutes by the numerically superior Royalists, Fairfax's tiny band fell back through the village and made good their escape. But a handful went to earth in a local tavern and were soon too drunk to offer resistance. Flushed out by the Royalist huntsmen, they were led in chains to Devizes and displayed in the market place like dancing bears. The first of the New Model's members to be taken, they were vilified by the London press: *'These seven or eight, having preferred their bellies to their safety, were brought with such triumph into the Devizes, that when Aulicus comes to flourish it over, I doubt not but it will prove a great victory, for he hath few others of late'.*

Days later, Lloyd set fire to Bromham Hall, the peacetime home of Sir Edward Baynton. The house had been empty for some time and its destruction was deliberate vandalism to prevent its occupation by Parliament's troops. It did little to help the Royalist cause: *'His soldiers* (Lloyds), wrote one of those who lived nearby, *'rove about our country where our misery is such that we are*

*forced to pay them moneys to eat up our provisions or victuals,
oats, hay and such like...And to add further misery to our country,
the said Colonel Lloyd with a party of horse and foot came from
the Devizes to Bromham..., when they utterly destroyed by fire one
of the famousest buildings in these western parts'.*[1]

But Parliamentary behaviour in its tiny North Wiltshire empire
was no better. Weeks before, the County Committee had
authorised Devereux to raise £1,000 for the maintenance of his
Malmesbury garrison. Extracted from the local people, this
arbitrary taxation unleashed a howl of protest and a petition to
Westminster.

> *'Your petitioners have ordinarily given free quarter to
> the forces of the said garrison,'* it complained, *'and their
> plough (teams) have been pressed at all seasons both to
> carry stone and timber and other material for the
> fortifications...without any payment for the same...And
> whereas your petitioners hoped (as the fruits of these
> great expenses) to have been protected in some measure
> from violence and rapine, yet the enemy have always
> compelled the country to pay contributions and other
> taxes, and also have continually plundered and
> spoiled...'*[2]

This was perhaps the most galling period of the war. Garrisons
generally lived off the immediate neighbourhood, parasitically
draining the local community of its life blood and means of
self-survival. In areas of agricultural plenty, the soldiers of these
strong points lived comfortably, stocking their larders to overflow
with little concern for those forced to provide. The men of
Chalfield, for instance, dined like princes. Between January and
June 1645 the 200 troops of this Wiltshire garrison consumed

---

[1] Waylen, S. 'History of the Devizes'.

[2] Ibid.

1,900lbs of mutton, 580lbs of pork, 1,600lbs of bacon and 40,000lbs of beef - more than a pound each of meat a day! In addition, they drank an average of two and a half pints of beer daily, and ate more than 8 ounces of bread, 12 ounces of oatmeal, nearly 3 ounces of cheese and 4 ounces of peas. Few civilians or soldiers on the march could ever hope to dine like this, and garrison troops consequently fought hard to defend their posts and protect their bill of fare.

Frequently they underpaid the locals who supplied the goods, setting prices well below the market level, or even choosing not to pay at all. In vain did the oppressed complain, their pitiful calls for justice unheard or handled by the oppressors themselves. Warminster was plundered on more than one occasion, robbed of its removables by bands of fleeting soldiers. After one such raid, a Mrs. Carter bravely petitioned, claiming that horses and linen had been taken from her charge. But those accused cruelly petitioned for her arrest, charging her with slandering the good name of Parliament. *'Your petitioners are free from such a heinous crime,'* they declared, *'and as we conceive it reflects not so much upon us as upon the High Court of Parliament in whose service we have ventured our lives'.*[3]

Other atrocities were more personal, attacks on the privacy and bodies of the innocent themselves. Trooper George Long was never brought to trial, but the crimes of which he was accused seemed wickedness itself. Refused entry to a house by the frightened lady inside, *'the said Long immediately by force broke down a window leaf, which fell into the house upon a pail of water which fell upon the child which did so bruise the child that it fell sick and shortly after died'.* Long was then said to have bitten and scratched the mother, *'swearing in most execrable and ignominious manner she was a witch and therefore he would have her blood'.*

---

[3] 'Records of the County of Wiltshire'. Wiltshire Public Records Office.

Sometimes the innocent were seen as whipping boys when things went wrong. High taxation was often meted out as a form of revenge or punishment in areas which had assisted the enemy. Taxation was always harsh, but in those areas of overlapping occupation life frequently became intolerable. For dual control meant dual taxation and double plunder - and a cross too heavy to bear. Resistance inevitably began. In the Spring of 1645, men of town and country, rose in protest. Occurring almost simultaneously in the neighbouring counties of the west, the risings of the 'Clubmen' were raucous, poorly co-ordinated, and uninspiringly led.

Yet their goals were far from lofty, and hardly imposed a threat. Wishing only to be left in peace, these men of the soil had just one humble aim, to defend their homes and property against outside aggression. Assembling near Devizes under the leadership of Thomas Bennett of Pyt House, the Wiltshire men resolved to petition Parliament with a list of their grievances.

> *'We the miserable inhabitants of the county of Wilts, being too deeply touched with the apprehension and sense of our past and present sufferings, received only by these civil and unnatural wars within the kingdom: and finding by sad experience...the true worship of Almighty God, and our religion are almost forgotten; and that our ancient laws and liberties are altogether swallowed up in the arbitrary power of the sword...are unanimously resolved to join in petitioning his Majesty and both Houses of Parliament for a happy peace and accommodation for the present differences, without further effusion of Christian blood'.[4]*

---

[4] 'Records of the County of Wiltshire'. Wiltshire Public Records Office.

But their true mood was quickly evident. On their banners were inscribed clear warnings, aimed equally at the leaders of both the warring parties:

> *'If you offer to plunder or take our cattle,*
> *Be assured we will bid you battle.'*[5]

Described inaccurately as the war's 'third force', the Clubmen were largely indifferent to the politics of those at war, regarding as enemies only those who saw them as pawns without rights in this vicious game of war. For most, the regime of rustic toil and daily exactitude would be the same whichever party prevailed. Few of those bent over rustic ploughs or workshop bench cared much for the quarrels of war or felt the passions of its ebb and flow and wished only to be left in peace.

But their neutrality was frequently dishonoured. Regarded by both sides as allies of the enemy, they were viewed with deep suspicion by both the warring armies. *'They,* (the Clubmen), *have not yet declared for the Parliament or the King,'* explained the True Informer, *'we fear they are of the worser party - they smell so strong of malignancy.'*[6]

Fairfax was just as unkind. In a letter to the Commons in July, he wrote: *'They pretend only the defence of themselves from plunder, but not to side either with the King's forces or the Parliament's but to give free quarter to both. The heads of them all are so far as I can learn such as have been in actual service in the King's army, or those that are known favourers of that party...They meet with drums, flying colours; and for arms they have muskets...fowling pieces, pikes, halberts, great clubs and such like'.*

In the weeks that followed their inception, the Clubmen were to grow bolder and more insistent, clashing indiscriminately with the patrols of Cavalier and Roundhead on village greens or on wayside

---

[5] Sprigge. 'Anglia Rediviva'. Page 63.

[6] The True Informer. 'Parliamentary News Sheet'.

tracks. Just occasionally they served as mediators or policemen, forcing the warring sides to settle their disputes in more peaceful ways. *'They take upon them to interpose between the garrisons on either side,'* states one source, *'and when any of their forces meet in places where they have sufficient power, as Salisbury and the like, they will not suffer them to fight, but make them drink together.'* [7]

On June 13th 1645, the leaders of the Clubmen met the commanders of the Royalist garrison at Longford and the newly established Roundhead garrison at Faulston to arrange a treaty until such times as the countrymen's petition had been answered. To ensure the two garrisons' compliance, the Clubmen offered to pay both sides fifty pounds weekly while the arrangement held.

One man, however, continued to stoke their anger. Francis Dowett, once Ludlow's most favoured officer, was a particular object of hate. Snubbed in his application for a regimental command in the New Model Army, he had spitefully chosen to join the King. Sending his wife in front to Devizes to acquaint Lloyd with his decision, he led his troopers towards the town, informing them that their objective was to beat up the Royalist camp. Just outside, he tore away the veils of deception and invited his men to join him in the service of the King. Thirty of his men, half the total, followed him through the gates of the town in support of a rapidly dying cause.

His new role was to give him almost unbridled licence. Instructed by Lloyd to purge the countryside of Roundhead leanings and surplus cash, he plundered and stole at will. Angered by his menacing shadow, the Clubmen tracked his activities, broadcasting his movements on village bells. On 10th July, he advanced on Market Lavington. One of the townsmen, observing the major's arrival but unable to reach the church in time, picked up a mortar and pestle, climbed on the roof of his house, and

---

[7] Lords Journals, Vol VII, Page 484.

created enough noise to wake the dead. Minutes later, excited groups of the living had gathered to meet the threat, and the town bell was hurriedly rung to rally those who lived still further away.

Dowett was met by almost 1,000 protestors that day, men and women with sickle and hoe. He wisely withdrew, hurrying back to the protection of Devizes. With him were more than forty horsemen, many of whom had ridden with Ludlow and shared in his earlier adventures in the snow.

The Clubmen followed him on foot. Halting outside the castle, they called on Lloyd to hear their grievances. But they were greeted with silence and the haughtiness of one who could safely afford to ignore their empty threats. He, after all, was secure behind the walls of a mighty fortress with cannon loaded and aimed at their rustic breasts. They, by contrast, were like exposed and defenceless worms in a freshly ploughed field where hungry birds had gathered for a meal. His treatment of their woes did little to help the King's failing cause and merely stoked the fires of discontent.

This was to be just the most dramatic of similar incidents that summer. Most were far briefer, and few were violent or momentous. The Clubmen, flourishing throughout the summer's golden days, were to be as transitory as the changing season. Fading with the autumn leaves, the movement did not resurface in anything like its former colour during those last months of a failing war. And it was never a mass movement; perhaps less than 1 in 20 felt a call to the banners of Wiltshire defiance. Few were prepared to die for an unclear cause. No heroes were produced, no epitaphs written. The Clubmen made little impression on the remaining course of the war.

The trading community was more deeply involved. War had brought brief benefits to the county's cloth industry. Depending on national sales, it had profited from the demands of both sides for its product and had so far survived the ravages of vulture armies. London remained its most important market, a metropolis of insatiable needs and changing tastes. For much of the struggle, the route to the capital lay open. From Bradford and Trowbridge through Devizes and Newbury, merchants trudged the road to London, their carts and packhorses piled high with their valued wares. But as war became more intense and sentiments embittered, the road east grew as hazardous as the spice route to China. Merchants became legitimate targets, attacks on the innocent somehow justified by the altered rules of war.

Yet still they journeyed, bribing garrison commanders along the way to give them free passage. But tales of their mistreatment abound. Sir John Boys, Royalist governor of Donnington Castle, was amongst the most notorious of the stationary and unprincipled highwaymen who preyed on this traffic. In one well quoted incident, Devizes merchants asked Sir Charles Lloyd to be allowed to sell in London and promised to pay him four hundred pounds on their eventual return. The merchant party, however, was intercepted near Newbury by Donnington men and ordered to pay a substantial fine. Faced by ruin, the victims borrowed money from friends in Newbury to pay the fee and then continued their journey to London. Hours later, they were stopped again, this time by men from Wallingford. Unable to meet this second demand, they and their baggage were bundled into the castle, and the party only gained their freedom by promising to pay ten pounds for every pack of cloth they carried.

The New Model Army's arrival in the county at the end of June would terminate these acts of terrestrial piracy. Most of late May and early June had been spent in following the King around the Midlands. Royalist strategy in the early months of 1645 had faltered and Charles lacked the muscle to deal simultaneously with both the New Model Army and with the Covenanters in the north. But a Royalist army under the Marquis of Montrose remained unbeaten in the Scottish Highlands and many northern towns and castles still lay under Charles's control. At tense meetings in Oxford, Rupert had argued for an advance against the Scottish Covenanting army, claiming that defeat of the Scotsmen might restore the north to full Royalist control and even enable the King to combine with Montrose. Together the two men might work miracles. With the marquis at his side, he could gather up the Royalists of England's northern counties and then return south to meet the New Model on more favourable terms. Charles, often capable of penetrating vision, should have seen the folly of this suggestion. But increasingly pessimistic, he was beginning to bow to well argued rhetoric and listening to any proposals that might save his crown. On 7th May 1645, at the head of 11,000 men, he set out from Oxford on an uncertain expedition towards the north, provoking criticism in Royalist circles about the foolishness of abandoning his capital.

Fairfax and his Westminster masters took full advantage of the King's departure. By the 23rd, Oxford was under siege, while plans were forged to follow the King towards the north. Brief Royalist successes followed: the Roundhead investment of Chester was abandoned and on the 30th Rupert's men stormed Leicester. The Prince's predictions seemed to be correct and the King's dreams of eventual victory began to revive.

But indecision at Leicester in the days that followed gradually blunted the Cavalier drive. By the 7th June, the King's army had withdrawn to Daventry, dulled by dissension in the commanding councils. On the 12th, the New Model Army, hurrying north in pursuit, clashed with the King's outposts on Borough Hill and a major confrontation seemed probable.

On the 14th, the Parliamentarians drew up in force near Naseby, just miles from the king's positions. Charles had been wrong-footed and ensnared in a Midlands field. A major engagement, however, that day could have been avoided. The King was still free to withdraw and might yet have chosen to pursue his path towards the north. But the fateful decision was made to stand and by 8 a.m. his army had deployed across Dust Hill, less than a mile from his opponent. At 9 a.m. the Royalist forces advanced. *'When I saw the enemy draw up and march in gallant order towards us'*, Cromwell later wrote, *'...I could not but smile out to God in praises, in assurance of victory'*.

By evening it was all over. Charles had watched the unravelling of his army during the day from the rear of his army's positions. At one point he had tried to interfere, preparing to personally lead the Life Guard in a charge against the enemy. But there was to be no Hollywood type ending with a hero King leading his men to a brilliant victory. Robert Dalzell, the Earl of Carnwarth,had laid his hand on the bridle of the monarch's horse and *'swearing two or three foul-mouthed Scots' oaths (for of that nation he was) said, "Will you go upon your death in an instant?"'*

Charles and his cause could never recover. More than half his army evaporated in the closing hours of that summer day and, with them, 100 standards, 200 carriages and the entire train of artillery. His nerve, too, lay shattered in the battle field's dust. He retired that night to Ashby-de-la-Zouch, a broken man with shattered hopes. The deciding battle had at last been fought.

Fairfax could now turn his full attention against Goring's forces in the west, effectively the King's last remaining army in the field. Initially heading south-west to the relief of Taunton, he entered Wiltshire's north-east corner on the 27th. The Royalist garrison in Highworth church lay in their path and was now to feel the sharp edge of Parliament's new weapon. Major Henne, the garrison's commanding officer, had constructed a line and drawbridge around the church, placing a detachment of soldiers under Lieutenant-Colonel Sir Thomas Nott in the village to divert the attackers attention. Assaulted by Fairfax's skirmishers, these defenders put up only a watery resistance before falling back to the Major's more solid lines. Nott was amongst the few victims in this short brush, killed only seconds after the fight began.

Positioning his cannon to face the west door, Fairfax sent an officer and a dozen men to demand the church's surrender. But Major Henne at first refused. A volley of cannon shot, however, brought him to his senses *'...he took down his bloody colours, and sounded a parley and yielded upon quarter*[8]. Holes in the

---

[8] Sprigge. 'Anglia Rediviva'. Page 60.

stonework to the left of the door mark the savagery of the brief Roundhead attack. Seventy men were taken captive and eighty muskets were found stacked within the church.

A few days later part of this invading force found itself ensnared by Major Dowett. Bivouacking near liberated Marlborough at the time of the fair, troopers of the New Model visited the town to join in the summer sports. Drinking heavily and conspicuous in their uniforms of red, they were to be an easy target for Dowett's watchful soldiers. For they, too, were at the fair, drinking in a tavern at the town's fringes.

The scene is almost imaginable. Deploying quietly at the edges of the open space, the Royalists crept inwards, choosing their quarry as they approached. Then a sudden flash of movement and a wild panic as the victims tried to escape, spilling carts laden with merchandise in their effort to get away. Few, however, succeeded. Minutes later they were being escorted to Oxford, their hands tied to the sides of a cart.

Highworth Church

Fairfax heard of their plight. But a far more menacing danger lay further west, growing like a tumour in the Somerset countryside. Goring was now in command of 8,000 men, and only prompt surgery and an advance by the New Model Army could prevent the Cavalier army's further growth. On the 30th, Fairfax briefly halted at Amesbury on his way to the west. Here Sir Thomas hung a deserter from his army in a display of discipline and called on the Clubmen to disarm. At Broad Chalke on 1st July, he was met by the Clubmen's delegates, who demanded that the garrisons of Wiltshire should be placed in civilian hands. Cromwell, possibly the last to hear this outrageous demand, was the first to lose his temper. Referring to the assembled Clubmen as *'poor silly creatures'*, he took their leaders captive and muted the voices that had spoken too loud. On 2nd July, Fairfax and his army left Wiltshire. In his absence, the more localised war in Wiltshire would resume again.

Parliament's garrison in Great Chalfield, having tasted the Cavaliers' weak venom during a brief siege in April, was the first to react. In early July, they pounced on Lacock, investing the abbey for a fortnight before retiring with their honour restored. But Boville's men were far from immobilised by this sudden attack, and scoured the countryside for sustenance and supplies. Perfect Occurrences provides some of the detail.

> *'This day there came other very good news out of the west...for the enemy's horse from Lacock, going out the Lord's day last to plunder...for that is their religion, their work of piety, charity etc., so barbarous and brutish they are...so that the enemy came for plunder near to our garrison at Chalfield, where they quartered very secure, giving themselves to pleasure (for all it was the Lord's Day) and plunder the country and abuse the people.*[9]

---

[9] Perfect Occurrences. 'Parliamentary News Sheet'.

Lacock Abbey

But Pudsey and his Chalfield men were watching keenly. Like an eagle from its eyrie, he sortied with his garrison, falling on the Royalist plunderers in the open countryside and seizing 95 horses. Boville's unfortunate men were forced to escape on foot, leaving many of their weapons on the road as they went.

News of Parliamentary success in the west followed rapidly on their heels. The New Model's great victory over Goring at Langport on July 10th removed the King's last dreams and signposted the path to Parliamentary victory. Bridgwater fell a few days later, its capitulation finally snapping Royalist communications with Devon and Cornwall. In the shadow of such defeat, any further Royalist offensives would appear as folly, merely delaying the day of reckoning and compounding the sins of the sinners. Yet some of the most virulent aggression was about to commence, produced by men who wished to salvage their self-esteem. Personal reputation, not hopes of a Royalist renaissance, would encourage these men to acts of violence in the service of a fallen monarch. Dowett chose to be one of these great adventurers.

19

'To view some brawling lines, come from a blockish pate'

APRICIOUS, a person of grandiose schemes, personal ambition and faultless arrogance, Dowett was about to set out on a personal crusade at the very time when other Royalist lieutenants were coming to terms with the kingdom's new masters.

Massey would soon experience the colourful major's showmanship. Encouraged by success at Marlborough and by Fairfax's departure to the west, Dowett decided to menace Hankerton, Charlton House and Newnton, each the base of semi-resident detachments of Massey's Gloucester brigade. Leaving Devizes in early July 1645, the Royalist forces were undetected until they had reached Lediard Tregoze. Parliamentary scouts then galloped hurriedly to Malmesbury, carrying news of Dowett's arrival to Colonel Devereux and his garrison. But the Parliamentary colonel took no immediate action to deal with Dowett, believing that his three detachments were sufficiently robust to deal with the Royalists' insipid threat. Instead he decided to snag the Royalists during their return to Devizes, and sent Sadler with three troops of horse to lay the Roundhead trap. This officer, who had served with such distinction at the side of Ludlow, was the almost perfect choice for such a mission. Selecting the high ground between Clack and Bradenstock Priory as the site of ambush, he dismounted his men and patiently awaited his quarry.

Dowett, as predicted, had already abandoned his ambitious project. Too close to Malmesbury anyway to be in any real danger, the three Parliamentary garrisons could easily combine to fend off an attack, and their merged strength would more than equal

Dowett's small force. The Royalists began to return to Devizes, looking for softer targets to plunder on the way.

One of Sadler's trumpeters caught sight of them at Christian Malford, and unwisely gave the alarm. The Royalists, sensing the danger, turned their horses and hurried away. What followed was one of the most glorious chases of the Wiltshire war. One hundred well-horsed troopers racing for home over mud-strewn roads, relying upon the skills of their horsemanship and the strength of their mounts. Only minutes behind, 200 equally matched Roundheads thundered in pursuit, carbines in hand and eyes fixed unswervingly on the men ahead.

The Cavalier horses did not fail. Slowly outriding their tormentors and convinced that Sadler had given up the chase, their riders stopped in a field near Rowde to rest and went to sleep in the freshly cut hay.

But the huntsmen were far too determined. Minutes later, Sadler's men fell on them, killing four where they lay and capturing fifteen more. Major Dowett unfortunately was not amongst that number. Mounting in haste and leaping a ditch, he and most of the troop reached the safety of the nearby town.

A Cavalier move against Chippenham followed soon afterwards. Constrained on all sides by the Parliamentary advance, Royalism in Devizes was in danger of suffocation, and the sudden push from Devizes was a bid for survival. Occupation of Chippenham was the ploy of the desperate, a frenzied attempt to link with Lacock and the other remnants of the Royalist west.

But it was seen also as a chance to settle old scores. Boville and Long, embarrassed by recent defeat, were probably co-authors of this plan to carry the war into Chippenham's quiet streets. On the 12th, Long and Dowett left Devizes at the head of a troop of horse and fifty foot, having arranged to meet Boville somewhere on route. Boville, still almost horseless after his humiliation at Chalfield, had only twenty horses. These he committed to a Captain Cook, declaring that he himself *would never cross saddle till he had mounted all his men on rebels' horses'*. He then set out on foot at the head of forty firelocks, almost the entire force at his disposal.

The Parliamentary governor at Chippenham, Lt. Col. William Eyres, had hardly time to prepare the defences. Ignored by both sides and never formally garrisoned until these twilight days of war, the town was viewed as a suitable base for intended operations against Devizes, and probably nothing more. Unlikely to face attack, its need for defences had been overlooked. Only flimsy breastworks ringed the town, as effective as a house of straw in a light breeze. Just outside the town and still unobserved, the Royalists surprised a lone soldier and forced him to reveal the details of the defence. From him they discovered that the Parliamentary horse had recently left the town and less than a hundred men remained. God and destiny had suddenly smiled, and the Royalists were quick to respond.

Reports of the fight are brief, as brief perhaps as the fight itself. Dowett attacked at the Bath Road, sending his men in lines against a moveable timber barricade. Long and Boville held back, waiting until Dowett had tested the defences. Then, launching forward from the opposite end of town, they tackled twin breastworks and the very heart of the Parliamentary resistance.

This was to be scaled-down war, with less than 200 men on either side. Parched by time and fatigue, the early war reservoirs of manpower had almost run dry. But the trickle that still flowed was as spirited as any of those earlier martial bands and heroes could still be made.

Filing through a narrow avenue, Boville's men quickly by-passed the outer breastwork. Clearance of the stouter inner work required greater effort. While Boville took possession of some nearby houses, Colonel Long's men mounted a bank, rode over the works, and charged into the market place. Two groups of Royalist attackers were now entering the town from opposite ends, and the Parliamentary defenders were sent scurrying for their lives along St Mary Street. Less than two hours of fighting had procured the town for the Cavaliers.

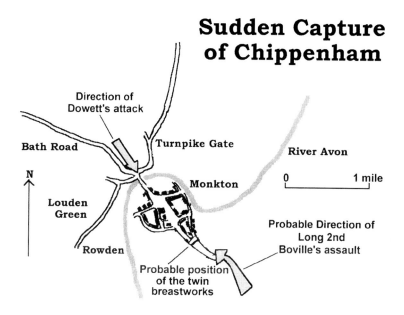

Sudden Capture of Chippenham

Direction of Dowett's attack

Bath Road

Turnpike Gate

River Avon

N

Monkton

0   1 mile

Louden Green

Probable Direction of Long 2nd Boville's assault

Rowden

Probable position of the twin breastworks

But then the Parliamentarians suddenly rallied, stiffened by the reassuring sound of trumpets in the distance. Believing that this might signal the return of their roving cavalry, they stood at bay for another hour, repulsing the joint efforts of Long and Dowett. Major Dowett's brother was amongst those killed, having *'received two shots and his horse three'*. Francis was luckier, a ball lodging in the collar of his doublet while the cheek of his helmet was shot away. But inevitably the fighting died down, and the backbone of resistance lay shattered in the urban dust.

> *'In fine (without further loss or hurt)'*, reported Mercurius Aulicus in its account of one of the last Cavalier victories of the war, *'those rebels in the street were killed, taken or drowned, and the town wholly mastered; wherein they took Lieutenant-Colonel William Eyres...and 80 prisoners besides, the rest escaped away in the dark...who left behind all their arms which were*

betwixt 2 and 300 very good muskets and firelocks, with
30 horse, all of which these gallant gentlemen brought
safely along with them, having killed the rebels' marshall,
1 sergeant, and 10 common soldiers, besides many
drowned; the inhabitants of the town not losing the value
of sixpence, though taken by assault.[1]

Boville had redeemed his vow. He could now mount himself
and his men on Parliament's horses and crow in triumph from the
walls of Lacock. Parliament's reporters were less buoyant, yet
caustic wit still flowed. Dowett was the principal target of their
derision.

'Major Dowett, they confess, was shot in the collar of
his doublet and the cheek of his casque,' sneered the
Kingdom's Intelligencer. *'Let him take heed the next be*
not his false heart...They tell us that Major Dowett did
excellent service at the turnpike. Oh! he is excellent at the
turnpike, or turncoat.[2]

Days later, Dowett spat back. With Long and Lloyd at his side
and one hundred horse at his rear, he fell on a Parliamentary
contingent at Aldbourne. Biased Royalist accounts talk of a
sensational victory. Whether Colonel Martin and his detachment
were part of Fairfax's army or what their exact mission was is far
from clear, but it seems probable that he was merely passing
through Wiltshire on route for most distant pastures. Briefly
stopping in Aldbourne to rest his sixty dragoons and 300 horse, he
was set upon by four waves of Royalist horsemen and forced from
his quarters in the town. A few horses and prisoners were taken
and Dowett was again triumphant.

---

[1] Mercurius Aulicus.

[2] Kingdom's Weekly Intelligencer. Parliamentary News Sheet.

This, however, was to be the watershed of Royalist success. On September 13th 1645, after storming Bristol, Fairfax called a council of war to decide his next moves. While the bulk of the New Model was mobilised for a further push to the west, units were detached to exorcise the remaining Royalist presence in Gloucestershire and Wiltshire. Colonel Thomas Rainsborough and three entire regiments marched against Berkeley on the Severn while Cromwell advanced at the head of four regiments, some 5,000 men, to tackle Lloyd at Devizes.

On September 17th, he reached Trowbridge, news of his movements sending shock waves of fear in the direction of Devizes. The Parliamentary press, of course, was quick to publicise these new events in the west, colouring its reports with blasts of pure rhetoric. The Kingdom's Weekly Intelligencer was particularly bombastic:

> 'Colonel Rainsborough the terrible is gone to assist at Berkeley Castle,' it reported that week, 'he will make the dust fly before long and their brains too; if they take not heed. The foot regiments of Colonels Montague, Pickering and Waller are at the Devizes....They of the town of Devizes said to our men, that the garrison prayed heartily to send them either an army of devils or 30,000 Turks, or they should never overcome these terrible Fairfaxians. '[3]

Lloyd had insufficient men to hold both town and fortress and went to ground within the castle. Dowett decided not to remain, weakly arguing that he would be of more service to the King in the open field. Abandoned in his hour of greatest need, Lloyd sent an urgent message to the King's Secretary, Sir Edward Nicholas, but his passionate appeal for help never reached its intended goal. It

---

[3] Kingdom's Weekly Intelligencer. Parliamentary News Sheet.

was intercepted on route, and Sir Charles was forced to stand alone.

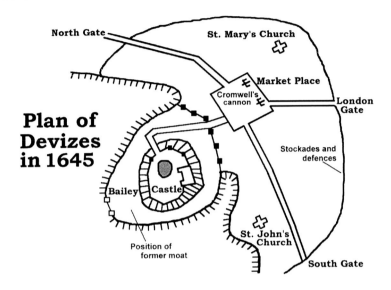

Plan of Devizes in 1645

North Gate

St. Mary's Church

Market Place

Cromwell's cannon

London Gate

Stockades and defences

Bailey Castle

St. John's Church

Position of former moat

South Gate

On the 20th, Cromwell mounted a battery of ten guns in the market place and paraded his strength in the fields beyond. The following day, a Sunday, he sent his formal summons, propping up the demand with poignant reminders of the King's recent defeats and the folly of further resistance. But this was just part of the established routine that now preceded any siege. The defender's delayed but defiant response was part of that routine too. Lloyd, like all other hard pressed defenders of the King's terrain and no willing martyr for lost causes, asked for a ten day truce and the freedom to send a message to his King. Other Royalist commanders were doing the same, and the King had become accustomed to these lame excuses from the fainter hearted.

Cromwell, reluctant to be the victim of circumstance when he could be the master of events, refused this straight request. Instead he offered to let the governor's lady, or any other woman of similar stature, journey to Oxford with news of affairs at Devizes.

Angered by this rebuff, Lloyd issued the standard response, a gesture of resistance and ill-placed defiance. Cromwell, he claimed, would *'have to win and wear it'*, (the castle). A dog was seen wandering the streets of the town. On its collar were inscribed some lines of rough doggerel. One of the garrison's unfortunate pets, it had been despatched as ambassador with a message of contempt.

Parliament's reply was equally scathing. Penned that evening, the author might have been Cromwell himself.

> *'Poor Cavaliers, it was my chance of late*
> *To view some brawling lines, come from a blockish*
> *pate,*
> *Wherein you call us fools: but stay,*
> *You'll prove the fools before we go away.'*

Lloyd had fewer than 400 men and probably the clear headedness to see that this was a conflict between rank unequals. The war, however, had been asymmetrical for months and yet had continued to glow, fed by the intransigence of diehard Royalists. And it was always possible that God might choose to favour him in his hour of need.

On Monday, 22nd September, the market place battery opened, keeping up its fire for 24 hours. Early the following day, a shell fell in the roofless keep where the powder had been stored. The resulting explosion killed several men, but miraculously failed to ignite the powder. Other near misses occurred in the hours that followed. John Gwyn, a soldier of the garrison, leaves details of one.

> *'...as I sat upon a small seat of sods, with my back to*
> *an empty cannon-basket...a sergeant that stood by calls*
> *me up in all haste, to show me three of the enemy that*
> *came to discover our works. I had no sooner started up,*
> *but he clapped me down in my place; nor was he no*

sooner sat, but a musket-ball struck through the basket into his head, and he died immediately. [4]

Throughout the Tuesday the cannon fire continued, a never ending tirade of punishment and near death to which the Royalists could provide no answer. Resistance crumbled along with the masonry and men huddled in groups and prayed for a miracle. *'The enemy, with incessant peals of muskets, great guns and mortar pieces, played upon us,'* wrote Gwyn, *'that it past us all day and night at our line, without the least reserve, that we could do no more.'* [5] That afternoon two officers emerged to ask for terms and the guns in the market place fell silent. Ushered to Cromwell's presence, they asked only that the garrison should be allowed to depart in peace and without fear of retribution.

Cromwell was surprisingly magnanimous. Punishment would be meted only against those who had changed sides, erstwhile Parliamentarians who had seen fit to desert the cause. They, and they alone, were to remain in the castle, to be detained indefinitely under the unwritten rules of war. All other officers, including Lloyd himself, would be free to depart. The lower ranks would be just as unregulated, permitted to leave, but with sticks instead of weapons in their hands!

The two ambassadors emerged from their conference and made their way, escorted by senior officers of the New Model, back towards the castle's still closed gates. The destiny of Wiltshire would depend on what was decided within. For, if Devizes fell, Royalism would be virtually extinct in the county, sustained only in Chippenham and Lacock, and in Longford's distant towers. Two days of deliberation followed. Like singers awaiting the final chorus call in a drawn out opera, Parliament's soldiers waited, ranging dangerously within reach of the castle's guns. Some

[4] Gwyn, J. 'The Military Memoirs of John Gwyn'. Page 64-65.

[5] Ibid.

played dice, others conversed, and an occasional cannon ball was loosed against the fortress as if to remind the garrison that a speedy reply was required. It came on the 24th. Lloyd had been reduced to the rank of a beggar, obliged to accept whatever scraps were offered. Ceremoniously the King's fluttering colours were lowered and his men marched out, officers followed by the men, the latter, as ordered, holding batons in their hands. Lloyd was at their head, mounted on his horse with sword at his side. Reining briefly in the market place, he acknowledged the victors and then rode off to seek reconciliation with his King. The capture of Devizes had cost Parliament just five men.

But condemnation awaited Lloyd in the Royalist capital. Sir Edward Walker was one of many diehard Royalists who publicly accused the Devizes commander of cowardice. *The loss of Devizes, in regard of the natural strength of the place, and the ability of the Governor in matters of fortification, was not as yet ever answered by him. But our misfortunes gave us not the opportunity to reward, and so we do not punish the loss.* [4] Valid comment perhaps. For within the surrendered fortress were sufficient provisions for one whole year, 120 fat sheep and 400 stands of arms.

Cromwell placed Captain Thomas Eyre in command of the town and set out to reduce neighbouring Lacock. Colonels Pickering and Devereux had already invested the place, and the ardour of the Royalist resistance had started to fade. On the 23rd, Boville answered Pickering's initial summons, admitting the hopelessness of his situation, but still breathing the fire of personal defiance.

'Sir, I confess my reason tells me that you being wholly possessed of the county, I cannot defend this place to a continuance; but must resolve to the utmost to give

---

[4] Walker, Sir Edward. 'Historical Discourses'.

the King, my master, a handsome account of his trust to me. I therefore desire...a parley that might discharge me with honour...and if the greatness of your power deny this, I can die handsomely, and by that, add more to your trophies than can a slavish yielding to your fetters.[7]

His second letter a day or two later was far more conciliatory. Pressurised by Parliament's manoeuvres in the meadows before Lacock and by the desertions from his own ranks, his mood had become melancholic and realistic.

'I ingeniously acknowledge many of my soldiers have deserted me, and by that lessened my hopes on account of his Majesty. I doubt not but you are tender of a soldier's reputation: my numbers are not great, nor will the allowance of arms to those few prejudice you, but infinitely add to your honour.[8]

So Lacock was added to Parliament's Wiltshire possessions on the 26th September, and another failed Royalist sought audience with the King. With Boville's departure from the county, the war left too, and peace descended in Wiltshire's northern regions. Chippenham's remaining Royalist strength melted away on news of Lacock's surrender, some of the garrison joining Boville on his pilgrimage to Oxford. Fairfax himself was said to be present to take Lacock's surrender and salute the enemy as they left. With Royalism virtually expunged, the spoils of victory could be returned to their rightful owners: the fat sheep of Devizes and the provisions at Lacock were amongst the first to be restored.

Peace in Wiltshire, however, would depend upon how energetically Parliament policed its lanes and towns. For, like a disease in remission, Royalism could burst forth again or be carried

---

[7] Waylen, J. 'History of the Devizes'.

[8] Ibid.

inwards from outside on the backs of an invading army. In Devon and Cornwall, it still survived, nurtured by a strong regional identity and the charisma of local leaders.

And it still survived in Southern Wiltshire too. Yet Longford Castle, the King's last prop in the county, had given no trouble and caused no offence, and might have been safely ignored. But Cromwell was determined to oversee its immediate destruction and set out from Devizes with this expressed intention. *'I hope,'* he wrote to Fairfax, *'the work will not be long. If it should, I will rather leave a small part of the foot (if horse will not be sufficient to take it in) than be deterred from obeying such commands as I shall receive.'*

Colonel Bartholomew Pell's Royalist garrison at Longford is described as villainous, even by those most sympathetic to the cause. Lord Coleraine, having a large family, had apparently moved into his steward's house in Britford, leaving Pell to adapt the castle to the needs of defence. Rose trees and ancient vines at the bases of the three drum towers had been savagely pulled up and the gardens desecrated to make room for outworks and earthen banks. Stands of ancient woodland had been felled, and the almost continuous sound of axes at work had prompted Lord Coleraine, watching the vandalism from his place of exile, to protest. He was, says Pelate, the family's personal chaplain, *'treated barbarously'* for his efforts, and destruction of the forest had continued.

Then, on October 16th, just as the park's remaining trees turned gold, Cromwell's cohorts arrived, filing almost ceremoniously through the parkland's gates and taking up positions of aggression on the higher land to the castle's north. For almost 18 months, the garrison had been waiting for this moment, aware that the unstoppable Roundhead wave sweeping from the north would eventually engulf them too. Slamming shut the castle's doors, they prepared to face the flood, determined to remain afloat for as long as God might give them strength.

But that would not be long. Cromwell had soon constructed a battery on Picks Mead and sent the usual demand for surrender.

On the 18th, castle and garrison passed quietly into Parliament's hands with hardly a shot in anger. One, however, had barely missed Cromwell. Fired from a southern window, the ball killed an officer at Oliver's side. The two men had been deliberating how best to storm the house. Providence, or Satan, had plucked the Roundhead commander from the jaws of death.

The King's last remaining garrison in Wiltshire had fallen. The house was cruelly punished for its non-resistance. Pelate has left his jaundiced account of what subsequently happened.

> *'...quickly repossessed by viler devils than formerly haunted. For instead of soldiers of fortune and some honest Cavaliers, there was put in by order of Parliament a knavish committee of clowns...who first pillaged the house of whatsoever the former guests had left or could be torn from doors or walls or windows.* [9]

Yet luckily the building survived. Cromwell, presiding over the complete collapse of Royalism in the county, could afford to be generous. News of the surrender travelled rapidly, sending a thrill of finality throughout the south. *'There was now no garrison in the way between Exeter and London,'* writes Sprigge, *'to intercept the passage, so that a single man might travel without fear of the enemy.* [10]

In those closing weeks of the Wiltshire war, one of Royalism's most insincere friends fell too. Having left Lloyd to his fate in Devizes, Francis Dowett had gone to North Wilts to raise a larger troop of horse and had then set out in another bid for belated glory. Basing himself at Faringdon in neighbouring Oxfordshire, and ready to wage a one man war against impossible odds, he chose to assault nearby Lechlade on November 20th. Here a small Parliamentary garrison under Colonel William Moore had recently

---

[9] Pelate, H. The Rev. 'The Longford MSS'. Archives of Longford Castle.

[10] Sprigge. 'Anglia Rediviva'. Page 156.

been installed to assist in the siege of Oxford. Held by Moore's men during the initial assault, Dowett struck again, trying desperately to reverse the drift of war and so lighten the mood of his downcast King. But Devereux and his men of Malmesbury were soon in pursuit. Marching hurriedly through the town, they encountered the Royalist marauders on the far side and the punishment commenced.

Minutes later, Dowett lay dead, felled by the ball of a well aimed pistol. Separated from his men by the fury of the enemy charge and facing certain capture, he had tried to escape by leaping a mud filled ditch. Royalism's evening flower had at last been picked and trampled in the mud. Few were to mourn his death. In fact, it was only to be mentioned as a passing comment in Devereux's official account to the House of Commons, of no more interest than the vagaries of the weather:

> *'Major Duett (or Dowett) with 120 horse and 100 foot went from Farrington to surprise our party of foot...whereup Captain Moore drew out to a wall 60 musketeers, who flanked the enemy as they came into Lechlade, and after an hour and a half's hot dispute betwixt them and the enemy, they repelled them out of the town...Close under Radcourt Wall they encountered each other, where our forces killed of the enemy Major Duett and twenty more upon the place...in this accident we lost not one man, only two hurt, not mortally I hope.'[11]*

For Parliament and its armies had probably long lost interest in Dowett and his mini-war. And possibly in Wiltshire itself. On September 27th Fairfax moved on to Warminster, attending Sunday church with most of his senior officers before travelling into Dorset to extinguish the last Cavalier flickers in the west. Unable to pay his troops for their recent sterling service, he was forced to allow

---

[11] Report on the MSS of the Duke of Portland, I, 376.

the men to live on free quarters during their two days' stay in Warminster and so indulged in a practice which he had openly condemned in others. Parliament had yet to find a legitimate means of keeping their army fuelled.

20

'This is no age for miracles'

NOR had the final victory been secured. Swept back across the borders into Oxfordshire, Royalism was like discarded dirt outside the door, trodden underfoot and probably of little relevance in Wiltshire's future affairs. But a sudden favourable wind might blow it back and the door into Wiltshire would have to be kept locked. On November 16th 1645 the Committee of Both Kingdoms asked the Wiltshire Parliamentarians to assess how many men would be needed to contain the shadowy Royalist threat. Existing forces were felt to be more than sufficient: Massey's brigade, increased in the autumn to more than 9,000 men despite the war's de-escalation, still manned the defences of Malmesbury, Devizes and Marlborough, with a detachment in place in Highworth Church. Longford Castle was garrisoned, its prime purpose being to protect the Commissioners, who sat in almost daily session at nearby Falstone House. But Salisbury and the woollen towns remained unoccupied and the carts and packhorses of Wiltshire folk would be the only traffic on most of Wiltshire's dusty roads.

Except near Calne. On 24th December Royalist raiders from the north swept into town, numbers uncounted and damage unstated, disturbing the inhabitants as they were about to choose the town's new burgess. But fears of a Cavalier revival were soon allayed. For throughout the winter of that final heave of war, Fairfax's army lay between Wiltshire and the King's forces in the far west while Colonel Edward Whalley and a strong force of cavalry was stationed near Oxford, policing the county's northern boundaries.

Peace, however, would come at a price. In January Westminster's commissioners assessed the county at £2,900 monthly, the burden of payment falling on exactly those who had been forced to pay before. Wiltshire and Somerset taxpayers were also held responsible for the maintenance of the Bristol garrison and the support of Parliament's forces on the county's northern borders. Yet Skippon, commanding at Bristol, was soon complaining that he had received nothing from Wiltshire and the port's vital commerce, he claimed, would be difficult to protect.

Royalism, unable to do much more, was now about to resort to lightning raids and guerilla war. On January 20th 1646, Colonel Sir John Cansfield and Sir James Long, hibernating in Oxford, irrupted across the county's border at the head of 1,000 horse and landed like vultures on Marlborough's walls, where three troops of Roundhead horse and 150 horse were now in garrison. Mercurius Academicus reports delightedly:

> 'Sir John Camsfield marched thither about eight of the clock that night, and with his Forlorn fell into the town, and after with the whole body of horse, killed seven of their foot soldiers that gave fire from the main guard, beat the rest of the foot into the church, took most of their horse, and thirty prisoners...which done, having summoned them in the church, they denied to render themselves; but about two or three hours afterwards desired parley, and presently yielded themselves with condition for their lives.'[1]

Amongst those taken captive were Colonel Eyres, governor of Devizes, and James Goddard, Treasurer of the Wilts Committee. Colonel Devereux was apparently also in town that day, but managed to escape through a back door!

---

[1] Mercurius Academicus, Cavalier News Sheet.

From here the Royalist insurgents moved to Salisbury. Perfect Passages, a Parliamentary news sheet, gives a caustic account of events: *'The Oxford horse, under the command of Sir John Cansfield, six or eight hundred, went to Salisbury, where they began to plunder that famous city which had been too good a friend to them.'* [2]

Mr. Gore, a county J.P., was dragged from his bed with only his shirt on, and forced to sit in the garden while his house was plundered and all his money removed. Forty long term Cavalier prisoners were then released from the city's gaol. Warminster, too, received a visit a few days later. From this town alone they took £1,000 - or so the biased accounts report! Eventually forced to a halt outside the town by Arthur Thislethwayte, the county's new sheriff, and a handful of locally recruited men, the raiders disbanded and hurriedly rode back to Oxford with money, glory and several stolen horses.

The near success of the raid worried the victors! Mercurius Academicus, a Cavalier news sheet exploits this well. *'By this it may appear that Colonel Whaley, of whom the London Mercuries have made so much noise, is not so strong or so vigilant to observe the motion of our Oxford horse.'* [3]

On 27th January, the Committee of Both Kingdoms wrote pessimistically to Fairfax, interpreting this savage rape of a county at peace as a major disaster.

'...their county is at present under the power of that party, and rendered altogether unable to furnish those recruits which are now ordered to be there levied for your army...We recommend this to your consideration and

---

[2] Perfect Passages, Parliamentary News Sheet.

[3] Mercurius Academicus, Cavalier News Sheet.

desire you to do therein what you conceive to be the best. [4]

Long's almost pointless act of bravado, however, was soon stripped of any meaning by events in neighbouring counties. On February 16th, Hopton's western army was destroyed beyond reform at Torrington in Devon and Royalism became an outcast beyond the Tamar. Cut off from Oxford by miles of solid Parliamentary territory, this western outpost of the King's empire could not hope to survive for long. *'The best you can hope for in the west is a reprieve,'* wrote Culpeper, one of the King's advisors, in a letter to a friend. *'The Scotch treaty is the only way left to save the crown and the Kingdom...this is no age for miracles, and considering the King's condition is such, less than a miracle cannot save him without a treaty.'*

In early March the shattered fragments of Royalist armies and garrisons were glued together by Sir Jacob Astley, one of the King's most reliable and steadfast commanders, and assembled for action at Bridgnorth on the Severn. But this rebirth of Royalist hopes was broken almost as soon as it formed: on the 21st Astley's force, some 3,000 men, was attacked at Stow on the Wold and the King's last field army was as transitory as gossamer on a dewy morning. *'Here certainly was a more than ordinary hand of God,'* wrote a commentator, *'which could not pass by without observance, being the last battle fought in England.'* [5]

Unfortunately he was not in a position to foretell events to come. Astley, now a prisoner, was to prove more successful at forecasting the future. Seated on a drum in the presence of his captives, he quietly remarked: *'Gentlemen, you may now sit down*

---

[4] Calendar of State Papers, Domestic 1645-47, Page 325.

[5] Rushworth, J. 'Historical Collections of Private Passages of State'. Vol VI, Page 140.

and play, for you have done all your work, if you fall not out amongst yourselves. [6]

The division in the victors' ranks would become increasingly painful during the weeks to come. But for now Parliament's political minds and military muscle remained firmly wedded, and the build-up of forces around Oxford continued. On April 10th the governors of Malmesbury and Highworth received orders to supply men to assist in the blockade of Faringdon. Fairfax, returning from the west in semi-regal style, halted at Salisbury on the 20th, remaining there just three days while the civilian administration at Falstone House turned to the subject of imposing fines on the proscribed. In place of the earlier see-saw of fortunes, the war's progress was just one way, an accelerating and probably irreversible path to rebel victory. On April 27th, at 3 a.m. in the morning, Charles left Oxford, disguised as a servant and with hair trimmed for the occasion, hoping to achieve some accommodation with the Scots. Yet, wisely pessimistic about his chances of reaching a settlement with these men of the north, he headed towards Lynn on the Norfolk coast, probably intending to find a suitable port from which he could leave for the continent if the Scots refused his terms. Days later, he was in effective captivity at Southwell in Nottinghamshire, and the proud King had at last been brought to his knees.

But not his family. At that very moment, one of his daughters, Elizabeth or Henrietta, was holding court at Wilton House, seemingly oblivious of her father's fate. Around her gathered a few of the county's Cavaliers, like colourless moths near a fading light. Days later the truth caught up and the young princess and her entourage were gone, hurrying to the south-west and an eventual boat to France.

Wiltshire's Royalists were not in the throng that hurried westward at her side. Preferring to come to terms with their new

[6] Rushworth, J. 'Historical Collections of Private Passages of State'. Vol VI, Page 140.

masters, and, sensing that an early apology might save their skins, they would turn to face the snapping hounds and petition for their estates. But Parliament had more urgent matters to settle and the machinery for the punishment of Royalist offenders was not yet fully in place. In their path lay an injured county, bleeding from the stabs of four years of war and writhing in the agony of economic and social collapse. Fields lay untilled for want of horses and men, wives wept for fallen husbands and children for their fathers. But few of these lesser folk lamented the absence of missing landlords. Yet the bond between tenant and landlord was the cement of the peacetime social structure and, without that stability, post-war society must inevitably unravel. Now it seemed that Royalist landowners might be permanently dispossessed and thoughtful men began to fear the consequences. *'...Men no longer know their masters,'* lamented a contemporary pamphlet, *'and we must fall apart.'*

In recognition of this dawning threat, the victors attempted to sew together the tears in Wiltshire's social fabric. In May a number of decrees were issued to restore the sense of pre-war order. Restoration of property to the innocent was deemed to be appropriate and orders went out to those in control. *'All such timber and other materials as have been taken away from any of the inhabitants of the said town,'* states the Commons Journal in its reference to Devizes, *'and are now remaining in the said castle, shall be likewise forthwith delivered.'*[7]

Others, just as forcefully, resolved to soften the scars of hostilities and revive the landscape of pre-war Wiltshire. *'...the castle hill and works at the Devizes and the works about Longford House...be forthwith slighted and that there be only one troop of horse kept in the said county, consisting of one hundred horse commanded by Captain William Ludlow.'*[8] Belatedly they also

---

[7] Waylen, J. 'History of the Devizes'.

[8] Calendar of State Papers, Domestic. 1645-47, Page 330.

ordained that 150 foot should be kept in garrison in Malmesbury, the only static force in the entire county.

Inevitably there would be the claims for compensation and retribution - and not just for the sufferings at the hands of Massey's men. William Dotteries of Stratford-sub-Castle was just one of many to demand a pension for his war-gained injuries. Having served in Parliament's field army in the south, he appealed to the county's justices for recognition of his efforts. County records speak of his attempt: '...*and at Newbury fight was mayhemed so that he has altogether lost the use of his left hand and is thereby disabled to do any work to relieve himself and two children.* '[9]

Some of the uninjured claimed compensation from the Justices for loss of livelihood. John Rogers, apprenticed in 1642 to a weaver, Thomas Harris, was impressed into the King's army in 1644, but, '...*having no affection that way got himself off and went onto ye Parliamentary army and there served until May 1645 after which time he repaired to his master and tendered his service* '. The weaver, impoverished by the demands of war, refused to take the young man back and successfully defended his stance before the Bench.

Widows, too, pleaded for financial assistance. Alice Dramont of Hornisham, whose husband was killed at Wardour, had lived since then in poverty with three small children. But her plight was to be made even worse: '...*she, being presently after the death of her husband plundered by the adverse party of that little she had, ...are now like to perish for want of food and to be turned out of door naked...* '. She received nothing in compensation.

With the fall of Oxford in June 1646, construction of the post-war order could commence in earnest. Disbandment of Massey's brigade would follow next, the consequence of Westminster's May decree. Ranging like Huns across Wiltshire's vulnerable countryside, Massey's men were clearly in danger of

---

[9] Records of the County of Wiltshire, Wiltshire Public Records Office.

inflaming passions and stoking the fires of rural unrest. Fairfax took up this point in a letter to the Speaker of the Commons. *'The complaint against Major-General Massey's brigade are still renewed, and indeed the burden is become insupportable: they not only tax the country, but by plunder, robbery, and other insolences, do so dishearten and affright the people, that it is feared many will quit their habitations if timely remedy be not applied.'*

Alarmed by his report, the House agreed on October 6th that £6,000 should be allocated from the fines to be levied on Lord Seymour and the leading Wiltshire Royalists to pay off Massey's men. Instructions were sent to the Wiltshire Committee to calculate the wages due to each soldier, a task that was to prove clerically too complex for the skills and labour available. Robert Nicholas, one of the subcommittee of Accounts for Wiltshire, wrote to London to complain.

> *'Whereas you directed a commission for Wilts, enabling a subcommittee to take the accounts in this county, the noble knight of our shire, Col. Ludlow, has very faithfully prosecuted the same, yet he found a great fainting amongst us, so that he could only swear five of us, and since then this business has slept; but it is a great pity that it should do so for it is one of the most important employments at this time.'* [10]

In an attempt to secure the dissolution of the renegade force, Fairfax, Ireton and Ludlow personally rode from London to Devizes in November at the head of two regiments of horse. Ludlow gives a brief account in his Memoirs of what they did.

> *'We are now by the blessing of God waded through the depths and difficulties of that business wherein we were appointed to be assisting to the General, in order to the paying, reduction, and disbanding of the brigade,*

---

[10] Calendar of State Papers, Domestic. Page 491.

*late under the command of Colonel General Massey,
there having been nothing wanting in his Excellency in
the fair and faithful management of this whole
work...according to which the whole brigade have
received their six weeks pay, the officers being engaged to
bring them to a second rendezvous in their course, as
before, when and where at the head of each regiment, a
proclamation is to be published and a pass to be delivered
to each soldier...the like is to be done today with another
regiment, and so with the rest till we have finished the
whole...* [11]

This tribute to the brigade commander was something of a
contrast with the savage criticism about to be levelled against
Massey by the politicians in London. The suggestion that he
willingly condoned his soldiers' savage treatment of the country
folk was to be partly responsible for driving him later into the arms
of the King. Hints of future tension in the camps of the victors
were now evident. Army and Parliament had begun to quarrel,
poisoned largely by a religious schism that seemed impossible to
bridge. The disturbance in St John's Church, Devizes, on
September 6th was typical of what the nation might expect. Mr.
Shepherd, a Presbyterian, was preaching as usual, reminding his
flock of their duties to God. A Captain Pretty, taking offence at an
issue of minor significance, ordered him down from the pulpit.
Throughout the county, ministers would be replaced by men of
more acceptable persuasion. The war of tongue and pen would
briefly replace the pike and musket. Then, in a dramatic replay of
those earlier days, the tramp of armies would begin anew.
Wiltshire, fortunately, would be largely spared.

---

[11] Tanner MSS, IX, Pag e 536.

21

'Favour and mediation for the obtaining of my liberty'

BUT old style Royalism by now had been rendered innocuous. Throughout the autumn of that eventful year, once proud Cavaliers were creeping homeward or seeking forgiveness at the gates of the victors. The machinery which would be used to administer their punishment had taken three years to construct. In March 1643 a Commons ordinance had decreed that all who had assisted the King politically were to be charged with 'delinquency' and their property confiscated by the committee of the county in which their estates were situated. But the doors of the Goldsmith's Hall in London, where the Committee for Compounding now sat in almost daily session, lay open to the truly apologetic: they had only to accept their delinquency and promise never again to take up arms against Parliament for the charge to be removed, and payment of a fine would generally secure the return of their property. A list of the sinners was promptly compiled. Presented to the Commons later that Spring, it contained 3,197 names nationally. Seventy-five were Wiltshire men, headed, of course, by the Marquis of Hertford. A late summer measure, passed in August, had softened this earlier decree, setting aside a sum from the fines for the benefit of the delinquent's wife and children. Fines were generally based on an ability to pay and property could even be returned on the down payment of just one-tenth of the total.

On January 30th 1644, the Houses softened still further. Hoping to attract deserters and cause a speedy collapse of the

Cavalier host, they offered pardon to all who would submit before a certain date. But few, it seems, were attracted by this generous offer and, temporarily at least, the Royalist ranks remained solid.

Yet Royalism rapidly crumbled to dust in the following year and the first of the delinquents was persuaded to yield. On 29th July 1645 Sir Francis Seymour, archdemon of the Wiltshire Cavalier hierarchy, wrote from house arrest in London to Edward Montague, Earl of Manchester, Speaker of the Lords: *'So that your Lordship may see that my failing herein was rather my misfortune than any wilful neglect. If this truth shall appear unto your Lordship, I shall hope to find your favour and mediation for the obtaining of my liberty, and that I may stand right in the opinion of that honourable House'*.[1]

He was promptly released. His fine was later set at £3,725 and his estates sequestered until payments were made. But his son, Charles, was treated more leniently. In a letter to the Compounding Committee, the Wiltshire Parliamentarians had this to say about the younger Seymour: *'Touching his delinquency, we certify that he was...a commissioner for sequestrating the estates of such as stood for the Parliament, but that he only once gave meetings with others of the commissioners, nor can we learn that he ever executed anything, but at that time did get many of the Parliament's friends freed from trouble...shortly after that commission was granted, he went out of this county to Oxford, where he remained till the surrender thereof, and he affirms he went thither on purpose to avoid any employment against this Parliament'*.[2]

A lukewarm Royalist, he was later to be fined a mere £80. The Seymour cases were amongst the first of hundreds to be heard before the London committee for Compounding and its daughter committees at Falstone and Malmesbury. Each assumed authority

---

[1] Waylen, J. 'The Wiltshire Compounders'. Wiltshire Archaeological Magazine.

[2] Ibid.

for its immediate half of the county, grudgingly working in the shadow of their London parent. Renting out sequestered estates or dealing with the offences of lesser men was their prime responsibility. Common men were sitting in judgement of their betters and the social order was being upturned. Thomas Hancock of Castle Street, Salisbury, was one of many delinquents who fell within Falstone's long reach. He was ordered to supply 50 quarters of malt to the Falstone garrison in penance for his war time crimes. Thomas Lawes, no less guilty, was fined £40, half to be paid when he felt financially able. Edward Knyvet, minister at East Coulston and protector of souls, was stripped of his living for his secular utterances. Storming in the pulpit after Lansdown's drawn battle, he had warned the congregation of his God-given right to hang those who enlisted in Parliament's thinned ranks.

On October 6th 1645, in a mood of unstoppable optimism, Parliament extended its arm of forgiveness still further. All those who submitted by December 1st would be allowed to compound on honourable terms. Michael Tidcombe, guiding light at the illegal assizes in Salisbury two years previously, was one of the first. In November 1645, he wrote to the House: *'Your petitioner therefore humbly prayeth, being heartily sorry for these offences, that he may be admitted to a favourable composition, and receive the benefit of the mercy offered to others, to free his person and estate out of sequestration '.*[3]

He was fined £450. The larger fish in Parliament's trawl were drawn to London to answer for their errors. But three of the five who topped the Wiltshire list were political minnows and their names rarely appear in the annals of war. Henry Danvers, a native of Dauntsey and servant of Kings, had gladly accepted the earldom of Danby, an offence for which he would now be forced to pay. Sir James Thynne of Longleat had been just as innocuous, a rural landlord with a penchant for drink. Sir William Button of Shaw

---

[3] Records of the County of Wiltshire. Wiltshire Public Records Office.

was still less, and his crimes are the actions of a man of forced leisure. His indictment was harsh and states his offences: *'That he voluntarily left his habitation, resided at Oxford, adhered to the King's party, and hath taken neither the Negative Oath nor the National Covenant'.*

The spiritually tainted, those labelled as 'recusants', were to be treated far more harshly. Amongst these were the Papists, men so vile that not even money could wash their souls clean of the crimes they had committed. Men found guilty of delinquency could atone for past sins and might one day again sit in the halls of the favoured. But the devilish lapdogs of Rome, *'abominations in the sight of God'*, could expect no such mercy and would be condemned to *'roast in hell for the impurity of their deeds'*.

Thomas, Lord Arundell, second baron of Wardour, was mercifully spared this fate. Dying at Oxford in 1643, his name fails to appear on Parliament's hit list. But Henry, his heir, faced the full weight of Parliament's revenge. Three-fourths of the estate was sold, parcels of land that straddled three counties. William Arundell of Horningsham and Woodhouse, Henry's uncle, was the most hounded of all. Unflinchingly Papist and a declared delinquent, he had garrisoned Woodhouse with Irish men and obstructed Parliamentary rule.

But he seems also to have been accused of things which he might never have done.

> *'Mr. Arundel came to his house at nine or ten at night'*, states John King of Horningsham, servant to a Mr. Beard in his testimony to the commissioner, *'and, with a sword in one hand and a pistol in the other, asked what rebel rogues he kept in his house...He then demanded a green-grey cloth of Mr. Beard's...and this he did because Beard was well affected to the Parliament.'*[4]

---

[4] Waylen, J. 'The Wiltshire Compounders'. Wiltshire Archaeological Magazine.

An Edward Adlam also gave evidence, probably paid handsomely for damming the Catholic squire.

> '*Mr. Arundel was always at home when the King's forces were in the county, but never when the Parliament's forces were there. He sent ammunition to his tenants at Horningsham with directions to keep his house against the Parliament...he then said that he wished all his tenants' throats might be cut.*'[5]

Arundell was fined £334 and two-thirds of his estate was seized. Perhaps 10% of Wiltshire's lands changed hands in the three years following the war. Yet the social impact would be hardly noticed. And a decade later, when fortunes were reversed and Kings restored, much of this land reverted to its former owners, and lordly ways were known again. Other surface scars of war were just as quick to mend: weathervanes on spires, felled by a playful passing trooper, were replaced, and grapeshot holes in doors and walls softened with the passing of time. The second and third wars were played in other theatres and Wiltshire was to pass almost unscathed through those troublesome times. Different masters for a while prevailed, but the dull monotony of rural routine, never really halted by the war's demands, continued as it had for decades past and would for years to come. Maidens courted on village greens and the slow economy of rustic life droned on, like an unstoppable engine with unalterable parts.

The deeper scars on hearts and minds took longer to fade. Two hundred of Wiltshire's sons probably died in battle, and as many more were maimed and mutilated. For the families of the unfortunate, life might never resume its pre-war pattern, and vagrancy or poverty would be the end result. Yet seen in the context of the county's thousands, they would be a mere drop,

---

[5] Waylen, J. 'The Wiltshire Compounders'. Wiltshire Archaeological Magazine.

reminders of the age just past and a burden on the parish rates. The war, with all its nightmare reality and shattered limbs, was to be as transitory as the passing seasons.